In Isolation

STANISLAV ASEYEV

IN ISOLATION

DISPATCHES FROM OCCUPIED DONBAS

Translated by
Lidia Wolanskyj

Distributed by Harvard University Press
for the Ukrainian Research Institute
Harvard University

The Harvard Ukrainian Research Institute was established in 1973 as an integral part of Harvard University. It supports research associates and visiting scholars who are engaged in projects concerned with all aspects of Ukrainian studies. The Institute also works in close cooperation with the Committee on Ukrainian Studies, which supervises and coordinates the teaching of Ukrainian history, language, and literature at Harvard University.

ISBN 9780674268784 (hardcover), 9780674268791 (paperback), 9780674268814 (epub), 9780674268807 (PDF)

Library of Congress Control Number: 2021948577
LC record available at https://lccn.loc.gov/2021948577

Commentary in the editorial notes and the timeline of events by Oleh Kotsyuba, edited by Michelle R. Viise

Maps by Kostyantyn Bondarenko, *MAPA: Digital Atlas of Ukraine,* Ukrainian Research Institute at Harvard University, https://huri.harvard.edu/mapa

Timeline design by Mykola Leonovych, background maps source: ZomBear, Marktaff, "War in Donbas," Wikipedia, https://en.wikipedia.org/wiki/War_in_Donbas
Cover image: Wilhelm Neusser, "Bus Stop / Yellow Cloud" (#2011), 2020. Reproduced with permission from the artist and Abigail Ogilvy Gallery, Boston, Mass.
Stanislav Aseyev photo courtesy of Radio Svoboda (RFE/RL)

Book design by Mykola Leonovych, https://smalta.pro

Publication of this book has been made possible by the Ukrainian Research Institute Fund and the generous support of publications in Ukrainian studies at Harvard University by the following benefactors:

Ostap and Ursula Balaban
Jaroslaw and Olha Duzey
Vladimir Jurkowsky
Myroslav and Irene Koltunik
Damian Korduba Family
Peter and Emily Kulyk
Irena Lubchak
Dr. Evhen Omelsky
Eugene and Nila Steckiw
Dr. Omeljan and Iryna Wolynec
Wasyl and Natalia Yerega

You can support our work of publishing academic books and translations of Ukrainian literature and documents by making a tax-deductible donation in any amount, or by including HURI in your estate planning. To find out more, please visit https://huri.harvard.edu/give.

  Translation of this book was prepared within the PEN Ukraine Translation Fund Grants program in cooperation with the International Renaissance Foundation.

 Publication of this book was made possible, in part, by a translation grant from the Peterson Literary Fund at BCU Foundation (Toronto, Canada). The Peterson Literary Fund recognizes the best books that promote a better understanding of Ukraine or the Ukrainian people, or whose subject matter is relevant to a global Ukrainian audience.

CONTENTS

FROM THE EDITORS

In this book, transliteration of personal and place-names follows a modified Library of Congress system for Ukrainian and Russian. With the exception of the name for Kyivan Rus´, primes for the soft sign (ь) and other diacritics are omitted (thus Luhansk and Lysychansk rather than Luhans´k and Lysychans´k), while apostrophes are retained (as in Slov'iansk and Pryp'iat). In personal names where a vowel follows a soft sign in the original, the letter "i" is used to indicate softness (as in Aksionov and Kiseliov). Toponyms are usually transliterated from the language of the country in which the designated places are currently located, including the Ukrainian letter "i" with diaeresis (ï), except for the capital of Ukraine, thus yielding Kyiv, Odesa, Lviv, Makiïvka, Avdiïvka, etc. Furthermore, well-known personal and place-names appear in spellings widely adopted in English-language texts (thus Yanukovych rather than Ianukovych and Moscow rather than Moskva).

Editorial commentary and the timeline of events leading to and during the war in Donbas were prepared by Oleh Kotsyuba and edited by Michelle R. Viise. Translator's notes were prepared by Lidia Wolanskyj and Anna Korbut.

In the course of translation and editing of the book, the author approved revisions of a number of passages and turns of phrase in portraying certain female and male protagonists, including those suffering from addictions, referring to geographic locations and stereotypes associated with them in Ukraine and Russia, and comprising metaphors that would be alien to an Anglophone audience.

Road signs for Makiïvka and Donetsk, with
Msta-B 152 mm howitzers on the road.

PREFACE

By the time the Ukrainian edition of this book came out, I had already spent a year in a special prison "for exceptionally dangerous persons" in the city of Donetsk. I had been locked up there for my political views and for the articles I had published in the Ukrainian press about life in the Donbas. My prison was located on the grounds of Izoliatsiia, formerly an insulation manufacturing plant; today it has earned a bitter reputation as a modern-day concentration camp. In part, that's where the name of the book *In Isolation* comes from; it refers to my imprisonment and contains the observations that I recorded while working as a journalist in the Donbas.

But the term *izoliatsiia* refers to more than just a jail. It also denotes the feeling that functions as the leitmotif of this book, the sense of aloneness and isolation I experienced every day, when forced to hide under the pseudonym Stanislav Vasin in my own land in order to be able to write about the things that you will find in the pages of this book. Despite my use of a pseudonym, I was still found out and arrested by pro-Russian insurgents and thrown into Izoliatsiia for twenty-eight months. This occurrence still holds some mystery for me, as my arrest was definitely no accident. To this day I have no idea how these people tracked me down.

Oddly enough, even after my arrest, while I was being held in a basement, my captors forced me to pretend for nearly a month that I was still free: to call family and friends, to keep posting comments to Facebook, and even... to write articles. In fact, the last chapter of this book, "A Knack for Losing Things," was an article written by me in that prison basement. It was included in the Ukrainian edition of this book by editors who had no idea of the circumstances under which I had written the piece. Indeed, when I asked my captors to give me a pencil and paper, they refused. I had to come up with the article overnight, which meant composing it entirely in my head so that I could quickly produce it in electronic form the following day and send it off to the editorial office. Curiously, my captors were not the least bit interested in censoring the content of my article: for some reason, it was more important for them that no one raise the alarm that I had been arrested.

During my stay in Izoliatsiia I came to understand that I knew very little about this war after all. From the minute the conflict began and up to my arrest, I did not leave the conflict area once for a prolonged period. I witnessed the operation of a separatist mobile artillery unit deployed right outside our apartment building, and I myself endured shelling by Ukrainian units in response. Furthermore, this war was the focus of my work as a writer and journalist. But it was only in captivity that I understood how minor all of this was compared to the world of underground torture chambers in Donetsk, where I found myself. It was here, in prison, that I witnessed dozens of lives broken, psyches destroyed by torture, and suicide attempts, but also the power of human will in situations that seemed entirely hopeless. All of this I described in detail in my second book, *Svitlyi shliakh*[1](forthcoming in English as *Torture Camp on Paradise Street*), which is entirely dedicated to the concentration camp in Donetsk where I was held.

Most of the hastily written dispatches published in this book were used as evidence of my "criminal activities" on the territory of the DPR (the "Donetsk People's Republic" or, in Russian, the DNR, "*Donetskaia Narodnaia Respublika*"), which earned me two prison sentences, each for fifteen years. As evidence of my "guilt" my accusers used the quotation marks that I put around the name "Donetsk People's Republic," even though my usage was politically neutral: the world community, including the Russian Federation, did not recognize the "republic." The pro-Russian leadership of the DPR, however, considered these quotation marks to be a form of extremism, one of the seven counts for which I was found guilty: for these quotation marks alone I was sentenced to five years. Another piece of evidence was the chapter "Donetsk: A Tour of Expropriated Places," a short piece included in this book in which I describe elements of civilian infrastructure like hotels that currently serve as military bases and are surrounded by barbed wire. This was interpreted by the local court as "spying," because it supposedly revealed military secrets, although all these buildings were (and are) visible to any passerby who happens to go through downtown by bus. This added another thirteen years to my sentence.

In general, however, the dispatches in this book focus mainly on social and psychological transformations on the level of both society and particular individuals who, regardless of their views, have found themselves isolated in this, or indeed any, war. This kind of isolation is not only cultural but also psychological, rendering people in the conflict zone incapable of experiencing appropriate emotional reactions, as, for example, when a child is crippled by a grenade. This very incident is described in the piece "Grenades Aren't a Big Deal Anymore: Everyday Tragedies in Makiïvka." Apathy and hopelessness are everyday feelings for everyone who lives in the heart of this war.

Without a doubt, though, one of the main themes of all my pieces was my isolation from most friends and even family who came out in support of the other side in the war—the separatist militants and mercenaries, and their masters in Moscow. Aloneness in one's views and the personal rift that has torn apart not just families but society itself demonstrates more than anything else just how strong the Soviet mindset remains in Ukraine. It is this mentality that Russian propaganda has played upon so effectively. "The Half-Life of the Sovok" and "Propaganda on the Streets of Donetsk" are about this issue; the essays are an attempt to comprehend not just the Soviet past but its latest transformation in Moscow's massive propaganda war. After all, the challenges that Ukrainian society has faced on the territory of the Donbas with the start of the war are not exclusively a problem for Ukrainians: the mechanisms of lies and disinformation that I bring up in my writing are used in a variety of forms in many wars around the world—military, informational, and hybrid. Herein lies the urgency of my book, as it attempts not only to raise the question of how individuals are to live in a suddenly risky situation, of their life principles and how those principles fare under difficult circumstances, but it also tries to illuminate nearly invisible things that in the end may cause people to become combatants without any political motive.

In December 2019, after a total of thirty-one and a half months of imprisonment and torture, I was released from captivity by the insurgents who are sponsored and directly handled by Russia. Only because I was released do I now have the physical opportunity to write a preface to this book.

Stanislav Aseyev
January 2021

PRELUDE TO WAR: MAIDAN AND THE REVOLUTION OF DIGNITY

2013

NOVEMBER

Popular protests begin in Kyiv, on Maidan Nezalezhnosti (Independence Square), after President Viktor Yanukovych cancels plans to sign the Association Agreement with the European Union, an abrupt pivot away from closer cooperation with the West that held the promise of closer integration with the EU and a continuation of democratic reforms in the country. The protests quickly spread across the cities of Ukraine and become a popular uprising dubbed the Revolution of Dignity, or the EuroMaidan Revolution, or simply the Maidan. The Maidan becomes the focus of an anti-corruption, pro-Western, and pro-democracy movement.

In response to these events, the allies of the president and his party, the Party of Regions, mobilize "anti-Maidan protests" in Kyiv and in Ukraine's east and south. Among the attendees of these pro-government, pro-Yanukovych, pro-Russian, and anti-EU demonstrations were people paid to participate and to attack the Maidan protesters.

FEBRUARY 18

2014

In the morning, Maidan protesters march to the Ukrainian parliament building in order to put pressure on the representatives to vote for a reinstatement of the 2004 edition of the constitution, which stipulated significantly weaker presidential powers. The march ends in violent clashes with the police and other state forces.

During the day, the special forces launch an attack at the Ukraïnskyi Dim (Ukrainian House), a base of operations for the protest movement, complete with a small hospital for wounded protesters, a kitchen, a cafeteria, and the Maidan Open University. After an initial wave is repulsed, police forces approach with armored personnel carriers and water cannons to attack the Ukraïnskyi Dim a second time.

Late in the evening, an attack begins on the Budynok Profspilok (House of the Trade Unions), another provisional base of the protest movement, which houses the main hospital for the protesters, a kitchen, a pharmacy, a distribution center for warm clothing, and sleeping quarters. During the attack, a fire breaks out on the upper floors of the building, killing an estimated forty to fifty people.

FEBRUARY 19

The Security Service of Ukraine (SBU) announces the beginning of an "anti-terrorist operation," which the administration of President Yanukovych uses as a pretext for a series of ominous actions:

1. All roads entering Kyiv are blocked.

2. Entry points to the Maidan are closed.

3. President Yanukovych fires the chief of General Staff of the Armed Forces of Ukraine, colonel general Volodymyr Zamana, and replaces him with the pro-Russian Admiral Iurii Ilïn. Simultaneously, the Armed Forces are subordinated to the SBU.

4. Channel 5, the television station supportive of the Maidan protesters and owned by oligarch Petro Poroshenko, is forced to discontinue its broadcast briefly following electricity cuts to the area.

5. The Kyiv subway system, used by protesters and their supporters to travel to and from the Maidan, ceases operations.

6. The SBU's response to the Maidan protesters unfolds in two sub-operations, "Boomerang" and "Wave," supported by close to 20,000 members of the interior forces, the Ukrainian police, special units such as the Berkut riot police, the interior ministry regiment Iahuar, the antiterrorism unit Omeha, and assault brigades of the State Border Service. Although the government initially plan to use units of the Armed Forces of Ukraine to quell the protests, the refusal of then chief of General Staff colonel general Volodymyr Zamana prevents them from doing that.

2014

FEBRUARY 20

Early in the morning, the special units and the police are pushed back from Independence Square by the protesters. Simultaneously, protesters and the press report shots fired by sniper rifles under the direction of state forces. Interim Minister of Internal Affairs Vitalii Zakharchenko orders the police to be equipped with firearms.

In the evening, an extraordinary session of the parliament is convened. The parliament passes a resolution condemning the actions of the security forces and outlaws the operation against the protesters. Seventy-three protesters and eleven security forces have been killed in the operation.

FEBRUARY 21

Leaders of the opposition parties of Ukraine and President Yanukovych sign an agreement for the political resolution of the crisis. The agreement stipulated:

1. The restoration of the constitution of 2004 decreasing presidential powers within 48 hours of the signing of the agreement;

2. Reform of the constitution by September 2014;

3. Snap parliamentary elections by December 2014;

4. The passage of new voting laws and the replacement of all members of the Central Election Commission;

5. An international investigation of the violence against the protesters by the state forces.

Although endorsed by the ministers of foreign affairs of Poland and Germany, a representative from France, and an ombudsman from Russia, the signed agreement is rejected by the protesters, who, after the previous day's bloodletting, demand the immediate resignation of President Yanukovych.

FEBRUARY 22

In the morning, Viktor Yanukovych disappears from Kyiv. The parliament responds by passing with an overwhelming majority a resolution declaring that the president has removed himself from office and withdrawn from the performance of his constitutional duties. The parliament subsequently schedules snap presidential elections for late May 2014.

On the same day, Viktor Yanukovych releases a television address in which he calls the events of February 18–20 a "state coup" and compares them to the Nazis' takeover of Germany in 1933. Yanukovych refuses to recognize the legitimacy of the parliament's vote. A later investigation would show that preparations for Yanukovych's flight from Kyiv had already begun three days earlier, on February 19. On February 21, Yanukovych is photographed personally overseeing the packing and removal of valuables and antiques from his lavish estate at Mezhyhir'ia. He leaves his home sometime in the next twenty-four hours, with last loaded trucks departing from the estate at 4 am on February 22.

2014

FEBRUARY 23

Opposition leader Oleksandr Turchynov, elected as the speaker of the parliament on the day before, is appointed by the parliament the interim President of Ukraine. Four days later, Yanukovych resurfaces in Russia. Later, in a documentary about the annexation of Crimea, Russian president Vladimir Putin retells the story of how Russian security services "rescued" Yanukovych and helped him make it to Russia, allegedly by sea from Crimea.

FEBRUARY 20–MARCH 18

In the aftermath of the tragic events in Kyiv, Yanukovych's disappearance creates a power vacuum. During this time, Russia covertly takes over Crimea and annexes it via an unlawful referendum and agreement. The Russian intervention takes place in stages.

February 23, *Sevastopol.* A pro-Russian demonstration takes place in the city where the Russian Black Sea fleet was stationed. The leaders of the demonstration, members of the Russian Block party, announce the formation of "self-defense units."

February 26, *Simferopol.* A demonstration in front of the Crimean parliament—the Verkhovna Rada of the Autonomous Republic of Crimea—takes place. The protesters, most of whom belong to pro-Russian organizations, demand Crimea's annexation by Russia. A counterdemonstration, comprising largely Crimean Tatars and pro-Ukrainian residents of the peninsula, takes place at the same time and demands the preservation of Ukraine's territorial integrity. Units of Russian military secret service (the GRU), arrive in Crimea from Toliatti. In Yalta, trucks with conscripted personnel of the Russian Black Sea fleet arrive.

February 27, *Crimean peninsula.* Unidentified military personnel without insignia—later dubbed "little green men"—appear at key locations in Crimea and begin taking over facilities. On the night of February 27, the buildings of the Crimean parliament and government are taken over and the Russian flag raised over them. The parliament convenes a session under the watchful eye of Russian special forces, and passes resolutions to hold a referendum in May 2014 approving the expansion of the republic's autonomy; to dismiss the prime minister of the autonomous republic, Anatolii Mohyliov; and to appoint a new prime minister, Serhii Aksionov, the leader of the Russian Unity party. A delegation of members of the Russian Duma arrives in Crimea and openly calls for Crimea's inclusion in Russia. Russian forces then take over the airport Belbek and the ferry in Kerch.

February 28, *Chonhar, Kherson Oblast.* At Chonhar and on other roads to Crimea, checkpoints displaying the Russian flag are erected, guarded by armed men in military uniforms with no insignia ("little green men"), and others in the uniforms of the Berkut and the Ukrainian police. On the same day, the

2014

Simferopol airport is taken over, along with the air traffic control station that regulates airspace over Crimea. Ten helicopters of the Russian military are reported crossing the border, a column of Russian armed personnel carriers is making its way to Simferopol, and five IL-76 military transport aircraft land at the military airport at Hvardiiske, in Crimea. Later that day, the office of the main provider of landline telecommunications, Ukrtelekom, is taken over and the master fiber-optic cable for the internet connection is damaged, cutting off cellphone and internet connections between the peninsula and the rest of Ukraine.

March 1, *Simferopol*. Serhii Aksionov, illegally appointed prime minister on February 27 by the Crimean legislature, appeals to Vladimir Putin to help "maintain order" in the region. Aksionov moves forward the date of the referendum on the status of Crimea to March 30. In the course of the next two weeks, Russian forces increasingly take over Ukrainian military and navy installations, government offices, and key equipment, while the interim Ukrainian government in Kyiv attempts negotiations to prevent bloodshed and loss of life.

March 11, *Simferopol*. The Crimean parliament passes the "Declaration of Independence of Crimea and the City of Sevastopol."

March 16, *Crimean peninsula*. The unlawful "Referendum on Crimea's Status" is held, two weeks earlier than Aksionov's adjusted calendar. The referendum takes place with a heavy presence of Russian or Russian-backed armed men and armored vehicles in the streets of cities and towns throughout the peninsula.

March 18, *Moscow.* Russian president Vladimir Putin and Serhii Aksionov sign an agreement on the annexation of Crimea by Russia. The annexation is condemned by the international community and becomes a major challenge to the global security system, particularly in view of the guarantees of Ukraine's territorial integrity given by the US, the UK, and Russia, in exchange for Ukraine's surrender of the world's third-largest nuclear arsenal in 1994 (the Budapest Memorandum).

MARCH

Pro-Russian demonstrations and attacks on government buildings take place in Ukrainian cities in the east and south of the country, including Dnipropetrovsk (now Dnipro), Zaporizhzhia, Melitopol, Mykolaïv, Kherson, Luhansk, Donetsk, and Mariupol. Orchestration of these events is generally attributed to pro-Russian and Russian-funded people and organizations in Ukraine, as well as Russian secret services with local participation, using methods of aggressive propaganda and informational warfare.

In Kharkiv, the building of the Oblast State Administration is briefly taken over and a Russian flag flown on its roof. In Odesa, a similar demonstration takes place on

2014

Kulykove Pole, a square in the historic center of the city. In Luhansk, the local Oblast State Administration is taken over several times, with Russian flags raised above it, then taken down, and the head of the Administration is forced to resign. Clashes between the pro-Ukrainian and pro-Russian protesters ensue, in which pro-Ukrainian protesters are attacked on various occasions.

With the Ukrainian military demoralized and disoriented after the defection of many general officers to Russia, Maidan protesters form the first volunteer battalions for the defense of Ukraine. Partial mobilization of the population for the Armed Forces of Ukraine begins.

THE LOST GENERATION
OF THE "FABLED *NOVOROSSIIA*"

These days, the cliché of the "fabled *Novorossiia*"[2] is alluded to more and more often in the Donbas media. What exactly makes it so fabled? Those who have maintained their ability to think straight despite the psychological pressure of this strange war will reply that its fairytale nature lies in the illegitimate government, in the lack of respect for international law, and in the very name, whose historical roots long ago withered in the soil of hard reality. But first, I should introduce myself: I may be the only person in contemporary Makiïvka who continues to live here with the blue and yellow flag[3] still fluttering in my head. Most pro-Ukrainian Makiïvites have left their hometown to become refugees,

Graffiti in Donetsk reading "*Novorossiia!* Putin."

pining away for their native corner on the pages of social media. I'm not ready to vouch for its accuracy, but based on the social sampling available to me today, among 100 percent of my acquaintances, relatives, and friends, there isn't a single one who would say they're against the "Donetsk People's Republic."

Beyond that, another number comes to mind: about 80 percent of my male friends and acquaintances are now serving with the *opolchenie*—the separatist "citizens' militias"—often in different units of militants that despise each other.[4] This makes the list of enemies of Ukraine far more extensive than we can imagine, because every one of these former plumbers, coal miners, and roofers has at least five to ten relatives whose attitude is exactly the same as that of their sons, husbands, and brothers. The point I'm trying to make is that the grassroots nature of the separatist militia makes the problem of the current war in the Donbas a far deeper one than people are used to thinking about.

Most people are used to considering all this the consequence of the Kremlin pulling the strings of local oligarchs and the intervention of regular units of the Russian Federation's armed forces, and only after that, the local population burrowed into their armchairs, watching the propagandistic LifeNews TV channel.[5] In fact, all these boys with orange-and-black ribbons[6] pinned to their fevered breasts live within 300 yards of my home. And the propaganda war is no more intense there than it is in my own armchair!

But the minute the bells rang out for the "Russian Spring,"[7] they all showed up on the city squares with portraits of Putin in wooden frames, for reasons that would probably need a separate chapter to explain. In any case, I want to describe how "the fabled *Novorossiia*," whose legend is becoming less fabulous by the minute, has been able to hang on here, in the vastness of our land, for nearly a year now, and to put down roots more and more deeply.

As of January 2015, the situation in the DPR looks like this: most of the industrial giants are closed, some of the coal mines have had their power cut and have been flooded, social benefits—with very few exceptions—are not being paid, and the universities and banks have all moved west to territory under the control of the Ukrainian government; in their place, the people here have been trying to set up some kind of surrogate along the lines of the "Central Republican Bank."

Most financial resources in the region are going to cover the war and to pay the fighters in the militias. For instance, my friend who is a private gets around 7,000 hryvnias [440 US dollars] for operating a Grad multiple rocket launcher.[8] It's true that "humanitarian aid" is being trucked here from Russia, but most of it is sold off at tables in "everything but the kitchen sink" bazaars, where it goes for ridiculously low prices to those who still have the means to buy anything at all—even at such reduced prices. Despite all of this, you won't find a single person on the streets of Donetsk or Makiivka who is not prepared to curse the "bloody Ukrops."[9] Why is that?

When I first heard someone use the term "Donetsk People's Republic," I remember how a feeling of perplexity washed over me rather than the urge to smile, and I thought, "What the heck are they talking about? What republic? What kind of nonsense is this?" But just a few months later, my entire family, to a person, put check marks in the box for "Independence" in the now-notorious "referendum."[10]

But this isn't even about my grandma, who thought that she was voting in a Ukrainian presidential election[11] (which actually took place, though much later)—the names "Hubariev"[12] and the abbreviation "DNR" (DPR) looked like gibberish to her—nor is it about my apolitical mom who checked the box for the republic just to avoid getting dirty looks from the neighbors. Many people genuinely believed in this "new bastion of the good" against Ukraine's "fascist capital."

But the very fact that "*Novorossiia*" became possible precisely here, on this soil, forces us to consider the lower strata of the social atmosphere where, beyond the nefarious hand of the Kremlin and despite the actual silencing of Ukrainian TV and the broadcasting of exclusively pro-Russian channels, there appear the faces of ordinary people whose responsibility cannot in anyway be written off as an "outside influence."

The backbone of the "militia" is formed by locals who lost their jobs because of the arrival of winter and continuing social upheaval. In addition to these are local riffraff with whom Mr. Strelkov[13] and his gang, while they were still active in Donetsk, dealt very harshly. We are talking about those addicted to drugs or alcohol who were given the choice of either building defensive fortifications, digging trenches, serving in the "*Novorossiia*" army, or getting snuffed out. Then there are the young guys from more-or-less respectable families who, to this very day, can count on their relatives to bring them borscht and hot meals in the barracks.

Of course, this has nothing to do with regular units of the Russian army, the volunteers from Russia, Czechia, and Serbia, or the Chechens. I can only speak about those who are walking around right now with a Ukrainian passport in their back pockets after changing the cover for one with a DPR flag on it.

Every one of these men has a dozen reasons for joining the separatist militants. Every one of them has gone through his own school of war and changed to such a degree that I can no longer recognize even those whom I've known for twenty years. Many of these men no longer see themselves and their future outside of the war, and should the shooting in the Donbas actually stop, they already have plans to migrate to the Middle East to fight in other armed conflicts.

While we are all busy following the movement of the tectonic plates of international diplomacy, we're paying far too little attention to what could turn out to be a much more serious problem than just shooting at each other right now: we are in danger of losing an entire generation on both sides of the front.

January 20, 2015
Radio Svoboda (RFE/RL)

The destroyed building of the new terminal of the Donetsk Airport.

THE WAR IN THE DONBAS

2014

APRIL 6

A pro-Russian demonstration takes place in Lenin Square in Donetsk. The Donetsk State Oblast Administration building is taken over by the protesters. In Luhansk, the building of the Security Service of Ukraine (SBU) is taken over.

APRIL 7

In Donetsk, a group proclaiming itself the deputies of Donetsk Oblast cities votes to declare the sovereignty of the "Donetsk People's Republic" (the DPR). In Luhansk, three thousand pro-Russian fighters attack and occupy the local branch of the National Bank of Ukraine, located next to the SBU building.

APRIL 8

In Luhansk, the formation of a self-styled parliament begins after a pro-Russian demonstration in front of the SBU building. Inside the building, sixty people are taken hostage by armed separatists and used as human shields against Ukrainian security forces. (All hostages are released by the end of the day.)

APRIL 10

In Donetsk, pro-Russian separatists announce that there will be a referendum to legitimize the DPR, and they begin forming an "election committee."

APRIL 12

Armed separatists attack and take over police precincts in the cities of Slov'iansk and Kramatorsk, and the city council in Artemivsk. Similar attacks are launched in Horlivka and Krasnyi Lyman. A unit under the command of Igor Girkin (Strelkov) takes control of Slov'iansk, Kramatorsk, and several other towns. The battle for Kramatorsk begins. (Ukrainian forces liberate the towns from DPR militants and Russian mercenaries on July 5.)

APRIL 13

Ukraine's National Security Council, without declaring martial law and with the involvement of the Armed Forces of Ukraine, announces the beginning of the Anti-Terrorist Operation (ATO). The situation in Ukraine is discussed at a meeting of the UN Security Council. The first battle takes place near Slov'iansk; here, the Ukrainian military engages Igor Strelkov's fighters. In Zaporizhzhia, an attempt by pro-Russian separatists to storm the city council is thwarted by pro-Ukrainian residents. In Kharkiv, pro-Russian protesters violently attack local pro-Ukrainian protesters. In Mariupol, the building of the city council is taken over.

2014

APRIL 14

In Donetsk, a majority of the local police members join the pro-Russian protesters. Checkpoints are installed on key routes and intersections and are controlled by armed men without insignia.

APRIL 16

In Donetsk, the pro-Russian protesters take over the building of the Donetsk City Council.

APRIL 17

A pro-Ukrainian demonstration takes place in Donetsk, with close to 3,000 participants. A large yellow-and-blue Ukrainian flag is carried at the demonstration as a symbol of Ukraine's unity.
Russia's president Vladimir Putin makes a statement calling southeast Ukraine "*Novorossiia*" (New Russia), while contending that Ukraine's eastern and southern regions were merely "transferred" to Ukraine by the Soviet government.
Quadrilateral negotiations with the participation of Ukraine, Russia, the EU, and the US take place in Geneva, Switzerland. In these talks, Ukraine demands that Russia cease all support for the separatist forces and withdraw its military, paramilitary, and mercenary units, and return Crimea to Ukrainian control.
A battle begins for control of Mount Karachun near Slov'iansk, a key location due to its high elevation and the TV broadcasting tower on the mountain.

APRIL 21

Pro-Russian activists in Odesa declare the establishment of the "Odesa People's Republic."

APRIL 27

In Luhansk, the "Luhansk People's Republic" is declared by those occupying the SBU building.

APRIL 28

A pro-Ukrainian demonstration in Donetsk is attacked by masked men armed with baseball bats, resulting in heavy injuries and the disappearance of some of the participants in the demonstration. The Donetsk police do not interfere as pro-Ukrainian protesters are being attacked. In Kharkiv, the tents of pro-Russian separatists are removed by the local police.

APRIL 29

In Luhansk, around 3,000 protesters led by armed men in military equipment, helmets, and bulletproof vests, storm the building of the Luhansk Oblast State Administration and take it over, raising the flags of Russia and the "Luhansk People's Republic" (LPR) over the building. The local police join the LPR protesters. The Luhansk TV station and the office of the oblast prosecutor general are taken over. Late at night the building of the Luhansk City Council is stormed and taken over by LPR militants.

HOW I BECAME A SHADOW
IN MY OWN LAND

When you start talking about your own life, what first comes to mind are the worn clichés that prop up your personal experience like a pair of old crutches in the corner. Things like, "I was born here," "I graduated there," "I got married then," "I have two kids now," and so on. These phrases always come to the rescue, don't they? But as for me, I can't even tell you my real name. On social media, I can't post my real photo and am forced to hide behind the not-especially-clever pseudonyms and masks to which my entire life has been reduced, all because the banners of the DPR unfurled over my land instead of the Ukrainian blue-and-yellow, and I now find myself in a kind of exile.

These days I'm Stanislav Vasin, the name under which I speak to you from these pages. And the first thing that I'd like to tell you is how it is that what once seemed impossible has become the way things are now. But my sense of incredulity, of the impossibility of this circumstance, maintains its hold on me, even though I have experienced life in Makiïvka every single day since the beginning of the ATO, the Anti-Terrorist Operation,[14] and should have become used to things by now. But the sense of unreality just won't go away.

What am I going on about? I'll tell you. It's the complete destruction of the shiny new airport from which I flew to Kyiv just two years ago. It's the wonderful restaurant in downtown Donetsk where a courteous elderly doorman used to hand me my jacket when I was leaving, now heaped with sandbags and frequented by men with grenades hanging from their belts. It's air spiked with explosions and the stench of burning buildings. And, finally, it's the people, whom the front has cut like a fault line, splitting up families and making adversaries of those who not that long ago were friends and colleagues. It all feels so unreal.

Two or three years ago, as I walked along the streets of Donetsk in the springtime with my college notebooks, I would have bet any amount of money that it was more likely that the whole world would blow up tomorrow than that I would come across a column of tanks, howitzers, and artillery here, rolling down Universytetska Street. What crazy circumstances could have brought them out here? It's quite unreal. And what appears before me now? Corpses on the sidewalk, terrified faces...

Last year, I witnessed all the major events in our region during the ATO, including the "parade of captives"[15] and the first March rally that, in fact, started the grand march of separatism through our land. I heard the groans of people whose bodies were scattered along the sides of the roads after the shelling of Donetsk that we all know about. Several times, I myself was *that close* to becoming just another statistic among the victims of this war.

What's more, I know quite well many of those who stood at the origin of separatism in Donetsk or who are now in the "People's Army of '*Novorossiia*'"—some of them as members of the "Cossacks," some in the Vostok or Somalia battalions,[16] and some in the local "police" or the SMERSH.[17] I see them almost every day—guys I once played with in the same yard when we were kids, or with whom I made plans not so long ago to go on summer vacation in Yalta.

All that is gone now. They're walking around in old "steppe" camouflage, tightly-laced army boots, a machine-gun strapped across their shoulders, and a knife at their right side. Most of them have filled their homes with entire arsenals, trophies claimed or just stolen, while they themselves have become a reflection of the war, having lost all sense of pity, empathy, or feeling in their trenches and dugouts. Every time I meet them casually on the street, I feel as though I should justify why I'm the only one in our building who, for reasons none of them can fathom, is still not part of the "militia."

Based on my own experience, I can say with confidence that the hardest thing about this entire situation is not the rattling of windowpanes by the Grads, or the melted snow that has replaced running water in unserviced taps. It's not even the blood and the screaming that fill the street from time to time. One can survive steep prices for everything and nights being hammered by Smerches.[18] What is worse is that which eludes the eye, that which hides from screens, lenses, reporters' cameras, or eye-catching, shocking articles: Namely, that over the course of a year of living under occupation, I've slowly lost nearly all my friends. Some have returned to their neighborhoods in closed caskets, while others have simply shut me out. The same has been happening with my family and loved ones: time has taught me to keep my mouth closed if I wanted to maintain at least a semblance of peace at home. Nor am I the only one who has become a virtual shadow in his own hometown, forced to hide my thoughts about the war: those who were once close to me have melted away with no less force and speed, disappearing with every day that this war continues.

Not a single day goes by that I don't ask myself—underneath the day-to-day problems and the moaning about sky-high prices and the barbed wire at checkpoints—how? How did this happen? I mean, this is Donetsk in Europe. That we should be living in basements dreaming of slitting the throats of those who, not that long ago, stood with us in the soccer stadium with the same blue-and-yellow painted faces... I know I will probably never find an answer. The question is far too personal, too drenched in the blood of my friends who took up arms for the sake of "Great Russia." I can list hundreds of reasons why they ended up in the ranks of the militants, offer endless theories about what was on the minds of Mssrs. Putin and Obama, or invent my own views on the problems of war. But who, if not I, should know the idiocy of such diversions when we kill ourselves trying to come up with precise answers to questions that make no sense—even as we recognize our own powerlessness to change anything?

I'll leave you for now with these thoughts. Perhaps next time someone will be luckier and will find at least the semblance of an answer to those things that I have been mulling over for nearly 300 days at this point. For now, I've probably said enough for us to get to know each other.

March 1, 2015
Tyzhden

WHO HAS JOINED THE DPR MILITANTS AND WHAT ARE THEY FIGHTING FOR?

It's no secret that a huge number of people of completely different sentiments, political views, nationalities and citizenships serve in the "People's Army of 'Novorossiia.'" It's often difficult even for those who serve in the "people's battalions" to figure out who is in these battalions and what their actual goals are. The militants themselves are sometimes surprised by the internal conflicts in these battalions, because such clashes have led to considerably greater losses than localized skirmishes with the Ukrainian armed forces.

This is a rough sketch of the "people's army," based on my impressions in Makiïvka as of January 2015.

KAZAKI

The name *kazaki*—Russian for "Cossacks"—can be applied to one of the biggest groups in the DPR; it is the one that most of the people I know from fairly respectable families have joined.

I'm deliberately not limiting *kazaki* to the mighty Don Cossack Host, as that group is mostly represented in the LPR. In our area, several groups operate that can be identified as "Cossacks" by the tall karakul lambskin hats with a yellow cross on top worn by their fighters.

All these "Cossack" unions have regrouped and reorganized themselves many times and their fighters likewise have drifted from one battalion to another. In a nutshell, joining the "Cossacks" is the way for the fledgling militant to get started, for it provides him with a barracks, meals, firearms, and a base camp in which to work up his shooting skills. The men from these groups who have fought since

DPR military recruiting office in Donetsk.

late summer 2014-these are the ones I'm aware of—have mastered a wide array of weapons, including Grad MLRS, systems that they are now trusted to operate. A rank-and-file militant in the three-person crew of a Grad multiple rocket launcher is paid 360 US dollars a month and has an official contract with the "defense ministry" of the DPR. An officer's salary starts at 500 US dollars.

THE OPLOT

The Oplot[19] is of the most privileged fighting groups and is loathed by the other DPR militants. From the very start it was the favored militant grouping of local criminals; now it is recognizable from the muscled dudes in Donetsk and Makiïvka sporting black T-shirts with the red-lettered Oplot logo. These are the guys who previously controlled local bus stations and engaged in racketeering back when Yanukovych was still running Donetsk. Later, men with fighting experience joined Oplot and it evolved into a force that has

functioned largely as a personal security detail for Oleksandr Zakharchenko[20] at rallies and public events.

Oplot fighters often took part in actual hostilities,
much to the annoyance of other DPR groups. In fact, one
militant told me, "They were too keen to save their own
skins and are not exactly raring to fight." Apart from this,
it was the Oplot who recently disarmed local checkpoints
in Makiïvka, which did little to improve their reputation.
Wages in this battalion ranged from 220 to 250 US dollars[21]
in the summer months. Today, a local channel called Oplot.
TV acts as "*Novorossiia's*" mouthpiece, broadcasting in the
DPR.

MECH

Mech[22] is a local Makiïvka group, formed by Igor Bezler[23]
with local men. Battalion members initially guarded checkpoints, then gained a reputation for their "curious" focus on
healthcare providers: they devoted a great deal of time and
energy to hijacking ambulances and raiding local pharma-
cies. The Mech militants I know have highly romanticized
ideas about the war and think of themselves as anarchist
revolutionaries. I have no idea how much they are paid.

THE "INTERNATIONAL BRIGADES"

I know of at least two such brigades. One is full of Serbs,
Frenchmen, Czechs, and some guys from Latin America.
The other one consists mainly of Chechens, Ossetians, Armenians, and Roma. The latter brigade stands out for its vi-
ciousness and uncompromising attitude in matters of war,
which the men see as the main purpose of their lives.

THE VOSTOK BATTALION

One of the best-known groups under the DPR "Defense Ministry," Vostok[24] consists of two groups: one is linked to Oleksandr Khodakovskyi[25] and the former Berkut special forces, and the other is made up of mercenaries from Chechnya and the Caucasus, but includes locals. In November 2014, Vostok members who fought at Donetsk Airport,[26] including one guy I know, were being paid around 200 US dollars a week. It actually wasn't such a big amount, considering that the airport was the hottest spot on the ATO map at the time and few men could handle active fighting for a whole month. Other DPR groups are not happy with this battalion; some militants have posted videos openly mocking Vostok's combat skills.

THE SPARTA AND SOMALIA BATTALIONS

These two battalions report to Motorola[27] and Givi,[28] probably the best-known men in the DPR army these days. Mostly deployed around the airport, Sparta and Somalia are also involved in prisoner swaps and issues linked to the rotation of the Ukrainian armed forces currently occupying the airport building. Sparta has many Russian volunteers.

KALMIUS

This group refers to itself as a "special unit." Initially, Kalmius[29] had the largest number of local volunteers, who fought without pay back in the summer months—something other battalions ridicule to this day, often referring to the Kalmius fighters as idiots. Because it was mostly made up of local recruits, typically coming from the coal mining community, this group was aggressive with the derelicts of Donetsk, shutting down a number of drug houses across the city.

RUSSIAN REGULARS

When it comes to the regular Russian army, I've personally seen three convoys of armored vehicles, KAMAZ transport trucks and artillery on the Makiïvka highway. However, I have not seen any regular infantry units from the Russian Federation in the times I've been in the ATO zone, perhaps because I have limited myself to the Makiïvka-Donetsk area.

January 25, 2015
Radio Svoboda (RFE/RL)

The "parade of captives" in Donetsk. Captive soldiers of the Ukrainian armed forces are led between two rows of militants armed with rifles with bayonets.

THE WAR IN THE DONBAS

2014

MAY 2

Clashes with pro-Russian separatists take place in Odesa, likely orchestrated by Russian security forces with the participation of local pro-Russian and Russian-funded organizations and individuals. A violent fire erupts in Budynok Profspilok (the House of Trade Unions), which has been taken over by pro-Russian separatists. In the fire, forty-eight people die and two hundred sustain injuries. Against the backdrop of these events, Russia questions the agreements reached at the quadrilateral meeting in Geneva and exits the negotiations.

MAY 3

Ukrainian armed forces establish control over Mount Karachun near Slov'iansk. Separatist attacks continue, resulting in the collapse of the TV tower.

MAY 6

Pro-Russian separatists install checkpoints controlling all traffic on the main streets of Mariupol, while briefly vacating and then retaking the building of the city council.

2014

MAY 9

In Mariupol, around sixty armed fighters attempt to take over the local branch of the Ministry of Internal Affairs. Fourteen tanks of the Ukrainian Armed Forces enter the city, and fire breaks out in the building of the city council and the local prosecutor general's office.

MAY 10

The Ukrainian government decides to withdraw National Guard troops from Mariupol in order to avoid further bloodshed and loss of life. The local police also leave the city. Looting of local shops is reported.

MAY 11

Unauthorized referendums are staged in select cities of the Luhansk and Donetsk oblasts for adopting independence in the form of the Luhansk and Donetsk "republics." Because the referendums are unconstitutional, their results are not recognized by either the Ukrainian government or international organizations. Leaders of the DPR retain the status of a "republic," while leaders of the LPR proclaim the sovereignty of the LPR the day after the referendum.

MAY 22

Battle at Volnovakha (located to the south of Donetsk, in the direction of Mariupol) in the Donetsk Oblast. Ukraine suffers its heaviest casualties to date, losing seventeen members of the armed forces. The Battle of Rubizhne (located near Sievierodonetsk and Lysychansk, to the northwest of Luhansk) is the first military engagement in the Luhansk Oblast. Ukrainian forces suffer three casualties, while the reported casualties of the separatists range between three and nine.

MAY 24

The LPR and the DPR announce the formation of a single state, "*Novorossiia*."

MAY 26

The battle for the Donetsk airport begins with Ukrainian forces taking control of the airport. (Separatist attacks begin with new vigor in the fall of 2014.)

EXECUTED AS AN "ENEMY OF THE PEOPLE" OF THE DPR

After more than 300 days of wandering lost through the streets of Makiïvka and Donetsk, I still haven't discovered any solid reasons that would explain the huge body of terror here. I really haven't. I mean, when you look at someone wrapped in a suicide vest who says he doesn't give a damn whether he kills one person or 500 million, you can disagree all you want with him, but you have to admit, he is being up-front about it.

Here, in the Donbas, you won't find such sincerity. Since the first days and minutes of the separatist protests, those who now proudly wear mud-colored balaclavas and DPR patches never have explained why they've transformed our land into a smoking ruin. From the very beginning, the notions of "friend" and "foe" in the Donbas has made it impossible to follow the first principle of war: to distinguish who is "us" and who is "them."

I don't support the DPR. That has been the case ever since these protest movements sprang up and this isn't the place to discuss my reasons. But when I look at my enemy, the separatists, those who have taken the lives of more than a thousand people, I don't see Nazi banners, I don't hear an unfamiliar language, and I don't understand why I should be afraid of that *russkii mir*,[30] whose makers come from the same people as all of my family. And there you have it, the same old trap that our entire region keeps falling into, over and over again.

Having managed, through force of will and mind, to keep the blue-and-yellow flag flying in my head, I keep asking myself: Whom am I supposed to fear? The Russians? Those who sat with me yesterday for Sunday dinner in Kursk? Or maybe it is my friends in the "militia," whose

The "parade of captives" in Donetsk, staged on Ukrainian Independence
Day, in which Ukrainian servicemen captured by DPR militants
were led through the city streets in a humiliating procession.

homes are within 300 yards of my own? Surely these ar-
en't my enemies? Surely these aren't people I might have
to shoot at tomorrow without hesitation—or are they? The
only possible answer is to tell myself, honestly, "Yes." This is
now our reality. How we got here is another question altogether. But if we want to keep thinking straight despite the
enormous pressure of propaganda, then we have to admit
that speaking the same language and living next door to
each other doesn't necessarily mean we are brothers. The
catch is that, even with the corpses and the weeping on Donetsk streets, most people in the Donbas still don't see any
clear threat, the kind of threat that you would feel in the
middle of an Arabian desert with a sword to your throat.[31]
But are we really that far from kneeling in that desert?

Having decided to stay in the DPR, I was determined
not to spend the war in basements and bomb shelters. After
all, you get the greatest understanding of events only when
you are in direct touch with what is going on outside your

walls. And so, from time to time, I wander around Donetsk for no reason at all; watching my city change before my very eyes is as necessary as it is unpleasant. A recent random walk not far from the Motel bus stop made me a witness to something I could never have imagined.

Of course, with the beginning of the war, a sense of the presence of death has been constant for those who live in this land. Yet, for most of us, death is an abstraction. Yes, you know that shells are flying all around, that somewhere at the Azot plant[32] or near the Donetsk airport people are dying, and maybe you yourself have spent time sitting it out in basements and seeing bodies in *rigor mortis* near schools or apartment buildings.

This one day, though, I was on my way back from my latest wander through Donetsk and was crossing the bridge between two bus stops: Pasta Factory and Motel. The residents of Donetsk know that this is a fairly lively part of town with constant traffic. To the right of the bridge are some small garages and a wooded area, and on the rails of a train track next to them I noticed two militants with a young guy in a tracksuit and no jacket. The young man looked exhausted and seemed to be having trouble standing up. What happened next took place in an instant, in the time it took me to cross the bridge. Without saying a word, without giving a warning, without the tiniest acknowledgment that this was a human being, —one of the militants pulled the trigger of his gun, there was a crack, and the young man fell. That was it. They shot him like an animal, without saying a word.

When someone shoots a person right before your eyes, let me tell you, it is a feeling unlike anything else you've ever experienced. I had effectively become witness to an execution. And the whole thing happened in a matter of seconds while I was crossing a bridge.

Maybe this was one of their prisoners of war or a saboteur that they had caught around the garages. Or maybe it was just some homeless guy who had managed to annoy the "defenders" and "fighters" of the Donbas. But the very fact that you could be shot in broad daylight right there in the middle of Donetsk, even if it was not on a main street but near a random patch of brush, brought me back to that infamous desert where a number of foreign journalists had lost their lives.

This is the Donbas, not Syria or Iraq. It is Donetsk, filled with people from a once brotherly nation. And that boy that was killed—he died not at the hands of Nazis, expanding their *Lebensraum* over the corpses of peoples and countries. Nor did he die at the hands of Chechens. Instead, the men who killed him looked like typical Slavic lads—just like their victim.

It's true that, back when Strelkov first showed up, people were being sentenced to death in Donetsk under laws from the 1940s. For the most part, the militants were executing their own: deserters, criminal elements who had merged into the "*Novorossiia*" army in the summer in huge numbers, and ordinary men who refused to follow Strelkov's orders. But in broad daylight?

After this incident, I felt that I had lost all understanding of what was going on in the heads of my kith and kin—heads that are still filled with thoughts of cheap Soviet sausage and the childish self-centeredness of "What does it matter, as long as there's no war."

March 7, 2015
Tyzhden

2014

JUNE 2

An unintended airstrike by a Ukrainian fighter jet damages the building of the Luhansk Oblast State Administration, killing eight civilians in front of the building. Civilians begin leaving the city in search of safety. The siege of the Luhansk Border Base on the outskirts of Luhansk by pro-Russian forces begins; the base is a key element in controlling the border with Russia. The siege ends two days later with the surrender of the Ukrainian troops and withdrawal from the base. The base with its ammunition is taken by the separatists, as are several National Guard and border bases near Luhansk and Sverdlovsk.

JUNE 3

The battle for Krasnyi Lyman begins. Ukrainian forces liberate the city within two days, although hostilities continue until June 19, when surrounding areas are finally taken by Ukrainian forces. Ukraine loses sixteen servicemen.

JUNE 5

The battle for control over the Marynivka border crossing in the Donetsk Oblast and the battle at the strategic mound of Savur-Mohyla begin. Ukrainian armed forces attempt to cut off insurgent supply lines from Russia. Fighting takes place near the towns of Marynivka, Dmytrivka, Stepanivka, Shakhtarsk, Snizhne, and Torez (now Chystiakove). The Marynivka border crossing is taken over by Russian regular military units in mid-August, and Ukrainian troops withdraw from Savur-Mohyla at the end of August.

JUNE 6

A Ukrainian military surveillance aircraft AN-30 is shot down at Slov'iansk. The first meeting of the Normandy Format (Ukraine, Russia, France, and Germany) takes place during the 70th anniversary of the D-Day allied landings in Normandy.

JUNE 8

Four members of a Pentecostal church, the Transfiguration of the Lord, in Slov'iansk, are captured and murdered by militants calling themselves the "Russian Orthodox Army." These murders cause a public outcry and are the first examples of religious persecution by the DPR.

JUNE 12

Ukrainian armed forces begin an offensive to take back Ukrainian territory in the direction of the border with Russia. Mariupol is freed from separatist and Russian forces.

JUNE 14

A Ukrainian military transport aircraft IL-76 is shot down in Luhansk, allegedly by the members of the Russian private military company Wagner, killing forty Ukrainian paratroopers and nine crew members.

JUNE 19

The city of Krasnyi Lyman is fully liberated from separatist and Russian forces.

JUNE 24

A Ukrainian military helicopter MI-8 is shot down near Slov'iansk, killing nine people on board.

THE CHECKPOINT: "I'M ALIVE BECAUSE OF THE WAR"

In this sketch, I want to share with you more than the situation that has developed at the separatist checkpoints set up all over the city, more than the little life that each checkpoint has, with its own laws and order. I want to tell you the story of a man whose fate shows that the war in the Donbas is far from a black-and-white affair, and is instead more of a kaleidoscope with a huge number of colored bits.

The fortified structures that the militants began to put up around our area back in the beginning of spring last year were and continue to be the main symbol of the separatist movement. It is precisely in these posts that the fighters for "a free Donbas" began their campaign, armed with no more than bats and rocks.

A separatist fighter with typical Christian Orthodox icons at an LPR checkpoint near Stanytsia Luhanska.

Set up on all the city's key intersections and main roads, the checkpoints have brought together individuals whose life interests are far outside the scope of any ideological goals. Most of the checkpoints are now controlled by fighters from the Vostok and Mech battalions, with a smattering of members of Oplot—none of whom have distinguished themselves by any special sense of duty or idealism in this war. Indeed, among local militants, the word "checkpoint" brings up only ironic smirks: as a rule, no military operations take place within city limits of Donetsk or Makiïvka and, with rare exceptions, any threat could only be posed by "saboteurs or diversionary groups" (a World-War-II-era Soviet phrase) of the Ukrainian armed forces.

This means that standing at a checkpoint is a profitable and relatively safe activity, offering opportunities, on one hand, to be paid officially by the DPR "defense ministry," and, on the other, to collect "donations" from those who happen to drive past in expensive foreign cars. This tradition started back in the day when the militias fought for no pay whatsoever and really had to beg from the cars they stopped.

From the time around the end of August to early September 2014, these spots were rightly called bazaars: by then, in addition to money, the militants were collecting literally everything that could possibly be of use to them during their arduous days at the intersections. This could include fresh meat, smoked poultry, bottles of wine or *kvas*,[33] or medical supplies, which might be demanded directly or in the form of money, with the phrase "Donate for my arm," and a militant's bandaged limb thrust through the open window of the car. In short, the demand for "donations" might be satisfied by anything found in a car traveling on the intercity highway.

Needless to say, at those places—the checkpoints—a pecking order had been established as to who had the right to levy "duties" on drivers, along with a table of rates for this kind of business, providing an income for those practicing the trade and their families. At this point, the checkpoints only stop passenger cars and trucks, letting *marshrutky*, the fixed-route minibuses, go by without bothering them at all.

Let me share a story of the kind of man you might have seen standing at one of these "bazaars" just a few months ago, with a machinegun in his hands and a karakul lamb skin hat on his head. This is the type of man you probably would have decided on the spot was the enemy, yet his threatening outward appearance and social attributes would have obscured his story.

This man belongs to those who, from the very start, were skeptical about the DPR and the idea of "*Novorossiia*." At a time when most of our mutual acquaintances were already standing at the crossroads or making their way in tanks to the Donetsk airport, he continued to work in a coal mine, where he held a rather prominent position.

Then one day came the shift where they were barely able to pull him out from underground because a battery was shelling them. The next day the coal mine closed down and operations stopped. He was left penniless, of course, and was unable to get a job even as a loader, because there were simply no jobs in our region. After a week of heavy drinking, he found himself one morning lying handcuffed on a wooden pallet at the Makiivka train station. Not far from him stood a few militants in camouflage and some guy who was already digging a trench.

My friend was politely told that, as a useless alcoholic and drug addict, he had been arrested by the Makiivka commandant and brought there the previous evening. Now he was going to spend two days digging trenches together with other "social trash" like himself—that is, the man with the shovel. Not happy with this interpretation of things, Artem—for that was his name—announced that he didn't plan on shoveling anything and demanded that they remove the handcuffs and release him.

The militants actually removed the handcuffs—after which they beat him up for the first time, to such a degree that, as he described it, he lay unconscious on that pallet for half a day before slowly coming to. Not a man of great endurance, my friend nevertheless once again declared that it was easy enough for any five guys to beat him up and mumbled something about a fair fight. At this, the men beat him brutally a second time, using their rifle butts and tossing the shovel in for good measure, and said that if he refused to dig, the other guy who had been shoveling all day alone because of him would bury him alive.

In the end, Artem managed to dig part of the trench by evening, then spent a chilly night on the bare pallet. The next day, not having a single coin in his wallet, covered in blood and dirt, he walked from one end of the city to the other. After this, he had to drink bouillon through a special straw for two weeks.

As you can understand from this story, this incident did not especially increase the man's sympathy for the DPR and as of today he has moved to one of the oblasts in the middle of Ukraine. However, he managed to collect money for this trip by working at the Makiïvka checkpoint when, after healing up and wandering around the coal mines that were still working looking for a position, he was forced to join the DPR simply in order not to starve to death.

When I met Artem in the Vostok battalion and asked what he thought now about the war and the DPR, he admitted with a smirk that he was only alive thanks to the war and had no idea how he would otherwise find the means to survive right now.

It's clear that, nominally, he could be considered an "enemy of Ukraine," since working as a checkpoint militant was not the only option available in the circumstances that he found himself in, as one might castigate him.

A lot of time could be spent arguing over this. But the very fact that the DPR and all its army units are filled with people with drastically different backgrounds, often with no ideological stake whatsoever in this war, becomes that stumbling block against which many a foot will trip in the attempt to clearly divide those people into "us" and "them."

February 4, 2015
Radio Svoboda (RFE/RL)

2014

JULY 5

Kramatorsk, Slov'iansk, Artemivsk, Druzhkivka, and Kostiantynivka in the Donetsk Oblast are freed from separatist and Russian forces. A column of separatists under the command of Igor Girkin (Strelkov) is allowed to retreat to Donetsk, hiding behind a human shield of prisoners.

JULY 11

Positions of the Ukrainian armed forces and the State Border Service near Zelenopillia in the Luhansk Oblast are shelled by Russian regular army units, killing forty-four Ukrainian servicemen.

JULY 12

A fake report about a boy being crucified and his mother executed on the central square in Slov'iansk by Ukrainian fighters is aired on the main Russian state channel, Pervyi Kanal (Channel One). The report causes a public outcry. It is shown to be entirely staged as a means of informational warfare against Ukraine, particularly on the territory of the Donbas where Russian TV is watched by local residents.

JULY 14

A Ukrainian military transport aircraft AN-26 is shot down by Russian regular units in the Luhansk Oblast, about 3 miles from the border with Russia, using the Buk missile system, two crew members are killed.

2014

JULY 15

A series of battles for Snizhne, located to the
west of Luhansk in the Luhansk Oblast, begins.
After being retaken by the Ukrainian forces, the
city becomes the target of shelling by the Grad
multiple rocket launchers from Russian territory.

JULY 17

Malaysian Airlines Flight 17 (MH-17), a
Boeing 777, is shot down near Torez (now
Chystiakove) in the Donetsk Oblast by a
Russian Buk missile system, registered with a
rocket brigade of the Russian army in Kursk,
Russia. All 298 people on board the airplane are
killed, mostly citizens of the European Union.
The downing of MH-17 finally brings broad
international attention to the war in Ukraine,
resulting in additional sanctions against Russia.

JULY 21–31

Fighting takes place in Pisky, Soledar,
Dzerzhynsk, Debaltseve, and Avdiivka in the
Donetsk Oblast, and Lysychansk, Iuvileine, and
Popasna in the Luhansk Oblast. In a battle for
Shakhtarsk, located to the east of Donetsk,
thirty-two Ukrainian servicemen are killed.

HOW TO DEFEAT THE DPR

I would like to touch on several intertwined topics this time. Allow me to begin with one important question I often hear from fellow countrymen who became migrants and left this region: Why haven't you left?

Why indeed? Clearly, even though I'm on the side of Ukraine, I'm not actually involved in this war in any way—which, at first sight, makes my staying here, in Makiïvka, exposed to mortars and the Grads, absolutely meaningless and unjustifiably risky.

But the answer for me, my friends, is directly connected to what I see as the key weakness of the "people's republics." Unfortunately, this has been barely noticed by either

A local boy with the DPR militants as they stand guard outside a regional administration building in Kostiantynivka, Donetsk Oblast, seized in the night by separatists.

the Ukrainian government or Ukrainians themselves so far. Let me explain.

The point is that Makiïvka is a city with the typical proletarian mentality, rooted in categories of both labor and being coerced to perform that labor. I don't intend to ridicule this in any way because I understand that this mindset is what makes it possible for many of my compatriots to heroically—this is no exaggeration—continue to go down into the coal mines, even under the sound of whistling missiles and mines, taking the risk that they won't come back to the surface and without the least hope of getting paid in the end. These are conditions that would break your average Western city dweller from London or Paris within an hour.

When it comes to political choice though, my people, the people of Donbas, tend to think the same way they work, accustomed as they are to hard labor and a strong hand, and not feeling the pull of civil liberties. This partly explains the massive support for the DPR among locals. It was always like this: Stalin, Yanukovych, Putin, Zakharchenko—all these men personify the popular sentiments roiling in the collective consciousness of the Donbas.

But this is a very broad and deep issue, so I would like to focus on one aspect: I am profoundly convinced that the use of force cannot bring victory in this war, however unpatriotic this might sound. Here is the reason why.

Let me offer a specific example that I have mentioned in passing in one of my previous pieces. The psychological support for the DPR lives not only in the active militiamen who were recruited among the local population. Support for the DPR comes from their immediate families, as well; in fact, the views of family members are often even more radical than those of their sons and husbands in the militia.

The father of a good friend who is now a DPR "Cossack" keeps two F-1 grenades in the liquor bar in his apartment. His son gave them to him on one of his Sunday leaves. The lower drawer of the bar is filled with AK-47 cartridges.

Captured munitions or Russian weapons are kept as trophies by people all over the city; an account of such cases would fill a whole chapter. In truth, it probably would not be so alarming, if it weren't for the views of these people, which are—well, I'll just quote this man's explanation for why he needs an F-1 grenade: "If anything happens to my son and the 'Ukry'[34] walk into Makiïvka, I'll just go out into the street and blow myself up in the middle of them. I won't give a damn anymore."

Now, my friends, imagine that a couple of his brothers, his wife, and another son, who may not serve in the militia but has joined the local police—none of whom have any special feelings for Ukraine—all think more or less the same thing. Let's assume that this friend of mine in the militia, who serves somewhere in Krasnohorivka, dies in battle, killed by Ukrainian armed forces as an enemy of Ukraine. Leaving my personal moral perspective out of this, I ask you: What do you do with his family, and with the families of all the local militants; how do you combat not just the militiamen, but the multitude of their family members, as well—their fathers, mothers, and siblings, all of whom would take their places in the DPR ranks the next day?

What's more, I assure you that this is an example from a stable family—in fact, an extremely successful, prosperous one—in whose apartment you won't find drug paraphernalia or empty vodka bottles lying around. From the outside, these people look no different from any resident of Kyiv or Lviv, yet their attitudes are rooted deeply in the Soviet past—and probably much deeper than that, in all honesty. Surely the problem cannot be resolved by putting all four of them up against the wall and shooting them—and the same with the thousands who have not taken up machine guns, but who might?

An armed stand-off clearly makes sense when it is against a foreign military—Russians, Chechens, Armenians, or whoever else comes to our land. But when it comes to the militias formed by Donbas locals, the only real force against them is the people who used to live one floor up or one floor down from them, but who had an entirely different mindset. Yes, I'm talking about dozens, possibly hundreds of thousands of citizens with a pro-Ukrainian attitude and whose social media pages say that they now live in Kyiv, Berdychiv, or Odesa.

Only a real civic movement of people with local roots, represented by thousands of those who do not accept the "land of the DPR," and who are prepared to gather on the central square of Donetsk, can radically change the situation, showing that Donetsk has more to offer than the shameful "parade of captives," and that, once upon a time, there lived here people who walked to the banks of the Kalmius River waving Ukrainian flags, and enjoyed listening to Okean Elzy's "Almost Spring."[35]

True, it would have to be a huge crowd of people whose collective body would be impossible to shoot in the square or throw into a basement prison. When I see mile-long lines of cars at checkpoints leaving the DPR every time the sound of the Grads gets stronger, something tells me that this mass gathering would be entirely possible—if only these people remembered who they were and what they were fleeing from.

And that's precisely why I'm still here in Makiivka, and not shedding tears over the ruins of Donetsk with someone in a comfortable suburban apartment in Kyiv.

February 22, 2015
Radio Svoboda (RFE/RL)

YOUNG PEOPLE IN THE DPR AND THE LPR: WHAT DOES THE FUTURE HOLD?

Despite all the criticism and skepticism toward the self-proclaimed republics, a lot of young people have not only remained in Donetsk, Luhansk, Makiïvka, and other cities of the Donbas now under militant control, but also continued their studies here. Only now, the schools, vocational schools, and universities where they are studying are under "DPR-republican jurisdiction"[36] and promise to issue Russian-style diplomas.

This situation is quite ambiguous. It's not just a question of where those degrees will be recognized. On the one hand, those who decide to continue their studies at Ukrainian institutions, mostly by moving to other cities and oblasts, face an array of logistical problems, including housing, work, new living conditions, and so on. At the end of the day, these difficulties should be offset by the benefit these young people expected when they first entered university—a regular Ukrainian diploma. On the other hand, those who chose to stay and continue their studies in the emerging "republican" university departments and faculties in Donetsk or Luhansk risk ending up with a no-name diploma that won't be recognized in Ukraine and possibly not even in Russia itself. High-school graduates face a similar challenge: while students in the sixth, seventh, or eighth grades can hope that the passage of time will solve their problem, those graduating from ninth and eleventh grades now will face this problem in the summer, as a gift from the DPR "Ministry of Education," which considers these graduates its own.

Despite all this, on a relatively quiet day in Donetsk, you can see many students holding debates, conferences, and seminars as they did in the "good old days," and having

Children celebrate a farewell bell event at Donetsk school number 30, where
the DPR anthem is played for the first time instead of the Ukrainian anthem.

a coffee inside university buildings adorned with the flag
of "*Novorossiia*," which looks very similar to the American
Confederate flag.[37] These young people really do support
the DPR, for the most part, and are prepared to take any
degree offered by those in charge because they don't plan
to leave the "republic" to look for a job elsewhere.

Yet, there is another reason why some young people
from the Donbas make this choice. In the past, competition
was high for a state-paid spot in graduate school at Donetsk National University. After most young people left the
DPR, the number of applicants was halved, and the number
of available state scholarships increased significantly. As
a result, it is theoretically fairly easy to get into university
on a scholarship now. The only problem is, there is no budget. Like other social benefits, there are no stipends at all
and few are daring enough to actually pay for a degree at
a "republican" university.

Public schools are a somewhat different story, as
their teachers were officially under Ukraine's Ministry of

Education until not that long ago. After a persistent campaign in the DPR for individuals and legal entities to re-reg-
ister with "republican" authorities, these teachers found
themselves in limbo, with no social benefits from Ukraine
or the DPR. To be fair, the DPR did pay a one-time lump
sum of about 130 US dollars to public and vocational school
teachers, after which the issue was shelved.

Now, while post-secondary students, being older and
able to think for themselves, make a more-or-less conscious
decision to study in the "republic," school kids are basically
under the influence of their parents and teachers, some of
whom have been demanding that Ukrainian language and
literature be removed from the curriculum. Needless to say,
it will be difficult to find any Ukrainian patriotism in the
generation that is growing up in this environment.

Meanwhile, theaters and concert halls continue to operate in Donetsk, and a few clubs have even opened recently, taking most of the young people who have chosen to stay
in the DPR under their wing.

March 1, 2015
Radio Svoboda (RFE/RL)

2014

AUGUST 5

Mar'inka is freed.

AUGUST 6

The first battle for the strategic
city of Ilovaisk begins.

AUGUST 7

Battles at the Ukrainian-Russian border result in
the encirclement of Ukrainian units, which are
forced to retreat, and in Ukraine's loss of control
over about 87 miles of the border with Russia.

AUGUST 10

The second battle for Ilovaisk begins. Ukrainian
forces manage to cut off the supply lines
between the Luhansk and Donetsk Oblasts.

AUGUST 12

First reports arrive of a direct incursion by
Russian regular army units into Ukraine.
Thirty-four Ukrainian servicemen are killed.

AUGUST 14

The Marynivka border crossing is taken
over by separatist and Russian forces,
allowing an uncontrolled flow of goods
and people into Ukraine from Russia.
Ihor Plotnytskyi takes over as
the leader of the DPR.

AUGUST 18, 2014:

The Donbas volunteer battalion enters Ilovaisk
with the support of Ukrainian armed forces.

Ukrainian forces encircle Horlivka in the Donetsk Oblast and enter the city center of Luhansk. A convoy of civilians from Novosvitlivka and Khriashchuvate fleeing the war zone is shelled by separatist forces, killing eighteen people.

AUGUST 20

At the village Heorhiïvka to the south of Luhansk, Ukrainian armed forces defeat a company of paratroopers of the 76th Pskov Guards Air Assault Division of the Russian regular army.

AUGUST 21

Stanytsia Luhanska, immediately to the northeast of Luhansk, is liberated.

AUGUST 22

The first "humanitarian convoy" from Russia illegally crosses the Ukrainian border at the Izvaryne border crossing, controlled by separatist and Russian forces.

AUGUST 23

A Russian military company is defeated at Lysyche in the Donetsk Oblast.

AUGUST 24

As Ukraine celebrates its Independence Day, a "March of Shame" takes place in Donetsk downtown, also dubbed "the parade of captives." Captive Ukrainian servicemen are led through the streets of Donetsk in a humiliating procession between two rows of militants bearing rifles with bayonets. The parade is meant to create a parallel with the march of captive Nazi soldiers in Moscow in July 1944. On this day, four battalion task groups of Russian regular army with over 100 units of heavy weaponry equipment enter Ukraine, crossing the border from Russia and moving toward Starobesheve to the southeast of Donetsk, thus cutting off Ukrainian troops at Ilovaisk and encircling them. Pro-Russian separatists launch an attack from Donetsk on Dokuchaievsk (to the south of Donetsk).

AUGUST 25

Pro-Russian separatist and Russian forces take control of the strategically important Savur-Mohyla mound. The battle for Mariupol begins.

AUGUST 26

The battle for Ilovaisk continues, as the 8th brigade of the Russian army is defeated at Mnohopillia.

AUGUST 27

An attempt to break the Russian encirclement at Ilovaisk fails. Forced to retreat under heavy shelling by Grad multiple rocket launchers, the Ukrainian National Guard units lose sixty-three servicemen who cross the border into Russia and are captured there.

AUGUST 28

Novosvitlivka and Khriashchuvate in the Luhansk Oblast and Novoazovsk in the Donetsk Oblast are taken by separatist and Russian forces.

AUGUST 29

After a "humanitarian corridor" is negotiated by Russian president Vladimir Putin to allow Ukrainian troops to withdraw from the encirclement at Ilovaisk, Ukrainian troops are shelled by separatist and Russian forces and 254 servicemen are massacred during the retreat attempt.

AUGUST 31

Battles at Debaltseve and the Luhansk airport continue; thirty-five Ukrainian servicemen die.

THE DONETSK "UPRISING" A YEAR LATER: THE FUTURE OF AN ILLUSION

In a regular civil society, people's minds are usually troubled by issues such as abortion, the death penalty, euthanasia, corruption in government, and the freedom and effectiveness of the press. Some might see these topics as overblown, while others can barely have a cup of coffee without catching up on the latest news. But none of these matters trouble people's minds in the Donbas.

For as long as I can remember, I've always heard, "We don't make the decisions." All we could do was think about the price of butter or how expensive potatoes had become, while the powers-that-be had already decided everything for us. My friends, have you never stopped to think why this is so, why people whose strength of character and will enables them to descend half a mile below the surface of the earth while under artillery fire are so indifferent and apathetic to their own fate?

Don't rush to answer.

As I mentioned earlier, I've been witness to all the major incidents that took place in the Donbas in the past year: the "parade of captives," the first March rally, the corpses scattered on the asphalt after the notorious shelling of Donetsk. I watched the people in my region, destitute, crying, hating both you and me and everyone who was still with Ukraine, and kept having the same thought: What kind of people are these who live in the Donbas?

A strange question, isn't it? Despite the fact that I'm from here and I've spent my whole life in Makiïvka and Donetsk, it takes someone who has completely lost confidence in his ability to understand anything at all about what is going on around him to ask such a question.

The first time I asked this was at the March rally when my exultant fellow Donbasians elected themselves a "people's governor." And you know, I shouldn't even put that in quotes: Pasha[38] really was a man of the people, not because a majority of the people elected him, but because that majority was ready for the apostles to show up. That day, everyone who stood at Lenin Square was waiting for just one thing—for a character to take the stage, a wrinkled little puppet whose wobbly movements were controlled by strings, and who was supposed to relieve them of any responsibility for moving their own hands.

Yes, we all know now that the figure in question was Hubariev, but at that time nobody knew him and just about anyone who wanted the role of the new Stalin with the castings of the Donetsk blast furnaces on his chest could have scrambled up onto that stage with equal success. Essentially, it was a blank spot, a face in the hole board with an oval to be filled by someone taking comprehensive and uncompromising responsibility for the fate of the entire people.

Pro-Russia demonstrators celebrate and occupy the streets after attacking Ukrainian police and violently dispersing a peaceful pro-Ukraine unity demonstration.

I remember very clearly what happened that day, even a year later. The square was overflowing with flags—flags of the USSR and the Soviet navy, small DPR flags waved by kids running about and held by gloomy pensioners just standing around, flags of Russia and the Russian Unity party. People here and there were wearing Saint George's ribbons fastened to their sleeves and trousers. A few hours later, a few dozen rough-looking guys in camouflage would start shoving their way through the crowd to usher the future governor to the stage, shoving away local members of parliament who were already being called traitors. Finally, there he was, Hubariev himself, who would still be scrambling for a working microphone half an hour after he had reached the stage and trying to talk about "the treason of the junta" in Kyiv.[39]

The "elections" that took place that day may have been in the best tradition of Cossack democracy: after half an hour of extremely vague muttering by Hubariev on the stage, a man came out calling clearly and loudly for everyone to vote for Pavlo and elect him the new governor. Whether people were tired or just bored with such passive eloquence, everyone started shouting "Great!," "He'll do!" and "Go for it!" And thus the "people's governor" was crowned, to whistling and scattered applause. The rest is history.

What is interesting is that not one militant that I know now, who joined the "insurgency," was on Lenin Square that day. In terms of age and social status, the crowd had been on the older side and largely blue-collar, wearing caps and worn jackets, and looking extremely weary. It was quite obvious that they were all just so much Play-Doh, ready to be molded into any shape by those shouting at them "Fascism shall not pass here!"

Why did everything turn out like this? The thing is that we were taught to look at the world with a calculator. We were made to believe that everything could be counted and measured, shown in the common denominator of budget calculations: this is how it used to be, and this is how things still are now; it's not worth thinking about having anything more, or thinking about the future. "The Donbas is at work" is the phrase that will answer any question, whether it be about your crippled appearance after a twelve-hour shift, about the handful of coins in your wallet, or about your short-term future in some dusty workshop. It is the answer even to the Maidan[40] itself, where people dared to do the unthinkable: to convert working hours not into the number of screws they had drilled but into songs and warm coffee by the heat of a burning fire. That is a foreign language that we were never taught—and is that our fault?

Today, between the flying bullets and artillery shells, we are busy coming up with new slurs for those who still believe in the DPR. But what if the DPR itself is merely a reflection of a past that will not go away with the explosion of a grenade?

March 5, 2015
Radio Svoboda (RFE/RL)

A road sign for Donetsk damaged by shelling.

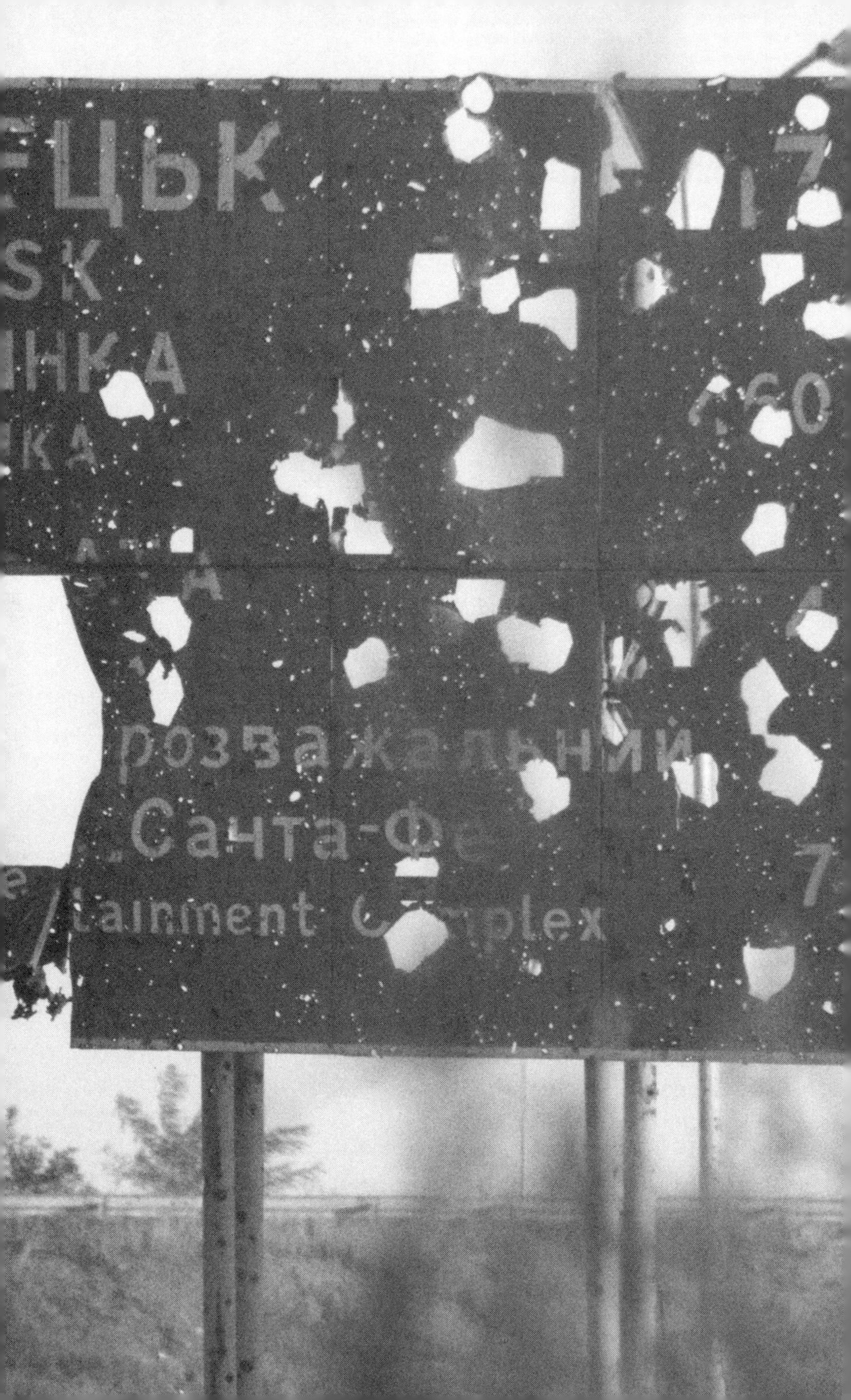
ЕЦЬК
SK
ІНКА
КА
розважальни
Санта-Фе
7
tainment C plex

AN EXCUSE TO PULL THE TRIGGER

Attitudes toward work in the Donbas completely determine how controversial the values and ideals from "mainland" Ukraine will seem. It is less a matter of wages than it is the ordinary coal miner's or steelworker's working and living conditions, conditions that don't allow a person to move beyond the mindset of an orthodox proletarian for whom only harsh working conditions bring a sense of pride.

Yet this is the very essence of the psychology of the people of the Donbas, for whom ideals like freedom and equality always came down to the choice of rope for their own noose. The mentality of a person who works twelve hours a day in very harsh conditions for a monthly paycheck of between 100 and 130 US dollars, often without any social safety net, turns into something that might be called masochistic, cursing this way of living and at the same time unable to imagine an existence outside of it. Is it so surprising, then, that this person couldn't care less about problems of corruption, freedom, rule of law, and democracy in their broadest sense?

As a result of the social upheavals in Ukraine in the winter of 2013–2014 and their continuation into the spring, many people living in the Donbas lost their jobs, which had a psychological effect: not only could they not buy groceries at the store, but they also saw a big part of their personal world fall apart. Empty words coming from their TV screens about the victory of democracy over evil did little to repair it. Without considering the difference in legal status, this situation bears remote similarity to Russia's emancipation of the serfs in 1861: after being granted their freedom, many serfs returned to their old masters, as they had no capital to become independent farmers, and some had no idea what to do with their lives next.

Moving on, I have to note that a significant number of today's militia really are men who live in the Donbas and who worked until the last possible moment with the shriek of shells flying over their heads. They joined the militia precisely because of what was going on outside. Only after they had lost their source of income and had a lot of time on their hands did many of them decide to join the militias and adopt clichés and ideas like *russkii mir* as expressions of their own experience. By the time the war broke out, many of those who worked in the Donbas had not received a single penny for their work, especially in the coal mines, yet they continued to go down below ground without the least hope of being paid.

Prior to the war, most of these men had taken over the local park and courtyard benches, washing down bottles of beer that they had just bought. Still, the very fact that they were prepared to adopt a system with a fairly rigid set of values, views, and opinions offered to them by the Kremlin explains the largely volunteer mobilization of recruits in the DPR ranks, which, admittedly, did not offer its rank-and-file a stable wage initially.

A fairly clear example of this is a militant with the *nom de guerre* Lis (Fox) who joined the *kazaki* just three days after he lost his job. Talking about his experience now, many months later, he says that he feels an amazing emotional surge only when he stands with an artillery round in his hands next to a field gun, because that feeling is stronger than his fear of his own death.

Fear as a decisive attribute of power is also ever-present in the minds of Donetsk residents and other people in the Donbas. Here you can distinguish a number of subconscious motives that spur locals to resist the government in Kyiv with everything they can muster, both mentally and physically.

First on this list might be the fear of change, which is partly entwined with anxiety over the loss of one's daily routine: work, home, work. Where, for most people, this is linked mainly with the practical side of the question—money and so on—for residents of Ukraine's eastern oblasts, this way of thinking has always coincided with their way of life and with a lingering Soviet mentality that is nothing more than a very longstanding tradition of giving responsibility for everything to a single individual, instead of deciding things for oneself.

The current information war has added its own characters to the long list of local stereotypes, where the elderly genuinely fear the "atrocities of Ukrainian Nazis," while the younger generation prepares sincerely to confront them in the battle for "a free Donbas." What mainland Ukraine simply laughs off—the myths about "crucified children" and mass rapes by Ukrainian soldiers—is becoming the new mental landscape in the Donbas and it is always two steps ahead of any rational explanations and arguments.

We should also keep in mind that the people who have fallen victims to this propaganda are inclined to believe this kind of thing in the first place. After all, not everyone here takes at face value the propaganda that Russian television channels broadcast.

In the end, the fact is that the majority of those Donbas residents who don't agree with the DPR and *Novorossiia* are the students, the teaching staff at post-secondary institutions, and artists: in short, the intelligentsia, which was not crushed by heavy manual labor and which has managed to preserve its capacity for independent thinking. Unfortunately, most of them have become migrants and have, with varying degrees of comfort, settled in other regions of Ukraine.

March 28, 2015
Tyzhden

2014

SEPTEMBER 1

Ukrainian forces retreat from the Luhansk airport suffering significant losses. Heorhiïvka and Lutuhyne in the Luhansk Oblast are taken by separatist and Russian forces.

SEPTEMBER 4

Battle for Shyrokyne in the Donetsk Oblast begins.

SEPTEMBER 5

The Minsk Protocol (Minsk I) is signed. The protocol requires a full ceasefire on both sides. On the same day, the Aidar volunteer battalion of Ukrainian forces is ambushed at Vesela Hora and thirty-five servicemen die.

SEPTEMBER 9

The battle for the Donetsk airport begins again with greater vigor.

SEPTEMBER 16

The law on the special status of the Donbas, required by the Minsk agreement, is passed by the Ukrainian parliament.

SEPTEMBER 19

A memorandum on the implementation of the Minsk Accords is signed. The memorandum requires of all sides a full ceasefire, a halt in place of all troops in their current location, withdrawal of heavy weaponry, and the creation of an eighteen-mile safety zone around the perimeter of the conflict.

THE VOICE OF THE DONBAS: HOW FIVE THOUSAND VICTIMS ARE "HEARD"

People who have lived for a long time in other oblasts of Ukraine and who drive into the DPR/LPR feel an almost physical change. This is not just because the scenery includes signs saying "Mines" or because men with knives, long beards, and machine guns accost them near the borders of the "republics." At this point, it is clear that reality has changed fundamentally; these residents are surprised to see that they are surrounded by a completely different world than in the rest of Ukraine.

As I have watched people's behavior in extreme situations more than once here in the Donbas, it is immediately obvious how much the war has changed things overall, turning people's priorities completely upside down. In the more than nine months of armed conflict with the DPR, Donetsk itself has turned into a different reality, even compared to what it was like here before the war. It is a world of dozens of tanks in the streets, deep trenches from exploding mines, traces of tank tracks on the asphalt right near the entrance to a café, buried missiles sticking out of the ground near playgrounds, daily searches, and suspicions of sabotage. Finally, there is the fact that none of your loved ones can guarantee that you all will survive to the next morning.

This is a reality where denunciations of family and friends have become the norm in the search for "enemies of the republic," where a nicely dressed eight-year-old child begs for "money for bread" on the steps of a Makiïvka supermarket, where the empty shelves at Amstor[41] mean you can't even buy a loaf of bread and have to make do with poor-quality substitutes like snack foods; where execution orders are handed out according to laws from Stalin's

A pro-Russia demonstrator holds an anti-Nazi sign in front of a barricade
outside the building of the Donetsk Oblast State Administration.

day; and where, even in "peace" time, grenades explode in
apartments, taking the lives of entire families. All this only
pushes people's thoughts away from the global-level considerations occupying the minds of most of those on the
"mainland."

For the most part, the population of Donbas has a fundamentally different mindset than the part of Ukraine to
the west of them, which has always accepted as self-evident
that the Maidan is the quintessence of democracy and freedom. The war has turned this divergence into an abyss. And
the point is not just that public opinion among Donetsk residents, specifically among those who stayed behind in the
DPR, swings between radical Russian nationalism and that
plaintive maxim "What's the difference, as long as there's
no war," even though war is already on their doorstep.
On the contrary, this position more clearly delineates the
specter of public opinion that currently meanders Donetsk
streets with little flags marked "Go, DPR!"

But let's ask ourselves, why are these people still here? Why aren't they running away from the artillery and the missiles (though many have already abandoned the Donetsk Oblast), but, on the contrary, keep going down into the coal shafts as before, under the blast of Uragans,[42] all while being paid a wage that is slightly more than what a generic new cell phone might cost today? What makes them live in apartments where the buildings next door often have no windows or walls? What exactly is this "voice of the Donbas" that was so often shouted about from the stands on the squares of Donetsk and Luhansk, and which has now moved to the walls of buildings along the main streets, in the exhortation "Let's make them hear the Donbas!"?

For starters, we need to say what this voice is not. It's certainly not the naive slogans about a "junta" and "Ukrofascists" that are repeated like a mantra in the DPR ranks. They had to work their way to that. Even the main "heroes of '*Novorossiia*'" like Hubariev and Pushylin[43] did not focus initially on how "fascism," if applied to Ukrainian realities, might be the perfect red flag to make the local population charge from corner to corner like an angry bull, hating first these and then those.

Still credit should be given to them. Coming up with the idea of using "fascism"—an absolute evil in the region, for a population that was mostly raised in the Soviet past and whose streets are still named after Feliks Dzerzhinskii[44] and Artem[45]—was simply brilliant. It has combined an entire cauldron of views with that indifference, apathy, Russian radicalism, anarchy, and the like that wash about in the ranks of "*Novorossiia*." Yet, the voice of the Donbas predates all this.

The yearning for a "strong hand," the rejection of basic democratic rules and norms, unmitigated xenophobia, both in politics and in the community, a general poisoning of minds with the idea and fear of "fascism"—this is what makes it possible for coal miners to keep going down into the ground, despite the holes in their pockets. This is what prevents hungry old people and impoverished teachers from coming up for air under the pressure of Russian propaganda pouring out almost round the clock from local channels and the press. This is why the monument to Lenin still struts about next to the monument to Taras Shevchenko,[46] and any attempts to change this situation will only run into even more stubbornness and resistance.

The voice of the Donbas has been sounding for nearly a year now and, thanks to it, there haven't been any architectural changes on the square in the center of Donetsk. Lenin is still standing, which can't be said about hundreds of burnt-out buildings and ruined lives. We've become used to think in facts alone, while the airwaves are full of the "eventfulness" of everything taking place. Yet, even in Donetsk itself, many people no longer remember why this war started: they think only of their own destroyed building, or perhaps of a father killed at Shakhtarsk. The DPR has managed to preserve in itself all hatred, fear, and stereotypes, while the local population finds itself in an emotional vacuum, where the least glimmer of a thought about possible action comes up against the cliché "No one has ever made the Donbas kneel down."

Even here, the "Russian Spring" is bailed out by that strange tendency among the locals to put up with everything from wage and pension arrears to shells and missiles flying into their apartments. This kind of "voice of the Donbas" is quiet, long-suffering—and absurd, believing in the now more than in the logic of the coming days.

April 19, 2015
Tyzhden

2014

NOVEMBER 4

Oleksandr Zakharchenko takes over as the leader of the DPR.

NOVEMBER 30

The siege of the Donetsk airport continues. Ukrainian forces retreat from the building of the old airport terminal and focus on defending the new terminal.

CHRONICLE OF DECLINE AND FALL: THE DONETSK OBLAST STATE ADMINISTRATION BUILDING

Initially, separatism was associated mainly with two places on the map in the Donbas: Slov'iansk and the Oblast State Administration (ODA) building in Donetsk. I found myself in the ODA several times, and each of those visits struck me as a certain stage in the history of Donbas—and the degeneration of those who were actively involved in it.

EARLY MARCH 2014

The first tense moments already made themselves felt on March 1, when a crowd of thousands of protesters came to the Administration building, which was then guarded by a few dozen special forces men. Despite the radical mood, those in the front ranks of the separatists stopped half a yard from the guard and tried to establish some sort of dialog with the men in helmets, who looked to be about 20 to 27 years old.

The older generation asked them to simply step aside voluntarily, and held back the more radically-inclined separatists, saying, "They're our sons too! Don't touch them!" These "sons" looked quite upbeat that day, even chatting a little with those who were trying to break through their ranks from time to time. The few pictures I managed to take show the benevolent smiles of the Hryfon[47] officers, even as they were surrounded on two sides by pro-Russian activists. As tensions escalated toward evening, a small group of separatists was allowed into the ODA building. While some separatists stood a little behind the guard, who had easily given way, the majority were still facing the line of special forces officers.

While what unfolded that day was clearly absurd, this turned out to be the most "reasonable" segment of the mass of separatists who spread across the entire Donbas subsequently. This is because most of those present were really Donetsk natives and joined the rally on the wave of political activism that had swept the entire country. Because of this, many were openly against causing any damage, however small, to the city, including the Administration building itself.

From time to time, someone in the crowd would yell, "Hey, why are you doing that?" when some of the separatists tried to storm the building or break windows with sticks. For some of the protesters, what was happening was already causing confusion over how things were supposed to unfold and what was supposed to follow.

I never did enter the Administration building that day, and I left Donetsk for Makiivka when Mayor Oleksandr Lukianchenko left the building, closer to evening. I returned and actually got into the building several days later, when a tent village was already set up around the ODA, and a "self-defense force" was inside, together with the Donetsk police.

When I entered, I was searched between the two sets of doors by separatists. Inside, I saw a very different picture: the young men from the Hryfon squad were sitting with their shields and helmets on both sides of the elevator, looking lost and lethargic. It was obvious from their faces how confused and unclear their understanding of developments was. Some of the men had already spent twenty-four hours there in full armor, literally sitting on their own shields.

APRIL 6, 2014

The next time I found myself in front of the ODA building was on April 6, when its courtyard was stormed. Separatists broke the iron grate, grabbed some of the shields from the special forces guarding the building, and took over the yard. Several flashbangs were tossed in and some windows were broken.

This time, the crowd standing around was hyper-aggressive and irrational. Where on March 1 you could hear people saying things like "Don't bust up the city" or "Don't do it like they did on the Maidan,"[48] today most of the protestors no longer cared about the consequences of their actions, and there was a clear order to storm the building. I remember one woman "protester" who stood there with a bottle of brilliant green dye that she poured on one of the guards while singing little ditties and egging on those who were trying to climb over the fence.

Pro-Russian demonstrators with icons and Russian flags on their way to a memorial in Donetsk.

LATE MAY 2014

My last visit to the ODA was in late May, when two lines of barricades had already been installed around the building. The first line of "defense" was made of torn up cobblestones piled vertically into a wall some 20 meters from the entrance. On top of it was some kind of wire, with rubber tires here and there. Right behind this was another wall, this one of tires. In the "courtyard" formed by these two walls, loudspeakers had been installed and stocky guys wearing balaclavas and unambiguous T-shirts bearing Russian symbols wandered around with bats in their hands. Some of them wore camouflage and gave off an unpleasant odor. Their hands and necks were a dirty brown after a week-long siege of the ODA building.

By then, tall barricades had been thrown up behind and at the sides of the building, too. On the very edges, hidden in a gap between old furniture and stones were tarred torches. Apparently, they planned to set the building on fire if there was a sudden assault. After the takeover of Slov'iansk, the mood in Donetsk was tense and people standing in front of the city's main building were openly discussing the future of the "great republic," handing out DPR flags and Saint George's ribbons, although most passers-by no longer dared to go beyond the first line of "defense" and come closer to the ODA entrance, let alone walk into the citadel that represented their future life.

When I spoke to a man standing by a tent set up that same day, I learned that Donetsk was already in constant contact with Slov'iansk and Strelkov. Of course, there was no actual coordination, but this self-anointed commander assured me enthusiastically that everything would be fine and that nobody was going to leave this position. To enjoy such a sincere exchange, all I had to do was pin to my chest the black and orange ribbon that was being handed out there. This made me "one of us" in the eyes of these people.

When I asked this man what they would do if an assault did begin, he answered that there were "enough resources" inside to stop the Ukrainian special forces at every floor.

That was my last visit to the Donetsk Oblast State Administration. After that, I did not even go into Donetsk itself for a long time, as it was gradually becoming a darker and darker city for me.

April 20, 2015
Radio Svoboda (RFE/RL)

THE WAR IN THE DONBAS

2015

JANUARY 9

The battle for Stanytsia Luhanska begins again.

JANUARY 13

The battle for the Donetsk airport continues; the airport tower collapses. DPR and Russian forces shell the Ukrainian checkpoint at Volnovakha using heavy artillery, killing twelve people.

JANUARY 20

DPR and Russian forces blow up the building of the new airport terminal; forty-four Ukrainian servicemen are killed.

JANUARY 21

The battle at Debaltseve continues. The battle for the Donetsk airport comes to a close with the withdrawal of Ukrainian forces, counting around one hundred casualties on the Ukrainian side.

JANUARY 22

In Donetsk, the Donetskhirmash bus stop is shelled by artillery fire and eight people are killed.

JANUARY 24

DPR head Zakharchenko announces an attack on Mariupol. The Skhidnyi neighborhood of the city is shelled, killing twenty-nine people.

JANUARY 31

In the battle at Debaltseve, Vuhlehirsk is taken over by DPR and Russian forces; thirty Ukrainian servicemen die.

FEBRUARY 9

The battle for the highway between Artemivsk and Debaltseve takes place; thirty-four Ukrainian servicemen die.

FEBRUARY 10

Several neighborhoods and the airfield in Kramatorsk are shelled by separatist and Russian forces using heavy artillery.

FEBRUARY 12

A new package of measures within the Minsk Accords (Minsk II) is agreed upon at the Normandy Format summit of Ukrainian, Russian, German, and French leaders, and signed by Ukrainian, Russian, DPR, and LPR representatives.
At Debaltseve, Lohvynove is taken over by separatist and Russian forces.

2015

FEBRUARY 18

Ukrainian forces withdraw from the encirclement at Debaltseve. Thirty Ukrainian servicemen die for a total of 179 casualties during the last month of the battle at Debaltseve.

FEBRUARY 22

A terrorist attack on the March for Peace in Kharkiv kills four people, including one minor and one police officer.

GRENADES AREN'T A BIG DEAL ANYMORE: EVERYDAY TRAGEDIES IN MAKIIVKA

Today, I'd like to share with you something that happened recently in a Makiivka neighborhood. It clearly shows how a war transforms ordinary civilians, never mind soldiers.

When Russia started actively supplying DPR militants with weapons, the completely unregulated DPR system ensured that illegal arms would flood the Donbas in almost unlimited numbers and find their way into the hands of locals, whether they were fighting or not. Buying any kind of grenades, assault rifles complete with full magazines, and other "trophy" small arms is no problem at all here. The system of distribution works like this: locals who have joined the DPR militias stock their houses and apartments with grenades and guns, which they obtain under the table from armories. Trophy weapons captured during combat operations with Ukrainian armed forces are sold to people who were not involved in the fighting but who want to buy something for personal protection. Some firearms are simply given to family members. My friend's father, whom I mentioned earlier, is a great example: he has two F-1 grenades tucked away in a liquor cabinet.

With the proclamation of a ceasefire in our city, the threshold of sensitivity to all kinds of emergencies has been lowered significantly. Before, during the fighting, a Grad explosion was greeted with no more than a bland statement of fact: "Grad." Now, in the silence of the ceasefire, any unfamiliar noise or explosion triggers keen interest, and a crowd of rubberneckers gathers immediately in the street.

A few weeks ago, tragedy struck a Makiivka family. A militant came home on leave and accidentally blew himself and his father up with a grenade he had brought home

with him on leave. A second incident happened almost before my very eyes. As it turned out, the reaction of the people who had gathered to watch the situation seemed even
more telling than the explosion itself.

That evening, a few militants who had come home on
leave gathered at a local gazebo. One of them brought his
two-year-old son along. Since I knew some of these people,
I greeted them and continued on my way. After I'd walked
a few blocks, I heard a deafening explosion.

It was so strong that I first thought another Grad rocket had landed somewhere nearby, or that someone had
shot a large caliber gun. Given the ceasefire, this was un-
usual in our area, so I decided to go back and see what had
happened.

Apparently one of the men had taken out a flash grenade and inadvertently pulled its pin. The grenade had produced a deafening blast and by the time I reached the spot
again, I saw that some thirty or forty people had run out of
their apartments, the DPR police were already there, and
the little boy was bleeding from both ears.

The toddler was standing by a bush screaming loudly,
while several of the adults around him were clearly disoriented from the shock. An ambulance pulled up just then
and took the little boy to a hospital while the "vacationing
militiamen" were put into a police van and taken in an un-
specified direction. But what caught my attention in all this
was not so much the blast itself, which was terrible enough,
but the bystanders at the scene.

What I saw was more than just indifference. Some
were standing and chewing on sunflower seeds, others
were smiling at a story about a similar incident that someone was making a joke of just then. Others were standing
there, knowing perfectly well that the militant had just
blown up the grenade himself without the help of "Uncle
Sam's bloody hand," but were blathering as usual about

An apartment building partly destroyed in a night shelling attack in the city of Horlivka (north of Donetsk) and blamed by DPR militants on Ukrainian armed forces.

how none of this would have happened if not for Poroshenko[49]—not the war and not the child drenched in the blood
in the entryway.

I spotted someone I knew in the group, so I went up
to him and in a mixture of anger and confusion asked him
outright: "Listen, why are they all smiling? What's so fun-
ny?" To which he replied, with a similar smile: "Grenades
aren't a big deal anymore."

Indeed, the level of sensitivity to the misery of others
that this war has caused is down to almost zero. And so,
people can watch grenades exploding next to them and
kids covered in blood almost with a yawn. When the war
first began, any shot, even from a machine gun, caused
panic among the locals and the smallest injury led to
screaming and fainting. Now, it seems that the only thing
that can move the hearts of these people is a Grad or an
Uragan raining down on them and forcing them to hide in
basements. Blood and suffering have become so routine on
the streets of the Donbas that locals are busy buying up
machine guns and fragmentation grenades on the black
market like their daily bread.

The postscript to this story is that the two-year-old is
likely to lose his hearing entirely, while his negligent father
was released and continues valiantly to serve, defending
the "holy fatherland" under the grotesque name of the DPR.

May 7, 2015
Radio Svoboda (RFE/RL)

2015

MAY 16

A battle between Ukrainian forces and an assault unit of the Russian military security service, the GRU, takes place at Shchastia in the Luhansk Oblast.

MAY 23

In the LPR, the leader of the separatist Prizrak battalion, Oleksii Mozhovyi, is assassinated after he accuses the leaders of the LPR of treason.

MAY 28

Russian president Vladimir Putin issues an order to classify the losses of the Russian military as "peacetime, while conducting special operations."

JUNE 3–4

Separatist and Russian forces launch a new attack on Mar'inka to the west of Donetsk. The attack is repelled by Ukrainian forces.

WHY THEY LIKE "TSARS" IN THE DONBAS

It's no secret that public opinion in Ukraine sees everything that is happening today in the Donbas through the lens of broad verbal caricatures, such as *"vata" and "vatnik,"*[50] "colorado,"[51] *"russkomirnyi,"*[52] and so on—clearly establishing in this way an ideological divide separating "us" from "them." But these terms are not merely a reaction to the separatists in the Donbas today; they have a history that goes back much further. We are effectively talking about archetypes in the public consciousness of the population of Ukraine's easternmost regions, where power has always been ascribed a sacral status, in stark contrast to its status in a secular democracy.

What we are really talking about is two fundamentally different models and views of government and its very essence, which could not possibly have arisen only now, as a consequence of current events. They have serious historical and psychological underpinnings. Moreover, this is true for both models. To my mind, the democratic model teaches individuals to look at the government, the main branches of power, and the head of state as hired employees whose functions are supposed to be completely regulated by the will of the "employer," meaning the people. No matter what wealth you enjoy, no matter what benefits you have from the position you hold, all this is only the consequence of the opportunities granted to you by the people themselves, and the official, just like the head of state, is only an expression of their will. In the democratic model, the psychological connections of its participants are also constructed differently, which makes individuals look at the government not as a top-down chain-of-command but as a horizontal one. This ensures that anyone can hold the highest posts in the land, thanks to the egalitarianism established in the time of the guillotine and the headless bodies of history's monarchs.[53]

Government is seen completely differently not only in the occupied parts of the Donbas, but also in the parts of the Donbas that are under Ukrainian control, and pretty much in all of Russia. This is a reflection of an old, deeply-rooted view of political power as a manifestation of divine will, something sacred; the head of state is perceived as anointed by God. Graffiti could be seen on Donetsk streets even before the war openly invoking this way of thinking: at bus stops, you could see the slogan "Orthodoxy. Autocracy. Nationality."[54] Of course, not all residents of Donetsk and the Donetsk area have embraced the idea of the sacralization of leader and nation. And yet, the icons of Stalin in a golden uniform on Lenin Square, the pensioners making the sign of the Cross three times whenever Putin's name

The building of the Polit (Flight) Hotel near the Donetsk airport, destroyed by heavy shelling.

was mentioned during the March 2014 rally announcing the DPR, and an almost uncompromising rejection of any changes to the political system, no matter what they might be—these are all an echo of the "golden-crowned" past, the image of which was the "Tsar-Protector," whom the people trusted absolutely.

Still, it is important to note the ambivalence toward power that has always been typical of our region and is today evident everywhere, including in conversations with local residents. Most of them were never entirely happy with the Yanukovych regime and the Party of the Regions, understanding perfectly well, even now, that those people had stolen public money and spread their corrupt network of cronies—often family members—across the entire country. But the minute you mention the Maidan and recent reforms targeting corruption, many of the ideological supporters of the DPR refer to the pre-Maidan period in almost sacralized terms. The past, no matter how tainted it was, will always win out over progressive change that moves the country forward. "Yes, it was bad," they will say, "but now it is even worse."

In the Russian Federation today, all these features of the Russian people's mindset are firmly ensconced in state propaganda, with the clergy kissing the hand of the "great tsar" (as happened in a well-known incident between Vladimir Putin and a priest at the Valaam Transfiguration Monastery on August 6, 2012), while ordinary Russians are genuinely proud of the "defender" sent to the Russian people by the Almighty Himself. In the Donbas, these motifs are reflected in a small way, manifesting themselves most clearly in the euphoria of the separatist "referendum,"[55] after which the people who voted for independence expected not just a geographic annexation of their territories by Russia, but the dissolution of the secular Ukrainian mentality within the holy circle of *russkii mir.* When nothing close to that took place and they did not return to their "home harbor,"

Russia, the image of the tsar was completely replaced by the metaphor of the "struggle against the traitorous junta." Meanwhile, the ideologists of the "Russian Spring" began to characterize the Donbas as the final bastion of Christian Orthodoxy and the battleground for the Russian people on the western edges of the "Great Power."

A scene from the 2009 Russian film *Tsar* by Pavel Lungin is very telling in this sense: the Russian people, dirty, hungry, and tattered, kneel before their "defender," Tsar Ivan IV, begging God with tears in their eyes that the tsar be forgiven, and then, together with this same "defender," crawl forward, calling for a new Orthodox metropolitan to guide this "great power." Today, in 2015, both in Russia and in the Donbas, all that has changed is the way of kowtowing to political leaders: the tradition of giving absolute power to the lord and master continues.

Of course, Zakharchenko, Plotnytskyi[56] & Co. are a far cry from crowned monarchs, a position that is basically claimed by Putin himself. But then they don't need to be crowned. In the Donbas it is enough that the local leaders establish a strong connection in public opinion with the Kremlin itself. After all, the crown of the Russian Empire will always be the ultimate guiding light for those fighting for a "free Donbas."

May 17, 2015
Tyzhden

WHAT IS UKRAINE TO ME? THE VIEW FROM MAKIÏVKA

I know this title looks like something from a fifth-grade assignment, but do not rush to judge me, friends. The themes I want to touch upon here are more than serious; I should probably start with the three myths that are still being broadcast on Ukrainian TV.

In almost a year of constant fighting, the destruction of buildings, and a *de facto* blockade of the region, a thought has arisen in many living in the "mainland"—one that is to some extent justified and is often broadcast in the domestic media. In a nutshell, it sounds something like this: "Granted, the Donbas is *vatnik*[57] country—everybody understands that by now. But after everything that has happened, the people of the Donbas, like characters in a Dostoevsky novel, have gone from feeling humiliated and insulted to feeling enlightened and remorseful. And now the Donbas is a cauldron of simmering social indignation that's about to boil over against the 'republican' governments." Let me put this quite bluntly: it ain't so.

Here's just one example. Given the widely publicized interview with a captive Russian soldier who claimed that seventy percent of the people in Makiïvka supported the "Ukrops," I am often asked: Is what he said true? I can tell you that no, it's a lie.

I don't know why his command told him that number—if they really told him anything of the sort. I know something else: when I go outside, I replay the one story in my head that I will start telling if any of these "patriots" reports me to the commandant here.

Obviously, I don't know all the thousands of residents in Makiïvka. But it is as dangerous to generate illusions during a war as it is to make tactical errors: nobody here stays up waiting for Ukraine's return with Ukrainian flags in their hands or singing Ukrainian songs at night, despite the fact that potatoes cost 28 Russian rubles[58] for a couple of pounds now. The pennies tossed by the separatists to pensioners, so that they might last another month or two, have lately been cause for euphoria and have started people thinking, "Finally we will be able to live better"—adding more ephemeral plusses on the side of the "people's republics."

What can you actually see in Makiivka? You see hundreds of cars whose owners have covered the Ukrainian flags on their plates with tricolored stickers. Dozens of *marshrutkas*—the minibus taxis—with an arsenal of separatist insignia, from Russian tricolors to patriotic slogans about the "Unbroken Donbas." People who have wrapped their passports in the "Donetsk Republic" covers sold at every corner. In a nutshell, a balance of 70 to 30 might well be true—only the *other* way around. I have to admit, though, that my personal sampling of the Makiivka locals I know comes up with even less optimistic figures.

This "uplifting" information works against us when it suggests the idea that we are one step away from victory here, as when my brother in Odesa doesn't understand why we "don't take it to the streets and tell them to get out," as though "we" wouldn't end up buried in plastic bags in the local woods. How many of those "we" still live here?

I've never agreed with those who pounded their chests somewhere in Donetsk basements during the shelling, screaming "We're heroes and the rest are rats who fled a sinking ship." Let's be frank: for many who left, this is no longer "their" ship. When it became obvious how the situation was turning, that Donetsk was ultimately drowning in a swamp of separatism and terrorism, many just gave up and said to themselves: "This is no longer Ukraine." I know such people. They have settled down more or less comfortably in Poltava or Kyiv and they aren't coming back, no matter what.

Nadiia Savchenko, a military bomber and helicopter pilot, one of the most prominent Ukrainian hostages captured by the Russian military. She was abducted from Ukrainian territory and tried in Moscow, Russia, on the charge of "illegally crossing" the Russian border. Savchenko was exchanged in a prisoner swap in May 2016 and went on to become a controversial politician in the Ukrainian parliament espousing pro-authoritarian views.

But there were the others, too, like the people whose one-year-old was sleeping in the next room as Grad missiles landed just outside their window. Can you blame them for abandoning such a "ship"? I can't.

And so, how many "we" are there? I assume that there might be thousands, but for the entire region, meaning the territory still under control of the DPR forces, the pro-Ukrainian population who have, in fact, not left for "mainland" Ukraine, are so scattered around the DPR that you end up with one pro-Ukrainian acquaintance per forty to fifty separatists.

I'm not saying that Donetsk does not have a few hundred people, myself included, who could go out on Lenin Square with blue-and-yellow flags. But the way things are today, this number is just a list of those who would fill a few rows at the local cemetery.

Let's go back to the title of this essay. This question—What is Ukraine to me?—has long gone the rounds among those of my relatives who are at least partly familiar with my views. Recently, my sister asked me that question after getting her Russian citizenship in Crimea. She honestly doesn't get why I still, as she puts it, "cling to Ukraine," a year down the line, while living in an area where everyone around me has the completely opposite view.

"What is Ukraine to you?" she once asked me. "What exactly? Flags on buildings, people in Ukrainian embroidered shirts in Donetsk, Ukrainian pensions for old ladies? You can have something like that with the DPR, just in different colors, but the soil under your feet is going to be the same, the same Makiivka. And that's all without people knocking down Lenin monuments..."

I listened to her carefully and thought that she had a point. Indeed, it's not the flag flying above Makiivka City Hall or the anthem on the main square in Donetsk that makes this land Ukrainian, although those are probably its outer attributes. It's also possible that they could perfectly well stop paying pensions in Odesa or Kyiv at some point, and Poroshenko and Iarosh would have hundreds of enemies protesting in front of the Rada building.[59]

In answer to my sister, someone who, until recently, had had the same passport with the blue-and-yellow flag in her pocket, I had to tell her that I didn't really know what Ukraine was. What I knew for sure was how it had ceased to exist: people woke up one morning in Makiïvka and no longer knew who they were—Ukrainians, Russians, or the "residents of people's republics."

I added that nothing could guarantee that those who called themselves "Russians" in Crimea today would not say they are "Belarusians" tomorrow, or stand at attention under Turkish flags. We can't run from one land to another all our lives, and we surely don't have that right during war. The state needs to remain in our heads, first and foremost. We can always figure out what to do with the flag and the monuments.

June 10, 2015
Radio Svoboda (RFE/RL)

A LETTER TO THE RUSSIANS

Allow me to remind you that I am a resident of Makiïvka. I have spent most of my life here, although I was actually born in Donetsk. Lately, my mind, like the minds of millions in our country, has been preoccupied with just one question: How is it that hatred, which sometimes requires entire generations to materialize, has grown in our soil in just a year and entrenched itself so deeply that it won't allow two unique peoples to move beyond the stereotypes that are being dictated by television today?

Of course, I don't expect an answer to this question and could probably not provide a proper one myself, either. But burnt-down buildings and rocket shells sticking out of the asphalt don't allow us to forego asking it at all. When you walk down a warm, sunny street and suddenly hear a mine explode and see dozens of people dead, after which quiet descends once more and the trams continue to run as before, it's impossible not to see the absurdity of this war—a war in which bloodshed is sanctified by ideas that never went further than the gates of a university.

Moscow views Ukraine today as a platform for dollar-driven American interests and Western values advanced to Russia's borders by ranks of missiles. And it sees supposed Nazism dominating our country. The Russian government sees in Ukraine not an original idea that is trying to find itself in the foggy aftermath of the Soviet era, but a threat to that same era, which was never erased in the Kremlin. Ice cream for nine kopeks and one-sixth of the Earth's land surface[60]—what more could one wish for in life, right?

But Nazism, the monster that is being used to terrify Russians so much, is typified largely by unity and blind worship of the one and only prophet who is supposed to

From left to right: Ukrainian pro-Russian politician Viktor Medvedchuk, whose daughter's godfather is Vladimir Putin himself; Russian Orthodox Church Patriarch Kirill of Moscow and All Russia; DPR head Oleksandr Zakharchenko; and LPR head Leonid Pasichnyk talk to the media following their meeting in Moscow.

lead the country to a grand dream. By contrast, where on earth can we find as diverse and varied opinions among citizens regarding their president as in Ukraine, where every new head of state is unlikely to do any better in terms of respect and success than his predecessors? And where in today's Europe can we find as blind faith in a leader and almost pious fear of him as in Russia, where the leader's hand is kissed by the clergy while the entire nation applauds any decision as though they were standing in a Soviet-style party hall the size of the entire country?

Dear Russians, when talking about Europe, it is you who say that the old gods have died and her new ones are not strong. You could be right, at that, if what you mean by "strong" is having strong moral values and goals. But then, what is so strong about Russia, which is trying to force us at the point of a gun to believe that the death of the Soviet Union never happened? Is dressing up Moscow, Tula,

Tiumen, and Petersburg in Saint George's ribbons and red Soviet flags anything more than paying homage to the past? Are you not just trying to resurrect that same thing whose death you mock in "rotting" Europe— a past that was unable to establish itself in sixty-nine years of existence?

By many socioeconomic parameters, Russia is doing better than Ukraine right now. While today the Russian nation is secure in its hard, protective shell of ideology, Ukraine has only a few delicate shoots of patriotism—albeit *real* patriotism—sprouting up from our soil. But if these signs of grassroots patriotism give you a reason to believe that forty million people have suddenly put on the Nazi swastika, I have to ask you: Who would want your version of prosperity, one that is based on endless delusion?

Dear Russians, right now, after a year of war in the Donbas, I'm absolutely certain that a person can wish for no worse enemy than history. No matter what we try to find in it, no matter what kind of episodes shape this mosaic of hatred, history itself is enough to leave a bad aftertaste of past offenses. There are some obvious things that we cannot ignore. Until you get it into your head that a Russian citizen has no right to come to a Ukrainian city, gather a group of mercenaries, and seize power and dig entrenchments; until you understand that the ethnic Russians in the Donbas are not those wretched cripples you see on TV, standing around their churches and wishing aloud for Russian Grads; until you accept the idea that the Ukraine of the past no longer exists (as I have had to realize myself); and finally, until you really hear the voice of those ethnic Russians in Ukraine who are not howling for help, but are crying for you not to help—until then all you will do is bring blood and suffering. Believe me, not one country in the world has been able to end blood and suffering through the violence of missiles.

We are still bargaining over the future. We are still shooting each other. Being in the very center of the Donbas and having neither a strong opinion about my present, nor a firm hope in my future, I just want to say that forgiveness is no less radical than war itself. If we manage to stop the war today, it is likely that we will find those who are able to forgive tomorrow. Therein lies my extremism, and I am calling on the Russians to make the same kind of radical choice.

July 26, 2015
Tyzhden

WHO LIVES OFF THE RESIDENTS OF OCCUPIED DONBAS?

A year after the occupation of parts of the Donetsk Oblast, a clear picture has emerged of all the social groups that not only survive in the DPR, but also feel quite at home here, in contrast to ordinary doctors, teachers, pensioners, and more vulnerable groups.

Strangely enough, at the top of this social pyramid are those who work in retail sales—mainly groceries. The non-food retail sector also has its privileged caste in the suppliers of niche products such as building materials or feed for livestock. In other words, those doing well are effectively monopolists in areas where, in the more competitive recent past, they struggled to make ends meet.

Whatever their social class, everyone needs to eat. Ukraine's deepening blockade of the occupied areas has enormously expanded the room for financial machinations and price-hiking, so that goods imported from Russia *de facto* duty-free are sold at inflated prices, while Ukrainian alternatives aren't available at all. Add to this the real cost of transporting goods from Rostov, Kursk, or even Moscow, which directly affects the final price. Meanwhile, the quality of food, especially sausages, is often dreadful, mainly due to certain schemes in use.

Russian suppliers are quite aware of the tight financial situation in the DPR and have a pretty accurate sense of the buying power of local consumers. High-quality food is an order of magnitude more expensive in Russia than products of similar quality in Ukraine, and transportation costs have to be added in. A simple calculation makes it clear that the price of a Russian sausage cannot be set several times higher than the average Ukrainian price, otherwise it wouldn't sell. Thus the products supplied are often of poor

Russian mercenary Arsen Pavlov ("Motorola") at his marriage ceremony
in Donetsk with Olena Kolenkina of Slov'iansk, which was attended by
DPR leaders Igor Girkin (Strelkov) and Pavlo Hubariev. The wedding
received a great deal of attention in the media. Motorola was
assassinated in his own apartment building in October 2016.

quality, so that when transportation costs and the local retail mark-ups are added, they end up at a relatively familiar
price point, although the quality is an order of magnitude
lower than what locals once bought for the same money.

Next comes some understandable confusion over prices in Russian rubles and Ukrainian hryvnias. In fact, most
produce at local markets is from nearby Ukrainian villages,
so the sellers are reluctant to accept Russian rubles. Still,
it has become common to see a Ukrainian price tag of 80
hryvnias and next to it a tag with 200 rubles, even though
the official "republican" exchange rate is supposed to be
2 rubles per 1 hryvnia. Most buyers figure the sellers are
shaking them down, but because of exchange rate differences between Ukraine and the DPR, sellers really do need
to demand a rate of 2.5, not 2, if they are to earn anything.
Because of complaints from consumers, the DPR recently

hiked the Ukrainian price to match the Russian tag, changing a nominal price of 80 hryvnias into 100 hryvnias.

The situation in the non-food sector is even more
complicated. The bulk of goods continues to come from
Ukraine. When the usual corruption regimen at block posts
is suspended because of fighting in Mar'inka, for instance,
serious shortages are common. At that point, buyers of livestock feed (to use the farming sector as an example) are
willing to pay just about any price for the desired bag of
compound feed. Naturally, as soon as this bag trickles into
the Donbas ghetto, entrepreneurial types jack prices up
sky-high until the situation stabilizes again, thus skimming
the financial cream off the patriots of "the people's lands"
(*narodnye zemli*).

Another class of local tycoons operates various unofficial currency exchange points, not to mention "cardhold-
ers" (which will be explained below), money-changers, and
basically anyone promising to help the unfortunate residents of the occupied territories leave the republics, withdraw money with their debit cards, and get an IDP (Internal
Displaced Person) certificate, or obtain a pass to leave the
ATO area. Let's look at these schemes one by one.

Due to a tacit ban by the DPR on the selling of hryvnias
for rubles at the "Republican Bank" and a number of local
unofficial exchange points, Ukrainian money can only be
bought from private dealers at markets or on the streets.
Obviously, they don't do this at a 1 to 2 rate in accordance
with DPR law. In reality, people are likely to pay 4.70–4.80
rubles or more for 1 hryvnia, depending on the amount
needed. Of course, the hryvnias are all brought into the
DPR from "mainland" Ukraine, which provides enormous
income for the "financial tourists," who earn their living by
buying goods for rubles that were exchanged at unofficial
rates as high as 1 hryvnia to 5.0 rubles.

A similar scheme plays out with the polite young
women stationed in cramped little corners and kiosks in

Makiivka, Donetsk, and Khartsyzk, offering to cash out Ukrainian bank cards. When this business first started, the fee for cashing out was ten percent. As the sale of passes increased and more locals could get out of the "zone" on their own, this source of income shrank, so that by now the offer has gone down to zero percent for significant amounts (around 5,000 hryvnias). The catch is that you still get your cash in rubles at the official 1 to 2 rate: for 5,000 hryvnias, you'll get 10,000 rubles. The fate of the hryvnias written off your account is easy to imagine: they end up on some account in Dnipro, where they miraculously convert into 11,000–12,000 rubles instead, depending on what the exchange rate is in a particular city in Ukraine and the difference with the rate in the DPR. The currency is converted once again. Less flush customers withdrawing small sums with their cards continue to pay high fees, but this is better than spending the same amount to try to travel out of the DPR and withdraw that same 1,500–2,000 hryvnias on your own.[61]

Getting a pass or an IDP certificate without leaving home is another goldmine in the "republics." Pensioners who have not yet decided to go to non-occupied territory (the Donbas outside the LPR/DPR) to get their pensions are offered all the necessary services: pay 1,900 hryvnias and in just fifteen days you have become the happy owner of an actual residential address somewhere in Kramatorsk along with a Ukrainian pension—even if you have to cash it out as described above. All this without leaving your apartment.

But this scheme also has its nuances. After the DPR began to pay pension benefits relatively reliably, far fewer people wanted to receive an identical amount in Ukrainian currency using such a complicated, tricky procedure. So, the IDP certificates are sought only by those who want to receive both a DPR and a Ukrainian pension. These cases are infrequent, but back in April 2015, the general confusion at the DPR pension fund resulted in many pensioners

receiving a "double" pension and believing that this pleasant surprise might continue indefinitely. Regardless, the
services for issuing passes, including electronic ones, now
constitute some of the most profitable business ventures in
the "republic," providing their owners with no less income
and as good a niche as the retail trade.

Passenger transportation is also part of this war-time
business. Monopolist carriers have jacked up prices for
travel out of the ATO area, and drivers make even more
money for carrying passengers without proper documents
through Ukrainian checkpoints. Initially, people had to
cross on foot, waiting in long lines in the heat, but quickly
crossing the contact line was "streamlined," and you could
negotiate with a driver who would take you whatever route
you needed without any documents and "leave" part of
that amount at the Ukrainian checkpoint. This business
has branched out into private carriers and taxis, which are
mushrooming and taking advantage of the bureaucratic
mistakes of the new Ukrainian government.

Few analysts covering occupied Donbas have focused
on this aspect of life in the republics, yet the DPR is not
only a haven for speculators and smugglers, but a mec-
ca for fugitives and criminals, who can join the ranks of
the DPR or simply lie low without fear that the Ukrainian
courts will reach them. Quite often, these individuals join
the ranks of the militias or engage in protection rackets,
thanks to their links to local criminal groups. Anyone with
debt or tax issues with Ukrainian banks, companies, or government agencies can also flee here to the DPR for a more
comfortable life without fear of being handed over to the
"enemy state."

Another social group enjoying a cut of the spoils of
happy life in the "republics" is the clergy serving the Russian Orthodox Church of the Moscow Patriarchate. Russian Orthodoxy has long been the *de facto* official religion
in the DPR and an inspiration for military feats "for the

glory of the Fatherland" among the fighters of the militias. This confession is now in great demand in the occupied territory. After Zakharchenko's announcement that there are only four officially tolerated religions in the DPR—Orthodoxy represented by the Moscow Patriarchate, Roman Catholicism, Islam, and Judaism—the smaller communities of other confessions are likely to leave the "marketplace" in the face of an increasingly rampant Muscovite Church and its clergy.

Wrapping up the list of the "republic's most fortunate" are the "militiamen" and anyone somehow linked to the DPR official entities. There's not much to say about the privileges these people enjoy, especially when ordinary residents—and even more so pro-Ukrainian patriots—remain at the bottom of social heap in the "people's republics."

July 6, 2015
Radio Svoboda (RFE/RL)

THE "ESPERANTO" OF VLADIMIR PUTIN

The war in the Donbas, with its thousands of victims and dozens of destroyed cities, has embodied in practice the theories of *russkii mir.* Since the outbreak of the war, diplomats have worked ceaselessly to find a way out of the stalemate that the two sides of the conflict have driven themselves into.

But the language of diplomacy spoken by European leaders to the boss in the Kremlin has only now begun to produce any results—after eight months of endless attempts to normalize the situation. Still, there has been no major breakthrough to this day and the conflict looks frozen rather than resolved.

This raises an interesting question. In possibly the most critical dialogues in contemporary history, are all the participants speaking the same language?

Once, on a Ukrainian talk show, well-known Spanish journalist Pilar Bonet[62] asked Ukrainian politicians a rhetorical question that, unfortunately, failed to get the necessary attention. Analyzing and criticizing Europe's response to the diplomatic moves "Great Russia" was making at that point, among other things, Bonet asked: "Could it be that Mr. Putin is the only thinking politician in Europe?"

When it comes down to it, clarity of messaging, an uncompromising stance toward Putin, and comprehension of his position could become the main means of disentangling of what's going on in the Donbas today. Bonet's thinking seemed to be that all of modern Europe's diplomatic moves were based exclusively in pragmatism and market economics—dry budgetary calculations. For European politics, diplomacy has long since been transformed into just another form of business, one in which minimal risks are figured

"Immortal Regiment" at the Victory Day parade in Donetsk.

out on a calculator. The future of European lands is discussed in terms of German pedantry and the cold logic of numbers.

The man running the Kremlin thinks entirely differently. Ever since the concept of *russkii mir* and "Great Russia" began to become tangible thanks to the actions of its primary proponent, an abyss has emerged that separates modern, civilized Europe and this man, whose ambitions do not fit into the simple logic of enrichment or territorial interests. Russian political and psychological reality is clearly taking on elements of fascism—the same fascism that the Kremlin has long been blaming on Ukraine's army and leadership.

Let us look at the key themes of *russkii mir*:

- the idea of the "special, historical mission" of the Russian people;
- the opposition of its cultural and spiritual environment to anything Western or European, as manifested in the idea of "Great Russia";
- the rejection of a number of international norms and conventions, and a challenge to the global system of

collective security by the occupation and annexation of a range of territories.

All this points to the reality that the Kremlin is not focused on trying to avoid sanctions or save the domestic economy, let alone to worry about the Russian soldiers dying in the Donbas.

We're talking about something fundamentally different—a difference that allows Putin to continue his devastating foreign policy and not consider any personal financial benefit or the reasons why outside forces are putting pressure on him. After all, a person who is standing at the pinnacle of modern geopolitics and sharing that spot with maybe five or six others like him is unlikely to care about adding a billion or two to his multi-billion-dollar personal wealth by shipping and selling coal from the Donbas or the remnants of scrap metal left from the factories here. Nor will he be especially bothered by his extremely low rating in Western countries.

The simplest calculation shows that constantly funding a huge army of militants, spending on social benefits for the "republics" far beyond what can be covered by local taxes, and even just a single day of Russia's presence on Donbas territory cost much more than any financial gain Moscow could possibly extract from this region. This was really Bonet's point: Putin's actions needed to be seen *through the lens of history* rather than just through the kind of business calculations that underpin the "deep concern" of his European counterparts.

Obviously, the war in the Donbas and Russia's policy of supporting the militants are politico-ideological choices springing from an idea, not pure pragmatism. But the question is, what is this idea leading to?

For now, Russia's entire propaganda machine, including elements that operate through local TV channels in the Donbas, is indoctrinating the Russian people and the local population here with an idea that is far removed from pragmatism. Nazism, fascism, and the illegitimacy of the Ukrainian government—all covered by Russia's "junta" rhetoric—are merely the visible markers that register Russian aggression and provide an image of the enemy's face.

The key idea is this: linked by the chains of *russkii mir*, the Russian people, in the broadest sense of the term, play a unique historical role as a counterweight to "decadent" Western society, which has been corroded by the ideas of sexual freedom, consumer economics, and distorted religious ideals. The image of Russia as a great state with a strong, intelligent "protector" like Putin holds minds captive from the top to the very bottom of Russian society, where the ratio of pensions to grocery prices is not much better than it is in Ukraine. This spurs ordinary Russians to think, condescendingly and disparagingly: "Without us, Ukraine is worth nothing."

With a nonstop flow of propaganda, Putin has created, effectively, an artificial media language, which is now spoken by the 140 million-odd people of the Russian Federation. The Kremlin's puppeteers have successfully ingrained a thinking in the masses that was previously cultivated by the founders of the Third Reich: "us vs. them," "friend vs. enemy," and "Russians vs. everyone else."

Why are we so shortsighted as to not notice this on the diplomatic front, as the enormous efforts of the German and French leadership fall apart when met with the cynical smirk of the Russian president? Perhaps he really is the only one today who understands that the various parties to this dialogue are speaking very different languages.

August 21, 2015
Ukraïnska Pravda

A LETTER TO MY COUNTRY

They say that humans do not exist outside of time. I would like this letter to be not some general impression of things, but a reflection of the time in which it was written. Because, just a year ago, these words would have been impossible, and one year from now, God willing, they won't be worth the paper they are written on. Allow me, as a person who has, in the process of making peace with war itself, mastered the art of war in its ugliest form—allow me to put together a few statements that most clearly express what is going on today in the minds of people who are Ukrainian citizens on the inside but who live surrounded by the ugly landscape of the DPR on the outside.

1. NOTHING HAS CHANGED IN MY COUNTRY.

It's hard to say this but, I'm sorry, that's how it is. The country's façade—redecorated with nice new police uniforms and the ever-present blue-and-yellow colors of our flag on everything but people's underwear—is not something that is worth giving up your life for. The only incontrovertible thing is this: pathways have opened for us but, so far, no one is taking them. After years of straining to reach the light, my country seems to have frozen in it. Corruption, obvious lies, protection from above, fisticuffs in the parliament, judges who can be bought off, and arbitrary laws—none of this has disappeared. But now it is "us" doing it. It would seem that the time that went by as we struggled will require more patience of us than the changes we fought for.

I can't help but feel that this could become a widely shared opinion for the next few years, during which our honorable political class will always use the need for more

At a base near Slov'iansk, members of the Ukrainian National Guard
carry munitions as they prepare to move in the direction of Donetsk.

time as an excuse. Of course, here, under the occupation,
the sense of justice is sharper; sometimes the few who today
view the Ukrainian "mainland" solely on their TV screens
desire to eliminate all kinds of things that someone in Kyiv
or Ternopil might not even have noticed. We see yesterday's
patriots being used to cut deals as those in power play with
them like a child with matches. It's worth asking if there is
a public desire for freedom as a goal, but no consideration
of the means necessary to achieve it. If that is the case,
then this is the worst dictatorship—one that no longer cares
about those who are still alive even as it hides its nature
under the sheet covering the dead—those same dead who
gave their lives on the Maidan, and the living who remain
here in the Donbas. Frankly speaking, though, most of you,
my fellow Ukrainians, have already thrown your handful of
dirt on us, as mourners do on a grave, which brings me to
my second statement.

2. MY COUNTRY IS MORE LIKELY TO GIVE UP
ITS CITIZENS THAN ITS TERRITORIES.

Again, let's be frank: the Donbas is just a mirage, while most of you are throwing stones of blame at those who leave the grey zone of the steppe. In the eyes of the rest of the country, we are already guilty, we have all been condemned to a certain degree, because we were unable to keep the Ukrainian flag flying over our land or prevent the deaths of thousands. We are guilty that someone in Cherkasy is shedding tears for a father or son, while those same deaths here in Donetsk are worthless because they are only imitations of the real thing—just phantom pain.

My fellow Ukrainians, be honest: Who among you has not had such a thought cross their mind at least once? We are afraid of them, afraid to say them out loud, and so the machine-gun fire says them for us. Between the young guy writing this letter in Donetsk and Ukrainian soldiers crouching in their foxholes there will always be a dozen excuses found to throw stones at each other. In this case, I ask you: What is the Donbas, after all? Because I don't believe that you just need our slag heaps, our huge manufacturing plants, the ideological rust that teaches us to love an abstraction of a country without a face or a language, a country that is deaf and mute. But who knows? Maybe that is precisely what Russia wants for us. Maybe they want even more hostility between us, who have a common goal: to see Donetsk Ukrainian. A state can think that way, but we shouldn't.

I don't want to compete in counting coffins. I don't want to know whether you fought at the front or once held a machine gun in your hands or slept in a basement to save yourself from whistling rockets. I don't give a damn about this. So much time and blood has flowed that death is unlikely to surprise anyone. That may be why I'm not that far from the truth when I present my third statement.

3. MY COUNTRY NEEDS FORGIVENESS; IT NEEDS TO FORGIVE ITSELF FOR ITSELF.

We have an external enemy. That much is unquestionable, clear, and understood. But are we going to continue to pretend that geographic origins are just points on a map and that a Donetsk coal miner is the same as a manager from Lviv? No. Cities determine ways of thinking, produce their own heroes, and shape different worldviews. To deliberately ignore this reality all those years was a huge mistake. Now, on pain of death, may God forbid anyone from suggesting that "one country" is just a slogan on a map and that we are actually so different that a map is the only thing to make us one in any way. After all, it is a disadvantage if we are afraid to acknowledge our difference. More than anything else, this fear is the "commodity" that has been traded on and successfully used against us by politicians for a long time now.

In the end, I want to say: Why don't we start by forgiving each other, without asking "what for," "why," "who's to blame," and so on? Why not start by forgetting who is a westerner and who is an easterner and start living in a new way, not on billboards with smiling paper faces, but in a truly unified country, where people are so different that they have succeeded when they are able to make themselves one? I would like to start with myself and apologize to all those who still have the honor of calling themselves Ukrainians, because I have a dream (with apologies to Martin Luther King, Jr.): I have a dream where I arrive in our country's capital and the word "Makiivka" doesn't mean anything, or it means no more than "Lviv" or "Frankivsk."

September 27, 2015
Tyzhden

THE HALF-LIFE OF THE *SOVOK*

"How much longer are we going to have to schlep the Donbas on our backs?" The longer the war goes on, the more often this question is asked in Ukraine.

At one time, the war was like a headache that you hardly noticed because of the shock you were feeling as if from an open wound. Now, as things enter a quiet phase with a nominal ceasefire in place, the public, especially the thinking part, more and more often demands an answer to this question. Because the Donbas means daily spending from the public purse, uncertainty about Ukraine's European future, and potential deaths and graves in possible future battles.

But the main thing is the uncertainty, especially with regard to those who still carry Ukrainian passports in their pockets while their hearts and minds hanker for the hammer and sickle and the red star. It is hard to quarrel with the fact that people with the mindset pejoratively referred to as *sovok*[63] reside mostly in the Donbas.

The uncertainty stems from the awareness of thousands of separatists with ideas of Communism, the Soviet empire, a massive revival of the Komsomols[64] in the occupied territory; and of the hundreds of people with Soviet flags ready to die in front of the Lenin monument on the eponymous square in downtown Donetsk just to ensure that it remains standing.

It is the streets named after Comrade Artem, the Red Army, the fiftieth anniversary of the USSR, the fortieth anniversary of the October Revolution, and the twentieth Congress of the Communist Party. It's also the DPR Communist Party, a serious force here. And all of this on a small portion of Ukraine, twenty-odd years after the colossal "evil empire" seemed finally to have sunk into oblivion. Or did it?

The current war in the Donbas is certainly a war with the past, among other things. Whatever the Kremlin's plans are, without widespread popular support at the initial stages, separatism would have been impossible. For instance, it's hard to imagine someone like Hubariev getting on a central square in Lviv and talking about Stalin, Lenin, or Putin to a storm of applause. Moreover, it was not just the old and retired people who gathered in March 2014 for the separatist rally on Lenin Square in Donetsk, as many tend to think, but also those between the ages of forty and sixty, who had lived a big chunk of their conscious life in independent Ukraine.

So what is going on? What does this term *sovok* really signify, as it drags Ukrainian society down today and tilts it to the southeast?

The infamous Lenin monument probably best illustrates how the words "Stalin" and "Putin" work on people, and explains the red-flag euphoria. This is the monument that some Donetsk locals have passionately protected from removal since February 2014.[65]

It is important to understand that, when people talk about Lenin and Donetsk, they aren't talking about Ulianov, the historical Lenin.[66] A quick survey on Donetsk streets would show that most residents know about as much about Ulianov as most Ukrainians know about Stepan Bandera—never mind Artem or the Baku Commissars after whom the city's streets have been named. Ninety percent of what they know is based on clichés found in the media; the rest they learned in school.

The Lenin that proudly towers over the main square in Donetsk and is now beautifully illuminated on the orders of the local "republican" leaders is not the Ulianov who founded the first concentration camps in Russia, presided over the Council of Soviet Commissars, or was the tyrant guilty of the deaths of hundreds of thousands.[67]

No. For them, Lenin is Kashtan ice cream for 28 kopeks and a warm May rally with their dads in 1979.

In other words, it's a deeply intimate personal past that has nothing to do with historical truth or reflections about civil war. Yet therein lies the deep connection that works so well in propaganda in the republics today.

Ideas have a limited shelf life, and they are easy to replace. Just like an isotope, all grand notions have a half-life. If all this propaganda had only been about promoting socialism or democracy with a Russian face, it might well have failed. But it is much harder for people to renounce a big part of their personal past when a huge hammer smashes down on the familiar stone image with a cap on its head.

Joseph Stalin portrait and a flag with Saint George ribbon's colors at the Victory Day parade in Donetsk on May 9, 2014. The totalitarian Soviet dictator was the mastermind behind the Holodomor, a genocidal famine in Ukraine and other parts of the USSR, that took the lives of millions of Ukrainians in 1932–33.

Sovok is more than values that live in our subconscious and present a danger to the unaware. Ideologically, it manifests in a focus on the "bright future"; the less effort it takes to get there, the brighter that future is. In this respect, Ukraine is united in waiting for that future to be brought to us.

The Soviet Union passed on two national ideas to the citizens of the "Great Russian" successor states: "Moscow is the Third Rome" and "I'm getting the hell out of here."

The former doesn't threaten us because that place doesn't exist on the map. As for Ukraine's EU membership, the impression is more and more that most Ukrainians consider it to be an exit door.

Should it then surprise anyone that even a Soviet people looking around bitterly at their surroundings always looked at the West through rose-colored glasses? Enemies could only be the people who lived in the apartment next door, not "over there," in the West, with all those Parisian promenades.

The ontology of the builder of a "red future" immediately switches to a ready-made object that has long passed the building inspection. The question then becomes, in this light, has the "civilized" part of Ukrainian society moved that far from the Donbas "savages" who hanker after the *sovok*?

Not really.

It's true that you are less likely to meet someone lamenting over the demolition of a Lenin statue the further west you go from the Donbas. But while those in Donetsk see paradise in the past, with its cheap sausages and inexpensive travel, those in Kyiv wait expectantly for paradise in the future, harboring a dream of Europe that is something close to a national neurosis. Europe, with its clean streets and decent health insurance, has become so desirable that the "European future" has taken on the shape of a halo, replacing the hammer and sickle with a circle of stars.

Unfortunately, we are still a long way from understanding that the EU with its relatively fair justice system, high standard of living, and respect for civil rights, is a club of the most developed states—not the source of limitless loans to help the dying. We are so desperate to rush through its door that we forget that Sweden was not transformed by Denmark into today's Sweden, and the Czech Republic did not sit back while Germany transformed it into what it is today. All these countries joined the EU because they had developed their economies and demonstrated respect for human rights.

As long as Ukraine's political ranks are filled with "businessmen," with habits formed in the murky 1990s, who merely change political colors every five years, and as long as the national dream remains a visa-free one-way flight from Kyiv to Berlin—preferably with no return flight—the sovok mindset of "I want it all, and now" will be impossible to eradicate, in both the west and the east of our country. Because we are merely replacing the myth of the happy communist future just around the corner with the myth of Eden somewhere on the Champs-Élysées.

October 18, 2015
Ukraïnska Pravda

Pro-Russia militants in Donetsk attack peaceful demonstrators rallying for the preservation of Ukraine's unity. The pro-Russian group, mostly youths in balaclavas, subsequently celebrated their actions by screaming that they had smashed "the fascists."

IRRECONCILABLE DIFFERENCES

In the last eighteen months, the war in the Donbas has been presented from many angles. Ukrainian experts and political pundits keep offering competing views as to why the situation arose and how it might be resolved.

A geopolitical vector is generally seen underlying what is happening in the region, and so the conflict is interpreted as a clash between the ossified Russian reality inherent in a fundamental rejection of all things Western and Ukraine's European aspirational efforts, which were halted with the occupation of Crimea, and the open, bleeding wound of the cities in the ATO zone. Put differently, by annexing the peninsula, Moscow gained a major bridgehead in the Black Sea region for the deployment of military force, while it put the Donbas on a short leash for the long term, which it can jerk to stoke up hotspots à la Marïnka,[68] should Ukraine make the least move to get closer to the EU.

However, in the DPR itself, hardly anyone thinks about what's going on in geopolitical terms, summing up their main complaints against the Ukrainian side in a few stale sound bites that nevertheless remain fairly relevant to this day. At the beginning, when the conflict had not yet reached its current massive scale, several attempts were made to set up a telebridge between Donetsk and Kyiv, to allow residents of the two cities to talk to each other directly, without the distortions and informational stereotypes inherent in media presentations. However, the attempt to find common ground always ended up the same: ten minutes in and both sides would be shouting at each other. Yet, over the course of this too-brief period of time, it was possible to catch a few basic beliefs that were so radically opposed to each other that there really was very little purpose in discussing them.

Belief 1: The Maidan was an unconstitutional over-throw that gave power to the "junta," a political group of individuals who took over in a revolutionary military fash-ion. None of the three conditions for changing the pres-ident—impeachment, death, or resignation—was present and so, from Turchynov[69] on, the entire government in Kyiv was illegitimate.

The paradox in this position is that, even in March 2014, at the infamous separatist rally in Donetsk, it would have been very hard to find a couple of dozen individuals who were actually demanding the return of Viktor Yanukovych; for most locals, he was no less repugnant than Turchyn-ov himself and hardly anyone considered him the head of state at that point. The controversy only became stronger with the passage of time, and when the official term of the self-exiled president came to an end, those who spouted this logic suddenly had no answer to the question, "Who then, in your opinion, is the legitimate leader of Ukraine?" I personally have heard some truly absurd responses to this question, ranging from "nobody" all the way to "why not me!"

The Ukrainian position is the exact opposite to this ar-gument. In the spring of 2014, a coup took place in a num-ber of cities in the Donbas and, having taken over illegally, a group of militants—which can also be read as a "junta"—came to power and all the "republican" authorities were therefore illegitimate.

Belief 2: The Maidan was a campaign completely or-ganized by the United States and involved paid protesters or people who were duped by Western propaganda. In Do-netsk, the Heavenly Hundred[70] have traditionally been in-cluded in the latter.

The slogan "The Donbas is at work" rather neatly illus-trates this opinion because, in the trains and buses that were taking gopniks[71] from Donetsk to show support for Yanukovych, not even one percent were truly interested

in schlepping to the capital. Most of the residents of Donetsk watched events unfold while sitting sullenly in their
armchairs after their back-breaking shift at work. Complete
apathy toward and distrust in the slogans being promoted
in Kyiv was the main feature of regional attitudes toward
the Maidan.

Here, too, the Ukrainian position was the opposite.
Events in the spring of 2014 in Donetsk were a campaign
organized entirely by Moscow, which put together a team
of well-paid operatives shipped in from the Russian Federation and locals who were duped by Russian propaganda.

Belief 3: All death and destruction in the Donbas is
entirely the fault of the Ukrainian Armed Forces and the
leadership of Ukraine.

Probably the most painful and irreconcilable issue,
this is also the most politically charged. With every death
and every burnt-out building in Donetsk and other cities,
a tsunami of propaganda has flooded the airwaves, pre-
senting the event—depending on the slant of the particular
TV station—in a polemical light. Far removed from any the-
orizing, this argument remains an impenetrable wall to this
day, standing between those who have buried a loved one
during the war, whether they live in Zhytomyr in right-bank
Ukraine, or Horlivka or Donetsk. The "argument of death"
makes people ignore the voice of reason and feel only hatred toward the other side.

Understandably, opponents of the "republics" adhere
to the opposite view here: all the death and destruction in
the Donbas is exclusively the fault of the militias and those
who support them.

And that's what the phenomenon that people call the
conflict in the Donbas looks like today—if we move it into
the realm of words and shut out the artillery and Grads for
a moment.

November 22, 2015
Tyzhden

A FEW FAIRYTALES ABOUT THE DPR

Whenever conversation comes around to stereotypes of the DPR in the heads of my fellow Ukrainians, it will usually involve people who get their information about the occupied territories from the distorted mirror of the press and who have never been in Donetsk themselves, or in other cities in the "republics" since they were taken over. Still, there are also those who have managed to learn a bit about the features of the "*novorusskii*"[72] way of life and are still convinced that, since the summer of 2014, nothing really has changed.

Let's call the first myth "them." Those who believe it typically are of the opinion that there is a certain critical mass of people united by a common desire to tear Ukraine down, and that these people live mostly in the DPR itself. In reality, there is no such thing as "them." In all actuality, there are only the following:

1. People who pull duty at separatist checkpoints because they are paid to do it, they don't have to risk their lives to do it, and they can benefit financially from the huge flow of vehicles.

2. Those who fled or quit the ranks of the militias and returned to their traditionally marginalized lives where they have become caught up in alcoholism and drug addiction.

3. An extremely thin layer of the ideologically inclined, who started back in 2014 with Strelkov in Slov'iansk, and who still believe in "a country from Odesa to Kharkiv." Another important characteristic of theirs is the inability to engage in anything other than war. This is what keeps them in the barracks to this day, despite

their thorough dissatisfaction with what is currently going on.

4. Finally, there are the completely cynical and transactional bosses, who don't give a hoot about any of the other groups and who have stolen everything that could possibly be taken, who have brought under their control all the cash flows of the region, and who are 100 percent carrying out orders from Moscow. Moreover, we're not just talking about Zakharchenko and his inner circle. It is worth considering also members of what one might call the middle class; they are about as interested in the war as the random man in the street in Berdychiv.[73] After all, it has already brought them its biggest perks in the form of stolen villas and other people's foreign cars. At this point, any widening of the war would merely expose these individuals to unjustifiable risk once more.

Of course, I haven't mentioned the broader mass of the militia, mostly standard hired labor who show about as much initiative as day laborers on a housing project. Somehow managing to survive from paycheck to paycheck, these people are basically mercenaries with local roots. Most of them admit quite openly that they don't give a damn about Odesa and Kharkiv, while many don't even think as far as the shores of Mariupol.

The other stereotype about "republican" territory is this: "No one is left there at this point," meaning that all the people with pro-Ukrainian views have completely abandoned their hometowns. Hearing something like this is especially upsetting and painful for two reasons: first of all, because it's not true, and second of all, because this kind of notion is often expressed by journalists who really did leave Donetsk some time ago. Percentage-wise, I think we can talk about at least 25 percent of *zalyshyntsi*, the "remainers," as being loyal to the Ukrainian government. Moreover, because of the latest games by the "republics" with elections and gas supplies, the number of those who are unhappy with the DPR has grown noticeably, even compared to this past summer.

Too often, this stereotype turns into another one: since "no one is left there," then we might as well cut off all ties with the "republics" because the collapse of food, energy and transport will supposedly ensure victory in the war, and "they'll be begging us to take them back." No, they won't. The DPR has switched to the Russian market by almost 99 percent, which means that not only basic goods are coming to Donetsk from there, but also delicacies like smoked salmon, squid, shrimp, caviar, expensive champagne, and wines. The same is true of non-food supplies, although prices are definitely hard on the wallet. Just about the same processes of reorienting to suppliers in the Russian Federation continue today in the fuel sector, while everyone who so wishes can easily enter Ukraine through Russia.

Security is another issue. A lot of people in the rest of Ukraine are convinced that the 1930s have returned to Donetsk and that people are being grabbed right off the street to be thrown into dungeons. There is some truth to this—but only in the sense that the DPR basically lacks any kind of legal system, and the justice you receive in a court in any dispute is determined by the presence or absence of a machine gun across your chest. You can be detained for looking in the direction of a "commandant" in a dubious manner, or you can be locked in a basement on suspicion of spying,[74] while any obvious displays of something Ukrainian—the flag, the national colors, and so on—are punished immediately. But everybody in the Donbas knows this very well, so you'll never see any blue-and-yellow insignia anywhere. Outside the buildings of the "interior ministry" or the "militia headquarters" you will only ever see one or two pedestrians walking by, while even among friends conversations tend to be restrained and cool, reflecting a mutual distrust and fear that someone might betray you.

Last but not least, a few words about Donetsk itself. If you were to draw lines from the Pivdennyi Bus Station to the Main Train Station, and then to the Motel bus stop, you would enclose a clean, well-swept, gleaming triangle where cafés, theaters, retail chains, and a few restaurants and nightclubs still operate. Beyond this triangle is the ordinary city that Donetsk was before this war. The closer to the outskirts you go, the more often you see broken up roadways and shelled buildings. And there is a sprinkling of districts like Zhovtnevyi, where there is almost no life at all.

In "republican" Donetsk, the population has shrunk severalfold. There is a permanent feeling of tension in anticipation of artillery fire and the occasional explosion. Worse, there is no legal guarantee of security whatsoever. But anyone who claims that the city has turned into a Stalingrad or into another Pryp'iat[75] simply doesn't know Donetsk at all.

December 13, 2015
Tyzhden

DONBAS: SEVEN HUNDRED DAYS OF SOLITUDE

February 1, 2016 marked seven hundred days since the first separatist rally in March 2014, which took place on Lenin Square in Donetsk.

Few knew then that the bland speech of the pale Slavophile Pavlo Hubariev, coupled with the fluttering Soviet navy flags, the tearful outpouring at the icons portraying Stalin, the Russian tricolors, and the men in striped navy-style undershirts would blend into a single patriotic stream of *russkii mir*, drawing the borders of the reasonable along the current line of contact between combatants and its checkpoints. But then the notion that knowledge is power doesn't seem to apply in the steppe. After almost two years of patriotic drooling over Russian flags and frenzied mantras calling on the Russian president to "come," the arrival has never taken place. Yet the patriotic drooling has not diminished, either. As before, life in the Donbas is still pretty much in "Putin, come!" mode, only that the shouting is a bit more muted, almost whispered, with a sullen glance at old Ilich.[76]

You would think that two years of wild inflation, permanent shortages, nonstop shelling, predatory exchange rates and prices, persecutions, hungry winters, and unanswered pleas for salvation directed at the Chechen mercenaries (whom the locals had greeted with bouquets on their first arrival) should have persuaded even the most hardcore supporters of the "Russian idea" that the national grandeur of Russia was not good for the health of those who dreamt about it. But "Donbas unbowed" is still replete with St. George's ribbons on the shuttle minibuses of Donetsk, *The Torch of Norovossiia*[77] is still available in city restaurants, and people continue to dream of having "their own" passports and—hope of all hopes—of integrating with "our native Russia" to rid them of the fiction of those three renowned letters, "D-P-R."

Indeed, the political preferences of those who did not wish for anything have clearly evolved. In March 2014, the people calling themselves "republicans" were bubbling with anger at the "Jew fascists," proud of their "young state" and the feel of a Russian passport in their trouser pockets. By 2016, the same "republicans" are filled only with the now-familiar wish for "anything but war." Yet, this mental watermark is actually not as naive as it may seem at first sight: it's far easier to break down the myths of Slavic greatness than to break down indifference toward either side. To a great extent, indifference and apathy, political amorphousness, and metaphysical pragmatism are endemic to the character of the local population. It took a colossal professional effort for Russian propaganda to move them from absolute zero toward the tricolor. At this point, however, the pendulum has swung back to zero again.

Of course, zero in the Donbas is always "anything but Ukraine." The locals may feel as much frustration as they like with Zakharchenko's cynicism while sitting around the table in the evening; come morning, like chameleons, they are back to wearing the colors of the DPR. In other words, discontent with the DPR does not guarantee love for Ukraine. Two years of round-the-clock professional propaganda that first had the "militias" falling in to "The Farewell of Slavianka,"[78] then burying members to the tune of Chopin, have led more and more often to the utterance by those who have lost family in the Donbas that "I will never forgive this." Multiply the number of unmarked graves near Donetsk by two or three and you will get the real number of individuals in every family in Donetsk, Torez, or Khartsyzk who will blame Ukraine if war flares up again in the Donbas. But why wait so long? A short conversation with the widow of a militant always reveals one thing: "My husband

From left to right: DPR "defense minister" Vladimir Kononov, Donetsk-born
Russian singer Iosif Kobzon, and the commander of the Somali battalion
Mykhailo Tolstykh (Givi) on Russian holiday known as the Defender of the
Fatherland Day, February 23, 2015. Tolstykh was assassinated in February 2017.

died defending his family and children." Only rarely will
you hear, "They should have never started this."

The problem is that those who initially joined the militia—and managed to survive these two years—reflect the social makeup of most of the Donbas: the marginalized workers. Without exaggeration, for twenty-three years, these
people felt like powerless beggars, migrating from the coal
mine to the factory with a wage just big enough to numb
their worries about the next day. To be fair, they didn't feel
any real difference when *russkii mir* first arrived, offering,
together with the usual vodka and *pelmeni*,[79] something
that they were unable to glean from the Ukrainian national
idea: hope. The hope that, from now on, things would be
different and that there was a chance to change everything.
As it turned out, things did really change for many former
fitters, master burglars, and one-time jailbirds: those who
managed to quickly figure out which way the different

winds were blowing in the "Russian Spring" are now cruising around Donetsk in SUVs or living in the nationalized (expropriated) mansions of one-time local prosecutors. Most have remained on the edge of the abyss, migrating from separatist checkpoints in 2014 to hot spots in 2015, and to their local hospitals' trauma centers in 2016.

This existential line offers a striking image of the fundamental ideas evolving here in the Donbas. The initial wave of imperialists who rallied for a "*Novorossiia*" from Odesa to Kharkiv with Strelkov at the helm was replaced by a calculating, pragmatic leadership cadre with Oleksandr Zakharchenko as its central figure. Strelkov's units, now cloaked in legend as "modern-day bogatyrs,"[80] were very quickly replaced with private military companies and nameless people like the notorious Wagner Group, MAR, E.N.O.T., and the Moran Security Group.[81] Soon enough, the remains of the former ideology-driven soldiers of fortune were found blown up in their own cars, with a bullet through the head right in downtown Donetsk, or eliminated like the notorious Troia battalion.[82]

By the way, that sensational event was only reported in the Ukrainian media. An incident of such an unbelievable scale, where over 100 men were wiped out in the DPR, did not make it to any local TV channel or the "republican" press. The only coherent description of what happened was in a letter from Evgenii Shabaev,[83] a Russian official representative of the Donetsk "Republic"[84] to "DPR leader" Oleksandr Zakharchenko, demanding an explanation for the "massacre in Ozerianivka."

It turned out that around a hundred men from the Troia battalion vanished in the most predictable way possible and in line with the best traditions of the local steppe: in bags. According to Shabaev, Russian patriots packed ninety-two of these patriotic bodies in plain black bags and moved them in two trucks in an unknown direction. There are few reasons not to believe him. His bold demand for an explanation had barely reached Zakharchenko when Shabaev suddenly was no longer the official spokesman of the Donetsk "Republic" in Russia and was persuaded to go into early retirement if he didn't want to join the ranks of the "Trojans."

The Prizrak battalion[85] and a slew of other LPR and DPR units are in a similar position. Their members are being dismissed in droves and sent on indefinite leave. Funding for the largest military corps, also, is far from ideal: the average pay for rank-and-file soldiers dropped from 360 US dollars per month in 2014 to 240 in 2015 and has sunk to 110–240 now, depending on the unit and the assignment. In other words, the idealistic believers in *"Novorossiia"* have been displaced by the enterprising advocates of "special regions" who see an opportunity for making money, which has totally confused the locals about the difference between the notion of a "republic" as part of Russia, and an autonomous region, as part of a "neighboring state," as the DPR boss himself described Ukraine in his latest press conference.

It's true that the back-and-forth of flirting with Kyiv and making forceful statements in favor of the DPR's independence, coupled with the "republican" leadership's lack of any evident strategic plans, the parceling out of key business sectors to the military elite, and, finally, the merciless crackdown on all dissent, have seriously undermined Zakharchenko's initial image as a kind-hearted strongman who held the people of the Donbas—portrayed as a hapless old woman in propaganda posters around Donetsk—to his breast. This has also cast a shadow on all the well-known militants loyal to him in Donetsk, especially the Somalia unit and its notorious commander Givi who not only avoided supporting Troia when it was being wiped out, but openly questioned the heroism and merits of its men.

Naturally, all this inspires some hope for the prospects of Ukraine, though, truth be told, one should not be too optimistic. The idea that Russia might fall apart in a few months because of plummeting oil prices, or that it might once and for all forget its satellite "republics" in the conflict zone, pushing them through the door of the Minsk accords and to the feet of the Ukrainian state, might present too high a price for Ukraine. It seems that Kyiv's politicians have failed to comprehend the key message of this war: the conflict in the Donbas is not a budget calculation or the result of someone's revenue predictions, based on a realization that the cost of maintaining an army here exceeds the income from the factories that have been cannibalized for scrap or the coal that has been shipped to Russia. Such considerations will never persuade Moscow to stop its war in the Donbas.

Indeed, a quick economic assessment shows that the cost of a week of Russia's presence in the "republics" does not compare to the minuscule income that the "local government agencies" manage to squeeze out of the few remaining businesses in the occupied territories, in taxes and other, less above-board, charges. This war is a long-term, well-devised metaphysical project whose roots bear no relation to the economic cost of keeping a Motorola and a Givi in Donetsk, or paying miserly pensions to the "republican" pensioners. Reinforcing the rigid chain of command of a military dictatorship, engaging in active propaganda, expanding local media, establishing an "Academy of Interior Affairs"[86] that trains those who just yesterday were Ukrainian students, proselytizing in schools and DPR-owned enterprises, and deepening economic relations with Russia—all this signals that the next two to three months will determine what the entire year will be like. As the key and only actor in this war, the Kremlin will, once again, determine the course of history, while, once again, all we will be able to do is adjust, however awkwardly, to Moscow's initiatives.

In fact, the collapse of Mr. Zakharchenko's image is not worth getting excited about. The Donbas mentality

flip-flops between deep bowing and complete indifference to those who get shoved aside by someone stronger.
When Strelkov, who had managed to become a legend in
just a few months, left Donetsk, many people, including the
militants, were in shock and thought that the Donbas was
once again being thrown under the bus. But if Strelkov left
without saying goodbye, Zakharchenko came in without
saying hello, never explaining who he was and where the
previous legend had vanished to. Dinner was served and
the locals ate it. The same will happen if Moscow decides
to replace Zakharchenko with someone less reserved: "The
Donbas is at work"[87]; don't ask unnecessary questions.

What is often referred to as the X factor should not be
forgotten in the Donbas, either. The idea that the Kremlin
completely controls the DPR and the LPR is not entirely correct. Clearly, Mozhovyi,[88] the Troia and Odesa battalions,
and a number of *kazaki* units that were summarily dealt
with not that long ago represented deviations from the pre-
set algorithm of actions. It's not even really about them.

"Eliminations" in working with local staff have been
an integral part of the young pseudo-states since the time
of Girkin and his trip from Slov'iansk to Donetsk, where
Khodakovskyi's militants were lying in wait at one of the
bases, ready to shell their own. The militants refer to these
events as "work issues"—provided that they aren't the ones
who end up in the black bags. There is an important point
here. Purging inconvenient units is not really part of the
Kremlin's complicated plan. In an environment where every competitor has a battalion backing him, the arms trade
that has been thriving since the massacre at Ilovaisk[89]—part
of it extending to the Caucasus, according to some sources—and the schemes that "filter out" supplies from Russia
in the form of kickback "taxes" paid to top people in the "republic"—both require a certain amount of well-armed support. Today, the DPR has only two such competitors: Khodakovskyi and Zakharchenko. Whenever someone pops up

talking about Holy "*Novorossiia*" and has plans to "clean up the Donbas," the opportunity presents itself to yet again for one group to weaken its partner in *russkii mir* without leaving traces that would attract the attention of Moscow. It was not a coincidence that it was Khodakovskyi's men who carried out the search at the Troia headquarters. They were, in fact, performing a reconnaissance for an assault, which Zakharchenko must have been aware of because he had attempted to prevent the search in the first place.

In other words, this is about your basic criminal underworld that has grown to the scale of a state based on a common ideological platform coming from the Kremlin. This means that the tactics of the local capos could easily prove more resilient than any overall strategy, even if it leads to a radical shift toward the Minsk accords.

As for the latter, we can now firmly declare that all the actors in this theater of the absurd are on the same page. Nobody—not the ideology-driven "republicans," not the small pro-Ukrainian element, not the militias, not the top leadership that at least nominally supports the Minsk process—seriously believes that the accords' provisions can be implemented. So far, even the initial agreements for a full ceasefire have failed repeatedly. What's more, Donetsk is busily preparing for "republican" elections, with ready-made candidates for the post of mayor and predetermined quotas based on who gets the top prize. Needless to say, Ukrainian laws and Ukrainian political forces will have no part in this process. Instead, they will yet again shake their heads at the treacherous terrorists who are violating Minsk.

In all fairness, the local people won't have much to do with this process either, and not just because, in essence, totalitarianism has been established in their "free country." Most residents of Donetsk had their fill after the previous election experience, when the city was plastered with ads saying that it was time for people to take the future into their own hands and cast a ballot for a "happy Donbas." Then suddenly it became clear that the election was off, canceled quietly, without explanation, the way the founders of the DPR have preferred to do things.

Only minor details remain on the sidelines of all the geopolitics: the homeless old people who have been swarming Donetsk stores again lately; the Donetskites who still think of themselves as Ukrainians and continue to believe that there should be no shame in living in their home city; those who can't leave for a variety of reasons; and, in general, all those whom the last two years have cast onto the shallow banks of history when the rest of the country adopted the extraordinarily unenlightened conviction that what has happened is exactly what everyone here wanted.

In 1967, Columbian writer Gabriel Garcia Marques first published his novel *One Hundred Years of Solitude*. In it, each of his characters, no matter what they did or didn't do, ended up surrounded by a solitude in which they spent the rest of their lives. Seven hundred days ago, the Donbas started drawing this circle around itself with its own hand, but it's clearly being completed by outside hands today.

February 5, 2016
Dzerkalo Tyzhnia

THE WAR IN THE DONBAS

2016

JANUARY 1

Separatist and Russian forces resume the shelling of Ukrainian positions using weaponry that is explicitly banned by the ceasefire agreements; ten Ukrainian servicemen die.

FEBRUARY 24

Ukrainian positions at the Butivka coal mine are shelled.

APRIL 30

A new agreement for an immediate ceasefire is reached by the members of the Trilateral Contact Group on Ukraine (comprising representatives of Ukraine, Russia, and the OSCE).

JUNE 29

The first major battle at the strategic town of Svitlodarsk takes place.

SEPTEMBER 1

Another agreement for an immediate ceasefire is reached by the members of the Trilateral Contact Group.

SEPTEMBER 21

An agreement requiring the withdrawal of troops and equipment at Zolote (deadline October 1), Petrivske (deadline October 7), and Stanytsia Luhanska is signed by the members of the Trilateral Contact Group.

OCTOBER 16

The leader of the separatist Sparta battalion Arsen (Arsenii) Pavlov ("Motorola") is assassinated in his apartment building in Donetsk.

OCTOBER 19

A meeting of the Normandy Format participants takes place in Berlin, Germany.

DECEMBER 24

An agreement for an immediate ceasefire is reached by the members of the Trilateral Contact Group.

DECEMBER 26

Ukrainian activists begin a blockade of railway communications with the occupied areas of the Luhansk and Donetsk Oblasts.

WHAT COMES NEXT?

Losing the Donbas breadbasket somehow did not end up destroying Ukraine. It turns out that the old lady is somehow managing just fine without us, the businesses of the big eastern oligarchs still exist, even under the DPR, and for the political elites, the occupation has proved to be a trump card that always draws a tear from the eyes of those who still believe in anything. After nearly two years, the refugees have settled into a new life and put down roots in new cities—and many of them have nothing material left in the DPR at this point. Today, most Ukrainians quite justly are more worried about their loved ones in the trenches than about having the Ukrainian flag fly over backward, pro-Soviet Makiïvka.

Sure, there are still some Andreievs, Ivanovs, Vasins, and other dinosaurs of the pre-tricolor era who have become exhibits in a museum you look at without understanding what they are trying to communicate. We keep them in our "thoughts and prayers," just as we do for the people of Crimea. As a nice gesture, we might even arrange another little blockade, as if to say, we are sparing nothing in the fight for your cause, beleaguered patriot of Ukraine, and at some point in the distant future, we will surely reclaim what is ours. In fact, it is nothing more than a delaying tactic, a largely ineffectual response to Moscow's well-planned maneuvers.

In a certain sense, we have become hostage to the impoverished—compared to the Russian version—propaganda that Ukrainian public opinion has managed to come up with: broadcasts around the clock about "victory" and reassuring repetitions that "everything is going to be great" that fog the critical faculties in assessing the real state of affairs.

And the real state is rather different. The prospect of taking Crimea back has been postponed until the death of Putin himself—which makes all these blockades a bit like shooting at a train with a slingshot. Meanwhile, returning the Donbas through military means will be impossible without making a complete wasteland—another Nagasaki—of all the occupied cities. The Minsk accords have no chance of raising the blue-and-yellow flag over the Donetsk Oblast State Administration (ODA) again, as "republican" government agencies and propaganda spread their roots ever more deeply, having engendered a kind of reflexive gratitude among locals, even in the face of widespread shortages, blockades, and sky-high food prices.

What's more, Russian propaganda has not lost one iota of its effectiveness, despite the complete screw-up with the false story of the crucified little boy.[90] No doubt, small crucifixes with babies will continue to please the eye of the unquestioning fans of the ideology of Great Russia. Indeed, an entire generation of the latter is coming of age: while valiant Kyiv promises for the eighty-fourth time in the last two years to launch a television channel for the occupied territories, a generation of Zakharchenkites, Komsomols, and young members of the Prizrak brigade is already growing up to write little verses to Uncle Liosha, aka Oleksii Mozhovyi. Will it be any surprise, really, when, in five years' time, this "poor kid, who's simply been brainwashed," takes up arms, together with thousands of other freshly-baked militiamen, to take vengeance for a father, a brother, or "Holy Russia"?

It's obvious that the winds of the Apocalypse have not been enough, so far, to resolve the conflict in the Donbas. It is equally obvious that there are not enough people here like me, people who feel the secret urge either to act to free Ukraine or who blame themselves for whatever happens. But those who have stayed are not the main victims of the easy sleep of our chocolate king,[91] who has managed finally to stop the endless flow of blood but leave the situation suspended in mid-air, all while assuring everyone of the positives of the situation, as if this were the final answer. The main victims are our Ukrainian fighters, who sit a yard below ground in freezing temperatures and wait for God knows what. These boys are the ones who have the right to ask the key question: How much longer, and what next?

Some may deny that there are also people sitting in the trenches on the other side, but this isn't entirely the case. The fact of the matter is that the mindset of the "republican" fighters is completely different from the Ukrainian army. Most of the tricolor trenches are filled with marginalized people for whom the coming of the war changed nothing, for the most part—men who had no future prior to the conflict and have nothing to lose now, either. The image of soldiers of fortune who live one day at a time and converged on the Donbas rightly reflects the current situation in the "republican" guards, brigades, and units. These are not people who left prestigious work and a fancy car in the garage of a nice house and are waiting impatiently for the situation to be resolved so that they can go home again. On the contrary, their life *is* the war, and they are prepared to keep sitting in those trenches forever. Of course, the Ukrainian army is not a bunch of knights in shining armor, but compared to the "republican" forces, their overall composition is much closer to the societal norm.

"The ATO will last a few hours, not a few months." That statement, coming from the lips of our president, filled many people, including me, with a naive hope; we associated that promise with a future "free" life. But what we got in reality was two years of never-ending battles, my continued dispatches from this parallel world, and a Donbas split between the local warlords, the late Mishka "Kosyi,"[92] Rynat,[93] "Zakhar,"[94] on the one hand, and those making money by bringing fresh boxes of Roshen chocolates into Donetsk in spite of any blockade. Meanwhile the locals, munching on the chocolates as before, still believe that they have a say in what is going on around them. What remains for those who are holding on to their country even more strongly than the state itself and have no desire to leave their homes for the sole purpose of making things easier for someone in Kyiv? "Hey, drop us a line sometime." That's what our government's commitment to the future sounds like.

February 21, 2016
Tyzhden

People queue for humanitarian aid in the town of Debaltseve, north-east of Donetsk.

LOWER THAN ROCK BOTTOM

I often find myself hearing comments along the lines of "You wanted Russia? Well, now you have it!" This comes from many of my fellow Ukrainians on the "mainland." I'd like to use this essay to disabuse them of the myth that Donetsk is now some kind of blend of Rostov-on-Don and Riazan in Russia.

First of all, the DPR has nothing to do with Russia. It hasn't for a long time now. And for any locals who are capable of even a superficial understanding of what's going on, this fact is no longer a secret. Russia left this place precisely when a huge crowd of completely deluded elderly ladies in lavender caps came out on Lenin Square with icons of Stalin in a golden uniform and a bald-pated Vladimir Ilich. In other words, when all is said and done—and as strange as this may sound—when it became clear that, in its purest imperial form, Russia never did manage to unfold in the steppes of the Donbas.

The point is that the only link between events in the Donbas and what goes on in Russia itself is the fact that both here and there, the darkest, deepest expectations and desires of the people's souls are being manipulated with extreme precision and subtlety. Both Putin and Zakharchenko are, to an equal extent, an extension of those very people, 82 percent of whom await manna from heaven in the shape of a strong hand. But that is where the similarities end. What Donetsk—and really all of the DPR—has turned into today is the 1930s, with the same ideology and the same social attitudes, and have nothing in common with the white kid gloves of Russian imperialism toward which Moscow is moving.

Let me give a few examples.

More than anything, fans of Russia in Donetsk insist on a loyalist media environment: 90 percent of Russia's media is in the hands of those who align themselves with the regime. However, Russia still has the Dozhd (Rain) channel and the Ekho Moskvy[95] (Echo of Moscow) radio station; it has Nevzorov[96] and Shlosberg[97] who sharply criticize the rulers in the Kremlin. Yes, they barely manage to squeeze into 5–10 percent of airtime, but they are there.

In the DPR, there's nothing. There is no opposition paper, no actual opposition, not a single television channel that won't sing praises to the regime about the opening of a canning plant or the latest record in milking "republican" cows. Instead, there is punishment in the form of execution by shooting for "spying and working for" Ukrainian special forces, a label that they will definitely stick on anyone who works for an opposition media outlet in the DPR.

A bit about this latest innovation. Execution lists and 30-year sentences cannot really be compared to Russian realities, even if we ignore the fact that residents who are especially inconvenient to the regime are "eliminated" without any court hearing under the guise of settling scores with "the Trojans"—familiar to all—and the huge number of "desaparecidos" here, even compared to the 1990s. No one can count on due process for any crime more serious than petty theft. The rest is based on who you know, cover-ups, greasing palms, and other tricks of the prison trade that have infiltrated all of long-suffering Donetsk.

When it comes to the only free window to world news, the Internet, "republican" computer geeks have done their dirty deed here as well; in the last two months, I have lost access by ordinary web browsers to mainstream Ukrainian media, including *Radio Svoboda, Tyzhden, Ostrov,* and *Dzerkalo Tyzhnia.* Of course, this ban is fairly easy to get around, but the fact is that this is a total dictatorship that interferes not only in the public realm—in social, economic, and cultural spheres—but also in personal communications.

The DPR has no equal for repression, either: lately, any dissent in Donetsk has been persecuted particularly harshly. Well-known individuals are being arrested and their lawyers barred, even when these individuals have not been formally charged. Moreover, there's nothing in the DPR criminal code that might get in the way of simply executing them.

In all these ways, Donetsk today resembles more Chechnya, with its traditional tribal mentality and respect for personal authority and the use of force, than it does the-more pretentious Moscow or St. Petersburg. After all, the aspirations of the people in the DPR and the LPR are quite diffcrent from the grandiose fantasies of many ordinary Russians, who nurture the dream of a tsar or "supreme leader" (in the words of Vladimir Zhirinovskii[98]) rather than the longing for a sausage sandwich wrapped in a Pioneer neckerchief.

These days I have to marvel at those who expected to see in the reddish-tinged politics of the DPR a repressed desire in the people to be disciplined by a strongman. At this point, you are bound to ask yourself: is there a bottom to this endless freefall into the abyss of the new Horde?[99] After all, all deviations from the plan have their limits. You can't spend your entire life praying to Lenin and defending ever-lengthening lists of people to be executed in order to "teach the enemies of the 'republic' a lesson." In practice, however, the bottom is nowhere to be seen and Russia's imperial past keeps growing upward from its Khrushchevian roots in the Donbas.

March 6, 2016
Tyzhden

CULTURAL LIFE UNDER OCCUPATION: THE CITY OF DONETSK

Life in the occupied part of Donbas, according to city dwellers, is marked by double lives—and on the territory controlled by the DPR, the cultural sphere is no exception. Most cultural institutions and events here are in Donetsk: in other cities, like Makiïvka, Khartsyzk, or Horlivka, the cultural horizon is limited to local "houses of culture."[100] In Donetsk, things are completely different: theaters, cinemas, and the Philharmonic are all working full-time, and are a decent indicator of what's really on people's minds here.

Needless to say, the DPR has imposed a strict ideological filter on cultural establishments on its territory. The official line of the DPR "ministries" of culture and education is that all manifestations of the Soviet past are to be cultivated. Any cultural events in Donetsk that are funded by the local budget—say, an art or photography exhibit—must reflect the "heroism" of Soviet soldiers and workers, and the "greatness" of Russian history. This is what you will see in local schools, universities, and ethnographic museums.

When it's a matter of financial interests, though, Sovietization is out the window. Counter to the official party line, Donetsk cinemas, the Philharmonic, and the city's theaters offer the same type of films and plays that were on show before the takeover. And so, in a sense, the commercial entertainment sector shows the real preferences of local consumers of culture.

At the Donetsk Drama Theater, plays by Dumas, Slade, Sinclair, Gibson, Hervé, and Claude Magnier are doing very well. Of course, Gogol, Chekhov, and Bulgakov are also performed, but with no ideological distortions, not even the slightest attempt to present Bulgakov himself from a Soviet angle. "The Show Must Go On" is especially popular, offering

Female DPR fighters pose on stage in Donetsk during a beauty
pageant to mark the upcoming International Women's Day.

an artistic interpretation and performance of Western hits
by Sting, Queen, Lara Fabian, and others. And yet, I know
for a fact that most of the performers and actors are pro-
Russian, and even active supporters of the DPR.

The situation at the Donetsk Philharmonic and the cinemas is much the same. All the billboards around the Philharmonic feature images of Zakharchenko and Stalin (in an
advertisement for a restaurant), along with messages like
"Our grandfathers won victory and so will we."[101] Yet, at the
end of October, the Philharmonic Orchestra will be offering the local audience a program entirely made up of the
popular Western hits of Freddie Mercury, Nirvana, and the
Scorpions. Meanwhile, Donetsk cinemas like the Zvezdoch-
ka and the Shevchenko play nothing but Western films. Indeed, moviegoers would not show up for anything else.

In short, Donetsk is living in a dual reality right now.
One reality propagates all things Soviet in the schools and
universities, where no alternative thinking is permitted. The
focus is on the younger generation, whose opinions have

yet to be shaped. The other reality is driven exclusively by the bottom line and reflects the actual Western preferences of local consumers. Nothing directly linked with Ukraine is allowed here, but there are no restrictions on anything Western.

October 7, 2016
Radio Svoboda (RFE/RL)

CITIZENS WITHOUT CITIZENSHIP

After the collapse of the USSR, many erstwhile Soviet citizens were unable to figure out who they were in the new reality. Similarly, in independent Ukraine, the longer the government failed to effectively promote Ukraine as a sovereign nation, culturally and politically emancipated from its Soviet past, the longer this ambiguity lingered in the people's heads. This was especially the case in the regions of Ukraine where notions of national belonging as such were alien to people despite a great number of ethnic minorities. Needless to say, in the independent Ukrainian state, the Donbas has been one such region.

Even after more than twenty years, Ukrainian identity has not put down deep roots in the Donbas, only manifesting itself to a significant degree in the minds of the new generation born in independent Ukraine. Then suddenly up pops the tricolor. If it had been just the Russian tricolor, the local mindset— still oriented on the old ideological notion of "the Soviet people"—would have remembered, somewhere below the surface, that "Soviet" in this game has really always meant "Russian." Unfortunately, what cropped up was not the Russian flag, but the tricolor of the "republics," an incomprehensible crossbreed with the American confederate flag, only without the standard stars on the blue cross. This provided little stimulus and the usual blather of patriotism got stuck somewhere between the imperial ambitions of Strelkov, who dreamt of a Russia from the time of Nicholas II, and the Kadyrovites[102] shouting *"La ilaha illa Allah"*[103] at the top of their lungs on Lenin Square.

And a year and a half later, these people still think of themselves as anything but Ukrainians. I say "these people," because I have in mind only the supporters of the DPR, among whom I count neither myself nor many of those who have stayed here with me, in Donetsk. I say "anything but" because they consider the question of who they are—DPRists, *novorusskiites*, New Russians, or people who happen to live in some no-name country—an open one.

Even before the war, Ukraine was nothing like Sweden or Denmark; we had problems enough before the DPR came along. But during conversations with today's "republicans," with civilians who have never held a weapon in their hands, there's a strong impression that instead of "Soviet people" a completely different type has emerged: a personality type whose ideology is a kind of Weeble Wobble doll that returns to the same position no matter how hard it is pushed. For example, you tell them, "Look, '*Novorossiia*' doesn't exist anymore and you're not even allowed to wear its stripes. Where's your great country from Odesa to Kharkiv? Where are the tanks that were supposed to take Mariupol? Where are Russia and the fraternal people who have been doing nothing but cannibalize the factories that

Putyliv Bridge near Donetsk Airport, destroyed by heavy shelling.

they didn't manage to cart away. Where is the Donbas version of *Krymnash*?"[104]

No, they respond, so what if *"Novorossiia"* has been betrayed? So what if we have miserable pensions and wages, and food costs more than in Ukraine? So what if we don't know what to call ourselves: "republicans," Russians, or New Russians? What matters is that it's not like what the Ukrainians have, because we're not them. This notion that "we're not them" has been inculcated for a long time here. When we talk about the Donbas identity, it is worth remembering that this involves not only the archetype of the collective mindset of the Soviet era, but also the Party of the Regions and the effective abandonment of all pro-Ukrainian policy for the entire time that Ukraine has been independent. It was not necessary to explain to anyone in Lviv who they were because they literally wore it on their brightly embroidered traditional Ukrainian shirts. Donetsk, on the other hand, has lacked this sense of national identity and has needed a pro-Ukrainian policy like a sip of water in the desert.

This does not mean, of course, that the resentments of some Donbas locals, compounded by stupidity, absolve them of their guilt. I myself have plenty of complaints about our state and sometimes don't understand in the least what's going on in the heads of people who supposedly respect the blue-and-yellow colors in common with me. Still, having lived now for a year and a half bombarded by a massive propaganda machine, having survived heavy shelling and experienced directly the misery of this once wealthy region, I have not allowed myself to take up arms and kill those whose passports are from the same country.

Incidentally, the passports of "these people" also have not yet been changed, although at one point it was fashionable to put them inside a dull tricolor cover in anticipation of the swift liberation of all the so-called republican lands. Not for the first time, Zakharchenko has announced the imminent issuance of the first "republican" passports, now scheduled for late March. But there is little euphoria about getting them, even if it turns out that the holders will be able to enter Russia with them, an expectation that this latest announcement clearly is playing upon. After all, not that long ago, this same Zakharchenko made fun of the issuance of passports by the leadership of the LPR, whom he viewed with condescension, anyway, declaring that he would not waste "the people's" money on a document that no one would recognize. But now everyone is in a rush to do just that. Whatever the case may be, the importance is not the passport's effectiveness as an official document, but instead its symbolic power as the latest way of cementing the madness and chaos of the DPR in people's heads.

With every passing day, the idea of a "republic" becomes more and more ephemeral. And with every passing day, the impression grows that this is all a nihilistic banquet of the damned for the "republican" elite, who control the lives of all those who still live in this benighted land. In any case, the party will end at some point; the graves will be overgrown with weeds, and those who are still walking the streets of Donetsk today thinking "Come, Russia," will once again draw support from the government that they consider hostile. But as they mutter about the traitorous president, they will receive a Ukrainian pension and enjoy regular prices instead of the Moscow-level prices in rubles.

March 20, 2016
Tyzhden

Coal miners near Donetsk are evacuated from under the Zasiadko mine after shelling caused a power outage.

HOMO DONBASUS, OR THE
CHANGES BROUGHT BY THE WAR

At one time, all roads led to Eternal Rome, but in Makiïv-ka, roads mostly lead north. It's not that getting around the city is so difficult, just that the main industrial plants lie in the north, so the commuter routes go there. It's also where one of the local "wonders" stands: an almost two-mile long concrete wall covered in faded whitewash and graffiti about "Donbas unbowed," which every worker sees every day. Whether you go all the way to the Makiïvka Steel Mill (MMZ), which stretches out over a three-mile expanse, or to the coal mines and the food storage facilities, you will see this canvas if you sit on the right side of the bus. The scenery often includes nondescript groups of people: tired faces, standard-issue worn-out denim or black jackets, and cheap plastic shopping bags. Huddling meekly around bus stops, they trudge silently home from their shift, just as you trudge silently to yours.

This is *Homo donbasus*, indigenous to this land. Some-how, this view reminds me of the walls where chekists used to line people up for execution. If, as you are riding, you chance to turn your head, you will first see a slag heap flash by on the left, then some giant concrete poles that have fall-en onto a concrete oval, and then, if you are on an adjacent route, the Kirov Culture Club.[105]

I began with this image for a reason: it's impossible to understand the transformation of the local mindset with-out this wall. One way or another, such walls are present in every city from Donetsk to Torez. The majority of the Donbas population is made up of working-class people who tumble out of factory gates after a 12-hour shift—not the journalists, writers and intelligentsia who have mostly sided with Ukraine. The thing is that, ever since the war started, people have been extending this wall farther and farther, gilding it and nearly turning it into a shrine. The Donetsk of Ukrainian days, with its songs about hard-working coal miners, has turned into a continuous ode to the fatigue that already fills every boulevard here anyway. In order to understand whether Donetsk is lost to Ukraine forever, we should first ask ourselves whether it was ever "found" under the coal dust, when the Ukrainian government was still in full swing here.

I often hear "But there are coal mines in Lviv, too," talking about the Lviv Oblast. It's true. But there, the link between risking your life for 115 dollars and the man at the helm is direct. In the Donbas, they don't believe in that. That coal mine is eternal, regardless of who runs it. Joseph Brodsky comes to mind. At 16, while working at the Arsenal defense factory in Leningrad, he witnessed a rally in support of Egypt and the struggle against capitalism—that was the reason given for calling the workers up for a *subbotnik*.[106] Then "a man stood up (those were very scary times, in 1956), a machinist from my shop, and said: 'What difference does it make whether my boss is a capitalist or a communist? It's the same devil, and I still have to get up at 7 in the morning.'"[107] That's pretty much how the Donbas thinks. That "machinist" hasn't gone anywhere. In the 60 years since then, he has lodged under the skin and been passed down genetically, along with facial features. People believe in him more than they do in God Himself.

This principle of profound disillusionment and indifference is something "we need to keep in mind in all these conversations about the New Society and Western models or devil knows what, already."[108] At the end of the day, "Listen to the Donbas," a phrase that is the same rake that hits your forehead every time you step on it, is not one of those naive slogans about your native language that really deserve to be taken ironically. It's the dialog between a worker who has spent a good part of his life a mile below the surface, and the man who has spent all his life calmly looking at sunlight. Down below, things look a lot simpler.

The war has simplified things even more. Donetsk today is, without a doubt, a different city. St. Petersburg has been turned into Leningrad again. Komsomols, pioneers, Zakharovites, butter with ice cream in packaging designed in the "stagnant 1970s," posters extolling the glory of the "republic" and milk made in the DPR workshops. But none of this is the main transformation. As always, what's visible to the eye is just a reflection of what's going on inside. An attentive observer will notice that there aren't too many actors on the "republican" stage. Yes, some have succeeded in blending into the "republican" colors and sincerely play the role of Pioneer leader or army political instructor to build up the "young states." Something different happened to the majority, however.

That "different thing" has washed away the remnants of those layers that usually define people. A referendum in Holland,[109] offshore scandals, government corruption—all the headlines in the Ukrainian world—are swallowed whole by the sugar in a sack of charity. Rynat Akhmetov's aid foundations gleaming across the city are now the beacons that define the lives of townspeople. If you see a long queue in Donetsk, it is doubtless leading to these offices or to branches of the "Republican Bank," luring people out of their shabby apartments under artillery fire. Nobody here cares that Akhmetov may have called the "republic" a disgrace, or that the sugar is "fascist" (that is, Ukrainian) and is—on some level—the price for everything that's going on now. That Akhmetov was also involved in building that damned wall, or that the views of devastation even in peaceful times were partly a reflection of the same obliviousness with which people are now grabbing up sacks of flour. No politics. No ideology. Nothing personal. Just you and your bag.

I once asked a pensioner about all this and his answer made things pretty clear: "Well, son, what are we supposed to be doing now, going to bed hungry?" Everything is mixed up. Today's Donetsk is certainly not Ukraine: any mention of the blue-and-yellow will be answered with a nod of the head pointing to the crater of a mortar round. All the same, there isn't much of the "republic" here, either. For the most part, the city reminds me of a hungry man in a refugee camp who is tossed a piece of food by warring sides, first one, then the other. He picks it up with burnt fingers, cursing both.

Today, hundreds of cadets with DPR "Ministry of Defense" insignia march to these curses. These boys were supposed to get Ukrainian uniforms one day, but now they proudly wear the "republican" uniform, soaking up the "republican" flag more and more with every passing day. It's not the land that's being irreversibly lost. Time is being irreversibly lost, time during which kids will be raised who won't remember Donetsk before the war. 10–15 years of a conflict like this is absolutely enough to lose the city and its inhabitants forever—something that will, in the end, leave behind more victims than the war.

But *Homo donbasus* just starts here. Where the Donetsk man who no longer believes in anything somehow continues to build his life on familiar soil, the Ukrainian patriot who has left the city is not quick to feel homesickness. These are two sides of the same coin, a monogram combining the desire to survive and the desire to live without being attached to anything.

And here is where the local cosmopolitans are sprouting like mushrooms. "It doesn't matter where we live, in Berdiansk, Kyiv, or Zhytomyr," they say. "We never liked this city, anyway. No point in being attached to streetlamps and stinky smog." Even so, Donbas cosmopolitanism is unique. This kinship to "free-spirited" citizens of the world among those who not that long ago proudly called themselves

Donetskites is really nothing more than a profound weariness with the back-breaking shifts at a factory after which you no longer cared about geopolitics, or revolutions, or even the ground under your feet.

At this point, a truly unpleasant image arises: thousands of dead supporters of *russkii mir* whose bodies will lie—are already lying?—all across a "free" Donbas, hundreds of thousands of adherents of Ukrainian "unity" who aren't willing to come back here, and a single, solitary slag heap blackening in the now-liberated steppe. The empty field that the "free," and therefore still ephemeral, Donbas risks turning into is just the consequence of a similarly empty field of consciousness that identifies with nothing: not the region, not the city, and not even this bench in the park. After all, there are parks in Berdychiv, too...

Maybe these people are the real Europeans, as comfortable living in London as they are in Berlin or New York. It's precisely their centrifugal force that will make today's Europe the Asia of tomorrow—and they are likely to be the first ones to leave the country, stepping over its corpse if necessary. Whether their thinking is sincere or is driven by bitterness and anger is a question too difficult to answer.

I've always hated Makiivka, this city that has almost become a living creature to me. But when I found myself in the capital for a short time, I realized very soon that the Makiivka in me hadn't gone anywhere, that it wasn't just some abstraction that could be replaced by a different set of letters. It's the grey and rusty factories, the weariness, skepticism and cynicism, the coal dust on teeth and shoes that doesn't wash off, even in the pretty cafés of the capital—they are still inside me, and they are still the same. Is it really possible to seriously say that all this will be "fixed" just as soon as you take your cheap reserved seat on the night train? Is there really no difference between the guy who grew up in the coal mines of Makiivka and the one growing up in the shadow of the Carpathians?

Notice that "I'm never coming back" sounds just as categorical as "I'll never forgive this." These are phrases of the same category. Stolid, short, and direct—the way people are used to speaking here. And so, the newly minted Donbas cosmopolites once more show their connection to the city either side of the Kalmius River that they are trying so hard to disown.

Of course, it's highly likely that these people will never come back. After all, coming back would be too much like the flight forced on them by the war: apartments sold in Donetsk and homes bought in the "mainland," kindergartens for their children, jobs and rebuilt careers, and, ultimately, a personal life bound to "that" place where the Ukrainian flag still flies. To abandon all this once again for the familiar park, even if there's no more machine-gun fire next to it? Hardly. And so, the city grows emptier by the day. In this way, the reality of one's personal life gives rise to the absurdity common to us all.

By the way, Donetsk had plenty of others who have emigrated at this point and are at least as interesting. I remember, back in May 2014, when separatism was just gaining traction and I was sitting on the Donetsk embankment with one of those who was typically called a "patriot." When I asked him, "Would you go fight?" he answered me in these exact words: "You know, I wouldn't fight for Ukraine, but for this riverfront? Probably." To be fair, that guy didn't end up fighting for the riverfront, or for the bushes—or for anything, for that matter. He succeeded in moving south, closer to Odesa. After all, the phrase "Ukraine above all" was even then alien around here, sounding something like a call to do a subbotnik against the United States. Around here, the concrete has always trumped the abstract, just like an empty fridge has trumped the geographic coordinates of a "unified country."

Be that as it may, for now, the Donbas is just a condom preventing the virus of *russkii mir* from infecting Zhytomyr or cities elsewhere in Ukraine—and no artillery will solve this problem. All talk of "slavery" and "cattle" by mainland Ukrainians who have never held a coal hammer in their hands, and, on the other side, the refusal by pro-Russian Donbasites to wake up from fantasies about the "Nazis" in Kyiv, are the footballs that Ukrainian public opinion has been tossing back and forth for over two years now. Sober thinking says that Donetsk is lost to Ukraine. Lost mentally, lost physically, with all the consequences that remain to be discovered. As our nation's thoughts gallop toward a European future, past the occupation of Crimea, past the loss of the Donbas, overlooking the mining of Volhynian amber[110] and the use of offshores—in truth, Ukraine looks more and more like a fatally wounded soldier reaching for a glass of fine wine.

In all this chaos and confusion, we have forgotten to mention one more genetic offshoot of *Homo donbasus:* those Ukrainians who remain here. There are still Donetsk Ukrainians, though with every passing day, there are fewer and fewer of us: some have emigrated, effectively leaving for another country; some have become believers in the "republic"—such cases are far from rare; and many still believe and keep up the fight for a Ukrainian future here. But the majority are simply waiting. They expect that their existence will be remembered, someday, and that it will not have been necessary to flee in humiliation from their native towns.

April 8, 2016
Dzerkalo Tyzhnia

ABOUT EASTER... AND MORE

The celebration of Easter and May 1 on the same day this year resulted in a very interesting test case: which competing color would dominate the minds of today's fans of all things "truly Russian"? Indeed, there are only two options: red or the mutable color of the "mystical religious fog," to use the words of a well-known academic who was abducted in Donetsk.[111]

The latter is, of course, not exclusive to the inhabitants of the snake pit called *russkii mir* and the DPR, but also is embraced by most of our fellow Ukrainians, whose virtuous consciousness associates the word "Paskha" solely with the eponymous treat;[112] no one knows the religious significance of the holiday or the origin of its name. But the DPR is the only place where Christian Orthodoxy has been taken to such absurd heights that the image of Jesus Christ on lapel pins may soon replace St. George's ribbons and the banners with the faces of DPR "heroes" and leaders. And therein lies the crux of the question: What is more important, the memory of cheap Soviet sausage to which the red flag of the workers promises a return, or the Resurrection of Christ?

Once again, the DPR has managed to create a symbiosis. But we need not be in a rush to judge these people whose consciousness has been subjected day and night for two years to an attempt to mold them out of reddish clay like puppets, complete with a dusting of Easter sprinkles that, one way or another, is part of everything that goes on here. Indeed, the role of the Orthodox Church of the Moscow Patriarchate in this conflict should not be underestimated. The fact that Mass in the central cathedral of Donetsk is paused whenever the main "republican," Zakharchenko, enters the sanctuary is evidence of the sacralization of the DPR.

Having created an image of the militants as "holy sons" with little icons in their pockets (and 50 Cent playing in their earbuds) as they guard the checkpoints, the Russian Orthodox Church of the Moscow Patriarchate has skillfully accommodated the socialist celebration with which it had to share a date on the calendar this year.

Still, it is not a fair competition. What can the bald-headed leader of the proletariat, lying under the roof of a sarcophagus lord knows how many miles away from the Donbas offer that would cast a longer shadow than the Easter service with its mandatory sermon about victory in the "Great War"?[113] Indeed, if you stood at the midnight mass anywhere in Makiïvka and listened thoughtfully to the droning of the priest, you would learn that we are all, for the third year running, "resisting ecumenical evil on our native soil." What's more, the fifteen-minute speech is so virtuosic and slippery that nowhere does it state clear-ly what precisely the "evil" is or who "we" are. In fact, no explanation is necessary: the answer is implied in the mil-itants quietly lining the walls of the church. After all, it is for them and their families that these words are being spo-ken, to strengthen them in their faith since, as we all know, "truth and God are on our side." In a word, Easter Vigil had smoothly segued into a Soviet-style course for literacy and indoctrination (*Likbez*), with quotes about bees and work-place discipline.

But the propaganda doesn't stop there. If you had decided to stay home and spend the night watching TV, you might have been no better off than if you had gone to church. Why? The answer is very simple: the dominance of Russian and "republican" channels ensured that every-one would watch the propaganda of the same Russian Or-thodox Church of the Moscow Patriarchate, only a more subtle version from professionals like Patriarch Kirill, not a pathetic amateur from the local church. In 70 percent of cases, local television broadcast the Divine Service from Moscow with commentary about the great "Russian spirit" and other "spiritually nourishing" treacle of which there is already more than enough in the DPR.

As morning dawns, the weary "republicans," refreshed and with brains thoroughly washed, suddenly remembered that today was also May 1, as it would happen. And not celebrating May 1 would top the list of Soviet sins. So, riding the spiritual wave of the night before and the Gospel readings, all of them were swept up in the more recent Soviet wave of *shashlyk*[114] and flags on the square in the spirit of "Lenin is still among us." "Back to the USSR" is the official

Trucks of a Russian "humanitarian convoy" heading for an illegal crossing of the border to Ukraine. The convoys were used by Russia to transport goods for civilians and equipment, arms, ammunition, motor fuel and oil for the militants in the DPR and the LPR. On the return trip, they often transported to Russia machinery stolen from Ukrainian defense factories and the bodies of Russian soldiers and mercenaries (*gruz 200*).

policy being promulgated throughout the DPR; the sudden appearance of the bearded faces of Marx and Engels next to the Crucifixion make quite an impression, like the confused language of drunken people in the streets responding to "Christ is risen!" with "Happy May 1st!" Still, some of the separatist leaders came up with the idea of combining these two sacred slogans while they were perfectly sober, as it happened in Luhansk. There, the head of the federation of the LPR trade unions addressed the workers with the words: "Christ is risen! Greetings on the International Workers' Day of Solidarity!" as if to say, "Take your pick."

Thus, in complete chaos and confusion, the once-again revived "Soviet people" of Donetsk, Makiïvka, Torez, and other occupied cities, finally arrived at the most important and most sacred part of the day: shashlyk. If only there had been a safe place to grill them; the DPR had been broadcasting nonstop about alleged Ukrainian saboteurs and the tripwires they had supposedly set up, especially in forested strips and cemeteries, which meant that most May Day celebrations were held in the bushes outside apartment building entryways where bottles of vodka and beer joined Easter bread and chunks of grilled meat—all of which will undoubtedly someday be added to the official DPR coat of arms.

May 15, 2016
Tyzhden

CHAOS IN THEIR HEADS: HOW THE WAR IS PERCEIVED IN THE OCCUPIED ZONE

The territory under DPR control is about to hold "primaries," a word you could be shot for. Why shot? Because anything linked to the West in any way is dismissed and rejected here. Here's one example of this: on Donetsk Day, when a Western hit was being performed, a group of young guys began to demand that the petite girl running around the stage with a microphone sing in Russian. I can't imagine how Freddie Mercury might sound in translation, but that's what these skinheads were demanding.

As the so-called primaries approach, posters have been plastered all over Donetsk announcing that something

DPR militants vote at a polling station in Kramatorsk during the unrecognized referendum on DPR's independence from Ukraine.

"grand" is coming, once again. In the DPR, they're especially sentimental about this word. Everything here is grand
(*torzhestvenno*): grand events, grand balls, grand concerts,
and grand ceremonial greetings—even the Greek food and
culture fair is grand.

All these ceremonies, the propaganda, and the atmosphere in general, generate a certain way of thinking in
people. Let me tell you about this one fan of separatism
I know. In some sense, he's a symbol of the turmoil and
chaos that has been churning in people's minds for two
and a half years now. First of all, he's a former militant. He
started with Bezler, then switched to the "official" military.
He later managed to safely resign from his illegal military
unit and is now working loading trucks. I know him like the
back of my hand and have known him for as long as we've
both been alive, so we have a pretty trusting relationship.
When I meet him in the street, I often try to talk him into
acknowledging what is really going on and what has been
for a while now. Yet every time I see him, this man tries to
justify why he's still on the other side—even as he drifts further and further away from the separatist narrative.

I have to say that the former militants among young
locals have a serious problem: their Ukrainian passports
have expired because they never updated their photo after turning twenty-five, so now they can't even go to Russia. They're locked inside a prison of their own making: the
DPR. Many are at the bottom of the social heap, and the
man I'm talking about is in no better position. But every
time I talk to him—I did so just the other day—he repeats
the same mantra: "Russia is my country." When I ask him
what is so awful about Ukraine after two-and-a-half years
of outright criminals occupying Donetsk (a criticism with
which, by the way, he agrees), with the Russian flag still
not waving over the territory, and when people like him are
tossed onto the slagheap of history, he mumbles something
vague about the Nazis who would have killed all Russians

here if people like him hadn't taken up arms. This man still wholeheartedly believes in the threat of Nazism and worries that the Lenin statue will be toppled.

One time I told him that only the very naive haven't figured out by now that there won't be any Crimean scenario here, that Russia isn't coming, that, as just one example, the Transnistrian conflict has lasted for over twenty years now, and that if he wants to wake up at the age of forty-six still loading trucks in Donetsk and holding a passport that only allows him to travel "abroad" to the LPR, then he can keep focusing his worries on the "Nazis." Unlike him, I travel around to Kyiv, Dnipro, and Poltava, not to mention the Ukraine-controlled cities on the other side of the front in the Donbas. And I can say that the population of those same cities along the line of contact changed by the influx of people from the country, people who care about as much about "Nazism" as the rest of Ukraine cares about, say, Albania right now. You can identify the rural transplants by their behavior and language (Surzhyk, as opposed to the Russian language of the city-dwellers), and from their tendency to leave litter around in the streets. But it is only here, in the DPR and LPR, that people fear the "Nazis," from watching Oplot.TV or Rossiia 24 around the clock, seven days a week.

For this reason, this former militant still wholeheartedly believes in the threat of Nazism and worries that the statue of Lenin will be toppled in Donetsk. He is firmly convinced that he would still be working on a loading dock, even if the Ukrainian government controlled Makiïvka now, which is probably true. Thus, he concludes, he hasn't lost a thing—and he hasn't let "the fascists" in, as he puts it.

This distorted perception of reality is typical of not only those who have been to the front, but their families, as well. Russian videographer Mikhail V. Polynkov's videos show this. Polynkov, a Russian mercenary and proponent of "*Novorossiia*," became known from his service under Girkin (Strelkov) in Slov'iansk. The locals in his videos, including the wives and mothers of dead militants, express thanks to Strelkov and to Russia for their bags of groats without recognizing or acknowledging that, as Strelkov himself has admitted, it was he who started the war.

September 20, 2016
Radio Svoboda (RFE/RL)

Wreckage of the Malaysia Airlines Boeing 777 plane (flight MH-17) is removed by a crane at the site of the plane crash near the settlement of Hrabovo, north of Torez (now Chystiakove), in the Donetsk Oblast. The airplane was downed on July 17, 2014, by DPR militants using a Russian-army Buk ground-to-air missile system, killing all 298 people on board.

WHAT PYGMALION LEFT UNSAID

In a famous Greek myth, the sculptor Pygmalion carved a statue so beautiful that he fell in love with it and longed for it to come to life. His desire was so powerful and obsessive that Aphrodite finally took pity on him and brought his creation to life.

This myth offers an instrument for performing an autopsy on the smelly corpse of the political reality here in the Donbas. The stench is getting stronger as summer draws near and "elections" are supposed to take place in the occupied territory. And, as we found out recently, the militants are demanding amnesty for themselves in exchange for releasing Ukrainian hostages. As in an autopsy, opening up just one part of the body can be enough to expose the pathology that corrupted the whole. And that's precisely what this amnesty reveals about the entire Minsk process.

Debate about an official pardon for those who "erred" has been ongoing for a long time now. As part of the roadmap of the Minsk accords, it has been a serious irritant, creating a headache for Ukraine, and providing the fans of Saint George's ribbon with a great excuse for manipulation. In the course of the Minsk talks, the head "republican," Oleksandr Zakharchenko, has made enough public statements to put together an anti-Minsk anthology. These include the mantra that Ukraine is a hostile state, that the DPR has no relation to it, that the Ukrainian parliament should amend the constitution to meet the approval of the "People's Council" of the DPR,[115] and so on. The recent demand for an amnesty is part of this, even as there is nonstop shelling around Donetsk Airport and Avdiïvka. Not to mention that demanding amnesty of a government that you do not recognize is like cheating on your lover with your wife. This situation is too much like that old joke, "She doesn't want it, and I don't, either."

At this point, the razor-thin edge that the Minsk agreement had to walk hit a brick wall with the amnesty issue—just like every other item in our national action plan.

Now it's time to take a little excursion through history. What kind of people are in the "DPR Armed Forces"? Answering this question makes clear just how far the idea of amnesty is from reality on the ground, and how far it is from the Minsk process, which itself reeks of the Belarusian political swamp.

In the summer of 2014, the valiant armies of *russkii mir* were made up of three categories of people: locals, foreign mercenaries, and Russian military regulars. In percentages, the share of locals has dropped dramatically since then; in line with the classical "great power" approach, the locals were used as cannon fodder to plug holes in the frontline throughout 2014 and early 2015-hence, the sad statistics. While the coffins of those who "came on vacation"[116] to fight in the Donbas have had the honor of being sent back to Russia and other thrill-seekers from the Russian Federation have been buried in local cemeteries, locals have often been buried in graves dug by an excavator in the area near the Donetsk coking plant. While locals are the only real candidates for amnesty, as no one has yet taken away their Ukrainian passports, the majority of them are indifferent to the prospect of an amnesty from the Kyiv government, just as they are unbothered by the government's renaming of districts in Makiivka.[117]

Why? Very simply, because most of yesterday's militants from Makiivka, Donetsk, or Torez left their units half a year ago, deserting or resigning, and diving headlong into the activity that unites the post-Soviet peoples most: long bouts of drinking. All of them returned to their prewar lives and now work twelve hours a day for about 90 dollars a month, earning enough to drink for the remaining twelve hours of the day and forget about tomorrow. An amnesty that opens a pathway to life in Ukraine changes nothing about this reality, which even the alcohol-drenched brains of potential candidates for an amnesty have managed somehow to understand.

Having suddenly found themselves turning the wheel of history in 2014, then returning to their familiar lives in the coal mines in 2016, the last thing that yesterday's coal miners think about is the prospect of a pardon and a new life, because they consider themselves neither guilty nor capable of starting that new life. In the two years of this war, I have hardly ever heard a sincere statement of repentance or any admission of having made a mistake. Many of those who quit the militias had a chance to turn themselves in to the SBU, the Security Service of Ukraine, under its pardon program. Instead, they preferred to load trucks and fix toilets, or whatever work they found in civilian life. This begs the question of why Ukraine has been unable to offer any qualitative difference between Ukrainian-controlled Bakhmut and occupied Makiïvka. Be that as it may, most of the local contingent don't care about the promised indulgence. There are some who wouldn't mind being pardoned, but only to be able to travel hassle-free to Bakhmut for cheap "Nazi" sausage.

The second group includes those who have come here as visitors: individuals in the Donbas on safari. Do not suppose that these are all Russians. The mix includes Serbian Chetniks,[118] "warriors of Allah," French socialists, and even a couple of Americans who consider Obama an international criminal, as reported by the pro-Russian LifeNews. There is also a very strange contingent from Latin America that, for some reason, consider themselves "warriors of Valhalla." In fact, these Brazilian Vikings have established themselves in *russkii mir*'s Makiïvka. Nevertheless, Russians make up the largest part of this group. It's almost impossible to sort these people according to any single criterion, except maybe to treat them as exhibits in an ideological cabinet of curiosities. It is even harder to sort out who has committed crimes and who hasn't, whom the limp hand of Ukrainian justice might eventually reach, and who will go back to hating Obama somewhere in São Paolo.

Finally, the touchiest point: the group comprised of soldiers in regular Russian units who romp around in camouflage without any markings and ask how to get to a bus stop that is 300 yards away. Although many of them are known by name, the demand for an amnesty for all parties to the conflict would turn a possible international tribunal into a one-sided game in which the cynical "They aren't there!" that we've heard about the Crimea takeover would become a mocking "Haven't you pardoned them all?"

It is understood that my reflections here only touch upon the formal aspect of this issue without even coming close to its essence. The devil is always in the details, and with war the details are truly satanic. A Makiïvka roofer who commandeered a Grad and killed a squad of our soldiers, then switched to a career loading cargo, was asked, "Did you feel sorry for the Ukrainian fighters?" He answered, "I felt sorry for the herd of cows we killed alongside their squad." Are details like this visible in Minsk, or are the politicians simply rearranging figures on a chessboard there without looking any deeper into the real rules of the game?

Sometimes I have the crazy impression that the only possible strategy against the Kremlin would be to follow its strategy—a possibility that Moscow does not seem even to consider. It is difficult to do, but imagine the impossible: we would actually implement Minsk within the insane interpretation imposed by the Kremlin: an amnesty in the midst of daily shelling, or elections even as railcars full of missiles arrive in Khartsyzk from Russia.

And this is where our myth comes into play. If we look more carefully, it becomes clear that, for someone obsessed with a goal, losing it is as fatal as reaching it. Any talk of amnesty, elections, or amendments to Ukraine's constitution has power only as long as these things are impossible, because that impossibility is the Kremlin's trump card. However tearfully Pygmalion begs Aphrodite to bring his statue to life, he is secretly prepared to beg for this for eternity. Which is the part of the myth that the Greeks discreetly left untold.

May 20, 2016
Dzerkalo Tyzhnia

EVENING STROLLS THROUGH
AN EMPTY CITY

War and occupation always offer a kaleidoscope of impressions that are so subtle and individual that to try to reduce them to a single whole makes no sense.

In the last two years, I have seen people who fall into a panic, cowering in their chairs with contorted faces at the least sound of artillery fire, and others who, on the contrary, run closer to see how a Grad works. The former hasn't turned on the TV since the start of the "Russian Spring," while the latter cannot let a day go by without checking "updates from the militants" as though in need of a drug. What's more, both the former and the latter could be supporters of the Russian or "republican" tricolor, or pro-Ukrainian patriots, although lately, being pro-Ukrainian has become more and more of a problem under occupation.

Indeed, you always find something that is common to all of them. First of all, it turns out that the "post-combat" atmosphere seems more oppressive than active shelling. The round-the-clock whistling of Grads and the sounds of explosions gradually train the psyche to experience them as normal. For me, one of the strangest experiences in my life was when a sudden decline in the frequency of the shelling led to a headache. When I went out on the street, I found myself irritated at the relative silence that hung over the neighborhood, with shots firing only sporadically in the distance, rather than close by, generating the clamorous background noise to which I had become accustomed.

In the end, the war has been felt in ways that are far from obvious. Far more oppressive is what I call the effect of strolling through an empty city. What I mean is that, toward evening on a Sunday, you can walk down a neatly-swept boulevard or square—behind the Viktoriia Hotel, say,

The building on Zlitna Street in Donetsk where DPR militants took up a position.

in the very heart of downtown Donetsk—turn around, and see not a single soul. Brand-new cobblestone and tidy trash urns will stretch before you, and every single streetlamp will be lit. Next to the park is a broad, long roadway that encircles Donbas Arena. You stand on a hill where stunning scenery unfolds before you, yet there is no one in it. No cars, no people—it is absolutely empty. It is eight o'clock in the evening and somewhere in the direction of the airport you can hear shelling but other than that you are completely alone. The city is a ghost town.

For those of us who still consider ourselves Ukrainians and express their own position in various ways, such as the author of this dispatch, for example, there is an added nuance to life in this ghost town. This has nothing directly to do with paranoia or the need to check both ways every time you open the door. To understand what I'm talking about you have to have lived here for a long time but crossed over to the Kyiv side for at least a day. The minute I cross that checkpoint, I feel an enormous psychological burden lift off my back and I understand the enormous pressure that I am living under in the DPR. Certainly, I don't think every hour about death or the likelihood of finding myself in a basement cell.[119] But it's worth stepping over into the rest of the country to realize that, in Donetsk, such thoughts hover in the back of your mind just as surely as the war hovers over the empty parks. Being outside the DPR is a fundamentally different psychological experience.

I know that even in Ukrainian-controlled Kramatorsk I could be robbed, or someone could try to kill me. But in Donetsk, that would be the norm; no one would pay for it unless you had connections with the boys in camo. Consider, for example, the recent takeover of one of the militant headquarters in Makiïvka. About a dozen militants were put on their knees in broad daylight by two dozen other militants just like them—only the latter were better equipped, driving armored vehicles, and carrying grenade launchers. The owner of the premises, who was renting it out, always used these boys with their machine guns to settle his own affairs. But along came some guys with heavier weapons and the owner ended up dead.

It might seem very strange, but one of the most serious challenges for people who have stayed here, under occupation, is the advice to leave. I am not talking at all about those who honor the "ideals of the republic": this group is self-explanatory. "DPR-republicans" would be only too happy, really, if no one remained here, as they keep trying, with dogged persistence, to persuade us on social media. No. I'm talking about being pressured by other Ukrainians—either those who are from here but long ago abandoned their hometown, or those who basically have never been in the Donbas. I am not referring to the difficulty of everyday risks like the ones I've described here. The requirements for handling them are pretty clear to all. The real problem is that the people who have stayed behind have to constantly hear about the consequences of what is termed their fundamental error: to remain in the land of the occupiers, which (say the critics from Ukraine) is just as wrong as to continue to trade with them. And there are many other arguments as well: why waste your life on things that cannot be recovered, why risk the psychological damage and the hopelessness of an existence in the shadows, where the best-case scenario has you remaining in those shadows. What's worse, this pressure keeps growing as the war drags on and on.

Finally, we might as well mention the obvious: the ubiquity of the pro-Russian propaganda that has never stopped. It affects even those who couldn't stand the DPR from the very start. One way or another, we all are subjected to this stream of information through the posters plastered all over the city calling on us to defend our homeland, or to honor the "immortal regiments."[120] Pictures of the "heroes" hang at the bus stops, and the phone numbers of enlistment offices as well as advertisements celebrating the "republican" achievements can be seen everywhere in public transport and the supermarkets, where you can always hear reports about enemy reconnaissance, saboteurs, and the "Nazis." This all acts upon a person as the thousands of drops of water that will one day wear down even granite.

June 12, 2016
Tyzhden

QUID PRODEST?[121]

I remember one of my few trips into Kyiv-controlled territory, back in the fall of 2015, when I came to the capital. In the subway, at one of the metro stops, I asked someone for directions and the man politely asked me where I was from. My response, "from Donetsk," clearly surprised him. But I was even more surprised by his next question: "So, how is it there in Donetsk? Are they still shooting or is it quiet now?" I remember thinking at that moment that he and I really were from different countries. I don't mean the country Ukraine, but the country of common sense. One of us clearly lived outside that state, although I never made up my mind which of us it was.

Those were my first twenty-four hours in Kyiv. I left Donetsk just a day earlier amidst a deafening thunder of night-time shelling around the airport and the repeated crackle of machine-gun fire during the four hours before dawn that I spent waiting in line at the checkpoint. The suburbs of Donetsk were shelled once again that day, and we once again lost men. The militants also reported three casualties. Waiting in line for hours in the middle of a field on a freezing cold night, many would not risk leaving their cars to relieve themselves because, instead of latrines, there were rusty signs warning "Mines." All this flashed before my eyes in a second as I tried to think of what to say to the man who had just asked me whether they were "still shooting" in Donetsk.

The war has never really penetrated the national consciousness of Ukraine. The ambiguity of this war has actually been fostered by the efforts of the DPR. Recent events, beginning on June 8 with one of the most serious escalations in the conflict this year, have been a perfect illustration of this. On June 9, a young woman from a Kyiv TV channel called me and asked naively: "Why is there such a fuss about last night in separatist social media? Is something really serious happening where you are?"

The previous night, Donetsk had been covered in a continuous curtain of noise: mines exploding in the suburbs, the air vibrating from shelling in the city center, and anti-aircraft artillery sending flashes into the sky right above my building as separatists tried to shoot down Ukrainian army drones. The power kept going out. We found out the next morning, when it was over, that it wasn't just Donetsk that had been affected: more than a dozen houses had been damaged or destroyed on the outskirts of Makiïvka, and the steel posts in the playgrounds in residential courtyards were riddled with shrapnel as if someone had burned holes into soft fabric. Fifteen civilians were injured and one woman had died. We lost several Ukrainian soldiers that night and another six a few days later, when their body parts were pried out from underneath the concrete rubble. The shelling got worse the following nights and some locals filmed a huge fire right outside Donetsk. That's how almost every night has been here lately. Is it "serious"? I would say so.

An equally fundamental question is *quid prodest*—who is benefitting from this? Who has been shelling Donetsk and Makiïvka again and again, deliberately aiming at residential areas? This might seem like a pointless question, one that you shouldn't even have to ask yourself; depending on your political colors, the answer will appear obvious. But those here who still consider themselves Ukrainians know that, after more than two years of occupation, the answer is really a kind of test of how well you understand this war.

It's no secret that militant headquarters are located mostly in residential areas. As one Russian journalist, Aleksandr Nevzorov, facetiously noted, these people hide behind hawkers of gooseberries and aproned market sellers.

A Horlivka resident in a house damaged in a night shelling attack
blamed by DPR militants on Ukrainian armed forces.

In late 2014, the heaviest shelling targeted the Horniatskyi
District in Makiïvka. The people here sometimes like to say
that Makiïvka is in the eye of the hurricane—that is, that it
is always quiet—but the Grad shelling of late 2014 was so
intense that, despite the dull roar of continuous shelling in
the distance to which people have become accustomed, locals talked about it for a week. I was myself just half a mile
away from where some of the shells had landed.

At this time, I was making a living loading frozen fish
at a store in Makiïvka. I had to get up at 5:30 a. m., but
this night everyone was awakened earlier. Just after one
o'clock in the morning, my room lit up as though it were
daylight. The old windows on the balcony, which weren't
your European vinyl type, sprang wide open, and the explosions outside were so loud that, half-asleep, I thought the
shells were landing right by my window. Within seconds,
I jumped from my bed into the hallway, lay on the floor behind the wall, and stayed there until the terrible noise had
stopped. I spent the next four hours fully dressed on my

bed, just in case the shelling started again and I had to run out into the freezing cold. But that was only the beginning of the day.

People in Makiïvka know that, until recently, there used to be a separatist checkpoint known as 4/13 close to the area that was shelled. The checkpoint was named after a fork in the road going to Khartsyzk and the village of Khanzhenkove. On my way to work in the *marshrutka*, the minibus shuttle, I passed that checkpoint and ended up under mortar fire myself. It was dark outside and all that could be seen or heard through the bus window were bright flashes and muffled pops. There was nothing we could do: we were in open steppe, with only a slag heap in the distance, so the *marshrutka* kept going, stopping and picking up passengers who entered the bus without a word. The only thing I noticed was a look of shame on people's faces, a sense that we were forced to feel a bit crazy, acting as if we hadn't noticed anything.

Why do I bring up these two examples? By the next day, the "republican" media was screaming about yet another bombardment by the Ukrainian Armed Forces. And they were right. A Grad hit near a militant base with a hangar full of equipment; the target was precisely the checkpoint we had passed earlier. In the end, the fusillade from the Grad partially damaged a residential building but only grazed the militant position and landed in a field without causing any harm to a military target.

Things like this happen all the time here; it seems to be inherent in this kind of war. The Lisove cemetery is pockmarked with Ukrainian shells simply because a "republican" self-propelled gun was shooting in the direction of Iasynuvata 100 yards from here for two weeks straight, taking the lives of our—Ukrainian—soldiers. The district of Oktiabrske, in Makiïvka, was recently shelled by Ukrainian armed forces. DPR propaganda reported that "a Ukrainian diversionary group" had been operating in the area and called in artillery on the neighborhood. Oktiabrske has no major military value and is about as threatening to Ukrainian forces as a village somewhere in China. Yet it was in fact in Oktiabrske, between residential buildings, that an armory had been established to supply DPR militants with ammunition. So, it really is all about how you look at this war.

Obviously, the events described above do not exemplify the war zone in its entirety. Some situations are worse. And they occur on both sides. For example, Grads were shelling constantly from a field by my window back in 2014, targeting the Donetsk airport. All I needed to do was to go out on my balcony to be 200 yards away from them. Sometimes, howitzers appeared and shelled in the opposite direction, targeting the city center. A friend of mine called me a minute after one such bombardment and told me that the house next door had been demolished and that he himself was lying on the floor in a bulletproof vest he had bought before the war. I told him that the howitzer was shooting from our field, that it was the DPR that was attacking them, but it was useless: he was convinced that it was Ukrainian armed forces. A civilian was killed on his street that night; the following day, calculated cynicism was unleashed in the press.

Death is the best propaganda, and Moscow knows this. While all Ukraine is trying to come up with some "honest answer to counter the lies from the Kremlin," the bodies are piling up around here. That is all that is needed. Whenever someone in occupied Donetsk, Makiïvka, or Torez goes to sleep still feeling indifferent about everything and everyone, but wakes up with no four walls and Grad shrapnel sticking out of their kitchen table, the ranks of "Russian Spring" followers grow yet again. All the more so, if they lose a loved one. It is impossible to persuade a person who has lost a daughter or a mother the night before that the DPR had a hand in it.

And what could be more convincing than the feeling that you must wear a bulletproof vest in your home? Certainly not the TSN News Hour on the Ukrainian 1+1 TV channel, where a smiling female presenter in expensive makeup mildly and calmly reports that "the militants have once again shelled residential areas in Makiivka." Indeed, no. No one in this area even hears her. Let's be realistic: that night on the floor will be picked up by Russia's best propagandists and spun so thoroughly that you will have no doubt that the shelling was aimed at the DPR rearguard by Ukrainian forces. They will convince you that the shelling came from outer space, if necessary, just so long as you never forget this night or that person's death. I kid you not—I know what I'm talking about. The guy who slept in his bulletproof vest that night still donates money to the "DPR Armed Forces"—the same people who almost killed him. And that was just a single night: no death of a father or a son, and by lucky chance his house was untouched, while not 100 yards away, another house was now a pile of rubble.

Has anything like this been done by the Ukrainian Armed Forces? Yes, it has. I spoke over the phone with a Ukrainian veteran survivor of Zelenopillia, where our boys were absolutely pulverized by Grads.[122] This guy was still recovering from what he had seen; he asked me if everyone in Donetsk believed that it was the Ukrainian Armed Forces that were shelling them. I said that most people did believe that, and that sometimes they were right, although it was unlikely that Ukrainian soldiers would shoot without having a clear target. I was amazed when I heard his reply: "You know, Stas, it sometimes happens." I was amazed by this officer's honesty and frankness, though not by the fact that such things happen. He told me that, after what the soldiers had gone through, many would just lose it, and often not wait for authorization from headquarters for a strike on coordinates.[123]

On what scales can this war be balanced? On the one side, the "republican" turns a howitzer on his "home city," with one shot burning down someone's house and ensuring donations from those who lie in their bulletproof vests next door. Or, on the other side, a Ukrainian soldier who has just witnessed his buddy torn into pieces (after you have scraped your best friend off a burnt armored personnel carrier, can anybody tell you what is immoral?)[124] blindly fires a howitzer round in the direction of Donetsk. It happens. But how can we pass judgment? We aren't there, next to those corpses and the smell that, they say, doesn't go away even after years of war. And that's exactly what the others will say when the shell lands next to them a minute later in Donetsk.

Death is inevitable in any war. But in few wars is it commemorated incessantly, with monuments to which flowers are brought every day, as happens in the DPR. Every death gets airtime: like the dead person's body, it is washed, dressed up, and turned into a made-for-TV product. Then it is commemorated, day after day, week after week, in reports on LifeNews and Oplot.TV showing close-ups of children in the trauma ward of a Donetsk hospital, their mothers next to them, tearfully cursing "Ukrainian Nazis," and broadcasting video of dead bodies in the burnt-out cities of the frontline. There is more: an "Avenue of the Angels" in memory of Donbas children who died in the war, posters of smiling boys with guitars plastered all over Donetsk, youths who are now members of the Immortal Regiment of the Vostok battalion. Even the birch trees planted in the central park of Donetsk commemorate the "fallen defenders of 'Novorossiia,'" as the granite plates carved with their names next to every tree attest. All this is a ready answer to the question of who will be responsible for taking away your apartment, your home, your job, and the people you love the next time a shell falls. The people of the DPR already know the answer, as do we—those of us who "remain" here among those who were "always" here.

The latest shellings in June rained down on Donetsk as people were gathering for a rally called by the separatist government against violations of the Minsk accords and the introduction of an armed OSCE mission. Such "coincidences" are not uncommon here. The two-year tradition of collecting "donations" has not changed; the collectors pour fuel on the fire and keep raking them in. The residents who know about upcoming meetings in the Belarusian capital or about the latest rally in downtown Donetsk put two and two together and stock up on water, because tomorrow there won't be any. Tomorrow, they will damage the pumping station, or flatten a few houses, or spread the false report of the crucifixion of another little boy. This is the fuel that keeps the war burning—that's pretty clear. But the fine line between those who benefit from it and those who are culpable is not always clear, and the main question of the war remains outside this division.

Sometimes people ask me what I would say if my mother, who works not far from the Somalia battalion headquarters, were killed during a shelling. What if they were shooting at the base and hit her, and I literally had to pick up the pieces? I don't know what to answer, but one thing is certain: I would not want people asking me.

June 17, 2016
Dzerkalo Tyzhnia

THE "REMAINERS": THE UNDISCOVERED BOSCH OF THE DPR

Donetsk today is a Hieronymus Bosch painting—or at least one of the contorted figures writhing in Bosch's Hell in a corner of the canvas. As you try to grasp the painting as a whole, with its multitude of figures, endless details escape you without which the essence cannot be fully comprehended. Just as the details of Bosch's painting had a greater immediacy for the audience of his day than for today's viewer, events in Donetsk carry greater significance for those living there than for people observing them from Kyiv.

It is Bosch's loss that he never knew Zakharchenko: with such a model, the great artist might have painted a dozen characters that will never be known to humanity. While it is true that you will not come across birdlike creatures feeding on human flesh in Donetsk today, instead, five hundred years of evolution has produced the local *Homo sapiens* recognizable by its characteristic orange shades, short hair, black T-shirt with the logo "I'm Russian" tucked into camo pants, and huge black combat boots; this creature parades about the central avenues and squares. Here, next to the central figure, you can see beggars sitting in underground passageways and parks, and a decently dressed young man forced to earn his living by singing a local hit about slumbering kurgans[125] in the city trams. This figure is even more striking because his singing is reminiscent of opera and his voice is incredible. In the corner of this canvas, you see a black Mercedes, finely dressed women holding Chihuahuas in their arms, and the smoke of a hookah bar spilling down the long boulevard. This would be "paradise"; it also goes by the name of Pushkin Boulevard, another panel of Bosch's painting. All these exotic characters dwell in a milieu of occasional shelling in the distance, expensive food, and well-armed gunmen prowling around the city in search of enemies of the people.

A hundred more details could be added: every inhabitant of the city will tell you something different. What even the most attentive observer will not notice in the painting, though, is the "remainers."[126] It is as if they weren't there at all. Bosch himself would probably have depicted them as otherworldly shades throwing into sharp relief the main subjects of the painting.

The category of "remainers" is quite peculiar: the war alone did not create the phenomenon. It has taken a profound amount of work for public opinion in Ukraine to separate them out from all the other actors in the conflict. They are the people who, rather than leave, "chose" to stay and sink to the bottom, and therefore are themselves to blame for their predicament. Of course, this does not apply to all characters in our painting, to continue exploiting this metaphor. Many residents of Donetsk, Makiivka, Khartsyzk, and other occupied cities will tell you that they have not decided to "remain"; they have "always" been here. "Those who have always been here" = "those who are loyal to the Kremlin." You find them all over the canvas.

The problem with "remainers" lies in the term itself. The very word "remain" implies the making of a choice, which, in turn, suggests that something is not right, and that there is an incentive to leave. This is about the people who have remained here, under occupation, despite everything, with pro-Ukrainian views, people who continue to live among the types described above. And this is anything but abstract. There was a time when a trip from Makiivka to Donetsk was a bit like a trip from the occupied territory to the "mainland" today. On Hornostaievska Street, which separates Donetsk and Makiivka, there was a checkpoint reinforced with heavy concrete barriers and occupied by a dozen armed militants. Trenches were dug and a machine gun was set up in the woods next to it. Grads hummed all around and a stream of black smoke poured out of the airport. Sometimes it happened that you were riding with two or three others in an almost empty bus and you would be checked more diligently at the checkpoint than you would be at the checkpoints on the line of contact today. They would ask about everything—your registered domicile, the purpose of your trip to Donetsk, your job, and so on—and with that interrogation there would be a search of passenger cars, confiscation of livestock and *kvas* "for the needs of the republic." This happened even though it is all of four miles from downtown Makiïvka to the city.

Donetsk in 2014 would have made Bosch jealous: a nearly dead city with endless artillery fire, stores shut down, and food shortages. There was no point in going there, which is why, in the summer of 2014, fantastical tales about Donetsk began to circulate in Makiïvka that resembled medieval legends, and the handful of Makiïvka locals who visited Donetsk reported in horror that "We're still pretty lucky." Indeed, few are capable of staying in the kind of place that Donetsk has become, and they have to understand what they are risking their lives for.

Be that as it may, this was when the main wave of emigration—or migration—took place. Everyone decided for themselves how they would relate to what they were leaving behind. Some—those who had families with small children and woke up to Grads operating just outside their windows—said that this was no longer Ukraine, and it wasn't just about the danger of living in a war zone. For these people, the problem was also the gleam in the eyes of neighbors who were convinced that Grads were necessary because "a Ukrainian Nazi" was standing just a few miles away. The fact that Grads were positioned in playgrounds and firing from them didn't bother them. This insanity catalyzed the first wave of emigrants who left the DPR for the rest of the country.

Today, many of these people say they will never go back. Firstly, they don't believe that their neighbors' eyes have become any clearer. Secondly, Donetsk no longer exists for them; rare visits to the city to pick up their things or a cat convince them that there is no longer anything Ukrainian left here. Thirdly, for two years they have been building a new reality from scratch: jobs, careers, homes, kindergarten for the kids, new friendships, and "clean air." This is how those who have fled *russkii mir* describe the ideological atmosphere in Kyiv and other cities. The Donbas no longer exists for them: their identity has been diluted and they no longer care where in the country they live. What is important is comfort; I understand them.

Having recovered somewhat from the shock of 2014, a second wave of people set off for the "mainland" as though wandering from purgatory to paradise. These people had lived a year under occupation and decided that this war would last forever. It didn't matter when it would end. Objectively, there is little hope for the next two to five years, and even then it will take years to rebuild what had been destroyed, including people's minds. This is a task for future generations; those who left after spending even a year in the DPR feel that the work would exceed their life expectancy.

Finally, the year 2016 has brought the outlines of the painting into view. Hardly any doubters remain. There are those who have "always" been here and those who have "remained" in spite of everything. The former are in their element, even if that element has turned rancid. These are the same people, as always—even before the war—walking around in their "I'm Russian" T-shirts; the same *Homo sovieticus* for whom the mere idea of Stepan Bandera[127] is more terrifying than the actual rockets landing outside their windows and homes; the same beggars on the square; the same beau monde in their Mercedes sedans whose wealth insulates them from reality now, as before the war.

These people can be discerned quite clearly: they are the visible figures in the canvas.

But what about the figures in the shadows, those who are hated here in the DPR, and misunderstood in "mainland Ukraine?" In the "republic," they are considered enemies. Zakharchenko talks every now and then about "selection," about a "just approach" in dealing with such people: some need to be put through the purifying fire of the "Ministry of State Security" (MGB),[128] while others might be "understood and forgiven."

Are things any better in the rest of Ukraine? Not really. The government has forgotten about the "remainers." It did so when it said that it could no longer guarantee their rights and freedoms for an indefinite period, effectively admitting its impotence. This means that, if you flee now, in 2016, like others did before you, you still have a chance. Otherwise, you are spinning the cylinder of the revolver every day and hoping the chamber is empty. The only advice you will get is to drop everything and start life anew, followed by the mumbled slogan, "The Donbas is still Ukraine."

Despite two years of being told to "get going," a cohort of people under the occupation has managed to stick to pro-Ukrainian views. This is a miracle, because DPR propaganda ticks along like clockwork, flawless and clear, day and night. Only those who have stayed can understand what it takes to survive "republican" TV and retain a sound mind. But the point isn't even this.

The presence of these people in the "republic's" infected body is like penicillin for the country. Yet it is not considered proper for "mainland" Ukrainians to acknowledge their presence in the occupied zone on talk shows or on the radio; we don't have solutions for them at this level, so it is easier to turn away. Basically, we tell them that it is their own fault, that no one is forcing them to be "there" rather than "here." Which is both true and false.

Here, Ukraine keeps stepping on the same rake by disregarding thousands of lives for which a standard answer does not apply. Some in the occupied territory are invalids or pensioners without family or friends. The same neighbors keep bringing them food because they have not gone outside for years. Leaving the DPR is not an option for them, nor is getting out to lodge a protest vote in the so-called referendum. Thus, they are automatically at fault for the results because they are still here. Some, in contrast to the internal displaced persons, repeat that this is their home despite the grotesque situation here, and that our defeat will not happen on the battlefield, but when the last people living with "the Ukrainian dream" in their head leave the DPR. Some don't understand how anyone can flee and leave forty, fifty, or sixty years of life behind. Sure, young are capable of that. But to start a new life at sixty—is there any law that can tell you where and how to start? To leave a job that you've gone to for many years—years that you no longer have? Or a family, some of whom, for reasons that only they understand, will never leave this place, so that you can then visit your wife or brother on special days, like they do in jail?

I also hear the question, "What for?" Ukrainians here don't understand why they should flee their home cities when the state was the one to desert them: the internal troops and special services armed with machine guns fled from the militants who, at first, had only clubs and stones. Now we are offered the same old prescription, the same rake our country stepped on once, and those who refuse to do so again are now being blamed for the problem.

Yet those who have stayed here are paying the price, not only in their quality of life, but also in their mental health and the diminution of their souls. One Donetskite put it very aptly, saying that he felt like he'd been on Novocain for two years and had grown numb to anything that happened around him. People may be immune to propaganda, but psychological changes are sometimes ir-reversible, especially in the younger generation, which was in its formative years when the war broke out. The apa-thy and indifference to sociopolitical processes that have always been typical for people indigenous to this steppe have reduced their aspirations these days to obtaining con-sumer goods, from new iPhones or brand-name shoes, and to the mundane "Let's just survive to tomorrow." This leaves a mark on people's capacity to feel sympathy; the suffering of others is just the projection of their own suffering, to which they have become indifferent.

But let's get back to penicillin. Few understand the ac-tual role of those who have chosen to stay in the "little land." First of all, in two years of occupation, the Donbas has de-veloped a unique blend of patriotism and pragmatism. Par-adoxically, the bullets and Grads that forced many locals to flee now force those who stayed behind to remain. The difference between those who left and those who remained corresponds with an emphasis on tactics or strategy. Flee-ing in 2014 was a tactical decision. As a long-term strat-egy, however, preserving Ukrainianness and a Ukrainian way of thinking, as well as a loyalty—an absurdly stubborn loyalty, heedless of the consequences—to the values that were here before the war, was the only way for this land to become truly Ukrainian. The Ukrainian flag that once flew over this land by itself did not make the place Ukrainian. Our country was not lost when the flag was hauled down from City Hall in Donetsk, nor was it lost at Slov'iansk. First and foremost, we lost the battle in our minds, when we fol-lowed a tactic of silence at one point or chose not to attend a rally at another point, thinking that someone else would defend Ukraine, even without us. That did not happen, and only a few people here can honestly say, "I did everything I could back then."

Yes, the Ukrainian army is now capable of defending our land. But there is still the problem of the cadets who

march to the DPR anthem today. The solution to this problem lies with those parents who, though they are bringing
up their children here and dropping them off to "republican" schools and universities each day, nevertheless remind the younger generation that the DPR is all a dream,
and that the people around them are in a deep slumber,
from which they will have to wake up some day. And, indeed, it is starting to happen already; in trams and stairwells I often hear someone say, "You were right about some
things back then."

Is this worth staying for, then? Two years of hate replaced by silence, and then, little by little, the start of a dialog. The pro-separatist shouts of "Glory to the republic"
are more often answered with "Yeah, we've seen your referendum already." This emergence of "your" is thanks to the
pro-Ukrainian "shades" on that Donetsk painting. It is easy
to look at reality at its most concrete, sincerely believing
that all that matters is the number of tanks on the frontline. The problems of the Donbas began here, though, in
the Donbas, and they must end here, too, however obvious
that might sound. It does not mean that only locals should
be at the front. But, if the front is understood as a battle for
people's hearts and minds, there are no antibodies other
than fellow residents to combat this virus. Your domicile
registration here and two years of shelling are what entitle
you to start the conversation. Otherwise, no one will listen
to you. Stay here and wait for the virus of *russkii mir* to run
its course, and then you will be able to say "This is our land"
once again. Most likely this, along with the unfortunately
necessary war, will be the start of a real reintegration.

In the end, we must not allow the government to brush
us off like it did with Crimea. As long as we are still here,
and as long as thousands of Ukrainians are still fighting in
various ways for the return of the Ukrainian flag, it will be
political suicide to seriously state that there is "no one left
here" anymore. This gives rise to the hope that, one day,

the voice of the Donbas will be heard, and it will not be the sound of the tricolor. This canvas is not finished yet. The artist's brush is still soaked in paint, and it is entirely up to us to decide whether we will become more than an indistinct figure in the shadows.

July 9, 2016
Dzerkalo Tyzhnia

SCREECHING IN THE THORNS[129]

Once upon a time, Joseph Brodsky described something remarkable in an autobiographical sketch. A blue horizontal line ran along the middle of the wall. Below it, the wall was painted green, and above it, the wall was whitewashed. Nothing more. "Nobody ever asked why it was so," he wrote. "And nobody would ever have answered."[130] This line ran along all Soviet walls, from school canteens to factories; at some point, this "landscape" became associated with NKVD prisons and basements, as well.

In Donetsk, that line has survived to this day.

To be sure, you can actually see it in the entryways and stairwells of buildings from the mid-twentieth century. Zealous residents will still paint the walls in dark green, drawing a thin blue line above it, even though the entrance doors have long since been replaced with modern ones that open with electronic fobs. Architectural design is not the point. Many of those who took to the streets in early 2014 will tell you that they sincerely wanted change here. They didn't need the blue line on the wall. They didn't need the Ukrainian blue-and-yellow flag, either. Their aspirations were limited to the desire for something new and to the feeling of euphoria for which many, at the time, were actually willing to give their lives.

But what Luhansk and Donetsk have turned into today, along with their "provinces," can be called the endpoint, even if the fairytale of "*Novorossiia*" lasts for many more years. Why? It is very simple: the Soviet-era blue painted line has come to run along everything. The occupied territories have finally lost their luster for even their most hardcore admirers, while the "republics" have plunged into

classic totalitarian repressions without differentiating between friends and strangers.

Even those who come from this environment struggle
to understand what's going on among the criminals who call
themselves the LPR/DPR. The lights of theater marquees
and the Philharmonic alternate with the flash of explosions
on main thoroughfares and purges among those who were
the pillar of the "Russian Spring" just yesterday. Donetsk
started a bit earlier than Luhansk, but this city is not to
blame for it. The Donetsk cohort was given a little push as
their Moscow handlers began tightening the screws on the
local "Chekists" and demanding results.

All this started with reports of yet another assassination attempt on Zakharchenko on August 22. Obviously, the
attempt failed, and the perpetrators were never found. Two
days later, on Ukraine's Independence Day, the Ukrainian
anthem sounded in Donetsk. What is more, it played in two
central districts, including the riverfront, where the writing "Donetsk. Ukraine. August 24, 2016" appeared on the
asphalt. The Ukrainian anthem had barely finished when
a powerful explosion rocked Donetsk's "government residential area," as locals call that area. This is the district
where the notorious Motorola and the DPR deputy prime
minister live. The city had barely recovered from this
blast when a new "terrorist attack" came on the night of
August 27. This time, it was at the "republican" recruiting
station, close to one of its military bases. Once again, reports mentioned a time bomb. In September, the threat of
explosions shifted to recruiting stations in Shakhtarsk and
Khartsyzk, where they managed to defuse the bombs. On
top of all that, a Ukrainian flag was placed on a slag heap
in Makiivka, blue-and-yellow leaflets appeared in Donetsk,
and the Russian tricolors were painted over right next to
the Ministry of State Security.

Some reasonable response had to follow to at least
give an appearance that law enforcement worked in the

"republic." And that response was found, though being reasonable was never a forte of either "republic." First, Eduard Basurin, the main spokesperson for Donetsk, announced that there was a terrorist group of three women, one of whom turned out to be a supporter of the "Russian Spring." Next, a "diversionary group" of underage children was heroically detained and charged with everything under the sun except perhaps the assassination of John F. Kennedy. Supposedly, these kids had been engaged from the age of fourteen in the bombing of coal supply trains and cars belonging to businessmen who owed money to Ukraine's secret services, spending the money they earned on saunas and prostitutes.

When that Hollywood plotline didn't seem impressive enough, they detained some of their own in Donetsk, throwing the Angels, a well-known "peacekeeping" battalion in the DPR, into the basement, together with its leader Aleksei Smirnov.[131] Smirnov was famous not only for his "humanitarian" achievements, but for a video he shot while at the base of the long-forgotten Troia battalion. In it, Smirnov claimed that Zakharchenko and the "republican" leadership were reasonable people and that all talk of Troia militants being taken away in black bags was a lie. Now, Mr. Smirnov himself has one foot in a body bag.

The "Ministry of State Security" came up with baffling charges against the Angels: the crime of illegally carrying weapons and using fake documents. Of course, the Angels had been cruising around the DPR for months committing those "violations" and no one had ever thought of arresting them. Today, in a video recording, Smirnov is genuinely repentant and calling on all citizens to hand even ammunition over to the "Ministry."

Still, even this isn't the height of the Donetsk repressions. Preparations are underway to issue a "ticket to the basement" to what should be an unlikely individual. Ievhenii Kosiak[132] was recently remanded to the DPR as part of a prisoner exchange and by now has become a household name in Donetsk. Shortly after getting out of SBU custody and returning home to the DPR, Kosiak was declared a "Ukrainian Nazi." A DPR parliamentary session issued an order to local authorities to "find, arrest, and try him." As one DPR member of parliament summed up Kosiak's fall from grace, "We traded an SBU agent for an SBU agent." It turns out that Kosiak had once arrested Pavlo Hubariev and now, sitting on the sidelines of history, Hubariev had his say about this in a blog. Incidentally, Hubariev is another personality who has been chewed up and spat out by the DPR. The blue painted line keeps running along that wall.

When it comes to repression, the LPR holds its own. As good young Chekists, they sped through the preliminaries and, within a week, resolved to bury everyone. Following the most mysterious coup in history, Plotnytskyi launched mass purges. As one Donetskite rightly put it, "I get the feeling that the LPR is in the Stone Age compared to the DPR. People are walking around with clubs, and there is no one in charge at all." There is some truth to this. The Russians who fought in the Donbas in 2014 and 2015 and had a chance to fight for both "republics" say that the LPR was complete chaos. Where the motley gangs of Slov'iansk, Makiïvka, and Donetsk were tied together by some common command and strategy, the LPR often had three or four *kazaki* units in each town, and they were subordinated to no one. In 2016, even after it seemed that a clear chain of command had been established, the LPR was stuck in this mode of operation.

Having managed over time to dispatch all of his rivals—some to Russia and others to the Donetsk cemetery—Zakharchenko set up a strict military dictatorship and made himself effectively the one and only "tsar" of Donetsk. In contrast, Plotnytskyi of the LPR had to make do in less fortunate circumstances. In 2015, he became bogged down in endless skirmishes with the local *kazaki* and had no one to turn to for help.

The LPR also has suffered by comparison with the DPR in terms of the cultural environment fostered in the latter. Despite all the 1937-style grimness in the DPR, art exhibitions still take place from time to time, theaters and orchestras still operate, and new restaurants keep opening. All this activity may be concentrated in a small area of downtown Donetsk, but at least an effort has been made to distract the people here. Amidst all the trimmed lawns and thousands of rosebushes,[133] who would see that what encircled them was really the dark-green of the NKVD prison?

Things are very different in Luhansk. The city and the LPR itself have been plunged completely into the darkness of the Soviet era. Even the party leadership is beggarly, and the *kazaki*—usually disgruntled—have grown tired of shooting stray dogs. Is it any surprise that the disaffected are purged from time to time on the pretext of "the threat of a coup"? Needless to say, no one quibbles when the conspiratorial "circle of persons" who have been deemed guilty have been supposedly plotting a coup since 2014, somehow meeting together undetected for two long years.

Among the first to fall out of favor in the LPR and end up on a wanted list was Oleksii Kariakin,[134] the now-former LPR Speaker. Supposedly, he managed to "use his personal weapon" and escape, but he did not get far: there were reports that the Russian Federal Security Service (FSB) picked him up in Rostov.[135] Plotnytskyi's advisor, "Comrade" Tsypkalov, followed Kariakin's path to the bottom, and, "having realized the graveness of his crime," supposedly hanged himself. Significantly, a major separatist forum published an account by a militant who reported that the "repentant" advisor had been beaten to death before a noose was placed around his neck. Meanwhile, Vitalii Kiseliov, known in the LPR for interrogating Ukrainian prisoners and for his signature Chekist cap with a red star, was dragged out of a cell one day and displayed, to prove that he was alive but under arrest. "Comrade" Kornet, the LPR "interior minister," was arrested, and LPR "legislative committee chair" Denys Kolesnikov was also tossed into a basement cell. After all, this is what happens when you put criminals and "politicals" in the same railway car to the Gulag. As in the prison transport, bowie knives and shanks continue to determine the future of the LPR/DPR.

Horrible as it is, all of this purging makes a certain sense politically, but for one minor detail: Why did Donetsk feel called upon to send the Sparta battalion under Motorola to Luhansk, even though Plotnytskyi had the Second Army Corps at his disposal and surely could have coped with a dozen or two "not quite patriotic" individuals? There are two possible explanations for this "aid" from Donetsk.

According to the first, Donetsk has been driving a stake into the LPR since the day a bomb nearly blew up Plotnytskyi in his own car, and Zakharchenko wouldn't mind "helping" the "republic" along, especially given the prospect of taking over an empty throne. When Zakharchenko sends Motorola to Luhansk and visits Plotnytskyi in the hospital, his real intention is eventually to take Plotnytskyi's place. Unsurprisingly, right after the attempt on Plotnytskyi's life, social media in the LPR was swamped with the message to Zakharchenko: "Sasha, take us with you," an open suggestion that the LPR be integrated into the DPR. But such an outcome is unlikely for the simple reason that both Plotnytskyi and Zakharchenko are puppets who can be replaced only at the behest of the Kremlin. If a *force majeure* like the killing of Plotnytskyi were to take place, Moscow would likely have a replacement ready. The same would happen in the event of Zakharchenko's demise.[136]

Most likely, though, the arrival of the Sparta battalion in Luhansk has a simpler explanation: Plotnytskyi has utterly failed to manage even those who support him, leading to a situation where he can no longer trust anyone, including the units that report to him. Hence the fear, the terror, and the arrests sweeping Luhansk today.

All in all, what are we left with? There is a legend about a bird that sings just once in its life. It leaves its nest and flies off to find a thorn bush and does not rest until it has found one. Once among prickly branches, the bird impales itself upon the longest and sharpest thorn. According to the legend, only then does this bird sing the most beautiful song in the world. As always, reality is more prosaic: the Donbas did manage to leave Ukraine and find a sharp thorn. But instead of a song, all that has come out of it is moaning and screeching.

October 1, 2016
Dzerkalo Tyzhnia

"PRIMARIES" UNDER THE OCCUPATION

Last Sunday, in the territories controlled by the DPR and LPR, this thing happened that Luhansk separatist leader Ihor Plotnytskyi apologetically chose to name using a "somewhat foreign" word, primaries. I can describe how it went in Donetsk, since I personally took part in this theater of the absurd.

I came to one of the polling stations to see what the heck was going on. First of all, I have to admit that, much to my disappointment, there were people there after all. I had naively convinced myself that, after two and a half years of falsification by the DPR, at least when it came to elections, things would be pretty clear to people.

About a month before the "primaries," all of Donetsk was covered in flyers exhorting people not to miss the vote. The flyers appeared in the windows and on the doors of restaurants and plastered all over public transport, homes, and stores, though I knew how the owners of apartments and establishments hated this charade. That was precisely why I thought that no one would show up.

Things turned out differently, though: at two-thirty in the afternoon, I counted fifteen people at one of the polling stations in a Donetsk school. Admittedly, they were all pensioners. In the school lobby, the DPR "police" were on duty and the platforms of the so-called primary candidates had been hung up. But what was interesting here was not so much the policies as the candidates themselves, who all had the beefy look of hitmen straight out of the wild 1990s. Naturally, I wasn't planning to vote. I was interested in something else. Given that I wasn't registered in Donetsk, I asked whether I would be allowed to vote here at all. I was immediately told that I would and that they had an auxiliary voter roll intended for just such a situation. The interesting thing was, I got to write myself onto the voter roll since there was no one at the "auxiliary roll" table, they told me to sign in on my own and wait. A few minutes later, some guy came out, took a look at my passport and, without even checking what I had filled in on the form, issued me three ballots. I went into the voting booth and stood around for a few minutes, then threw the empty ballots into the ballot box.

That was just the beginning of the fun.

About an hour later, I found myself in a different district of Donetsk, not far from another polling station. Just out of curiosity, I went into that one, too. I was allowed to "vote" here, as well. What's more, at this station, which is nowhere near where I live—let alone have listed in my passport—things were pretty pathetic. First of all, the group of voters here was even older, mostly women in their seventies, to whom someone was trying to explain what was on the ballots in the dimly-lit corridor. Second of all, they didn't even bother to check my passport here; I simply gave them a nearby address, signed the register, and got my ballots. I could have gone on voting like this all day.

Why? Because nobody cared who you were planning to vote for. There could be no ballot stuffing here simply because the stuffing had taken place a long time ago. Even the debates that had been broadcast the day before, between the incumbent "mayor" of Donetsk, Martynov,[137] and his opponent, were a Potemkin village. What was being evaluated here was something quite different: the "election" was set up to test the civic fitness of Donetskites after two and a half years of a complete circus—a test that once again, in my opinion, they failed.

October 3, 2016
Radio Svoboda (RFE/RL)

С Днем защитника Отечества!

Глава ДНР
А.В. Захарченко

A banner in Donetsk portraying Oleksandr Zakharchenko and Saint George's ribbons, ahead of Defender of the Fatherland Day (February 23).

PROPAGANDA ON THE
STREETS OF DONETSK

Visually, Donetsk today looks like a cast mold of continuous propaganda. No matter what district of the city you are in, you will see at least one billboard glorifying either the DPR or its leadership. The heaviest concentration of propaganda can be seen in the Voroshylov District of downtown Donetsk, the part of the city where residents go to relax and militant leaders like to hang out.

The propaganda itself has two main aspects. One manifestation cultivates the Soviet past, especially anything tied to victory in the Second World War. To this day you can see posters with slogans for May 9 all over Donetsk. You will also see them for Donbas Liberation Day. Clearly, a parallel is being drawn between the soldiers who defended this land in the 1940s and today's militants. Huge posters, sometimes the height of an entire tall building, portray Soviet soldiers embracing their wives. And over here, just a little lower, the same kind of image, but this one with local militants. And the message is: "We won then and we're going to win now." On some buildings, you can see graffiti of armed rebels giving flowers to kids or holding kids in their arms.

The second form that propaganda takes is connected with the current time, with the DPR itself, and with Russia. On many buildings in Donetsk, you can see the Russian tricolor and right downtown, up until recently, you could find posters saying "Thanks, Russia!" in gratitude to Russia for its "humanitarian shipments."[138] The rest of the propaganda is all dedicated to the DPR itself. Billboards glorify the separatist leader, Zakharchenko, around whom a personality cult has been built here, as you will no longer find any of the other militant leaders being portrayed. And everywhere you can see information about industrial milestones, happy families, and students promoting studies at DPR colleges.

However, there are some organizations that are given rhetorical space in the public arena—the Oplot unit, for example. There is now a "civic movement" by the same name. On one of the former student dorms in the very heart of Donetsk, a huge banner hangs for the Oplot militants. Indeed, the spot where it has been hung up might be called a "propaganda wall," as just to the left of the banner is an advertisement for Phoenix, a local internet services provider and the militants' mobile operator. And on the right, yet another piece of the propaganda mosaic: a portrait of Oles Buzyna,[139] with the date of his death and the words, "To win, you must not only be right but also strong." To increase the impact of these words, they have been painted bloodred.

As for Buzyna, the appearance of his portrait in the center of the city was a big surprise for Donetskites themselves, since most of them had never heard of him. And those who did recognize the name probably had no idea what he was killed for—let alone what views he held.

October 13, 2016
Radio Svoboda (RFE/RL)

OCCUPATION AS IT IS: KHARTSYZK

Life in the occupied territory is a bit like standing in the light of a dim streetlamp. When you are close to it, you get some light and can even distinguish a few things. But the further from the source you are, the more the light scatters, growing darker and darker.

All you have to do is drive a few miles from the center of Donetsk, where many cafés, restaurants, and theaters are still open, and you will see a very different picture, one with sporadic machine-gun fire, torn-up roads, craters from exploded mines, and people who look very poor.

The further you move away from the center, the more wretched the situation becomes. Khartsyzk stands on the periphery of the most neglected and depressed areas of the occupied territory. In some ways, the city manages to imitate Donetsk. In fact, the city center and the half-mile radius around the bus station is relatively quiet and clean. But Khartsyzk, not especially large even before the war, became depopulated after it began. Life here is centered around small oases: the local recreation center and the Obzhora[140] supermarket. Some locals even call the former ATB supermarket[141]—now called the First Republican—the "center of the world."

But the outlying districts of Khartsyzk are the perfect image of stagnation, and it is not just an economic matter. Because it has extensive industrial districts, Khartsyzk has become a boundless military base where militants house equipment and personnel. This activity is reflected in the local population: some of the men from villages like Komunist belong to illegal military units where they receive at least some kind of pay packet. The rest of the population spend their time drinking and earn money by scavenging defunct factories for scrap metal that has not yet been cut up and sold by the militants themselves. A majority of the industrial companies here have either been stripped to the walls or are working at half their capacity. According to locals, the Khartsyzk Piping Plant, which was once one of the most powerful enterprises in the Donbas, paid workers their July wage only in October. If you walk around the city, you will see almost no job offers among the notices on lamp posts; most ads are about services for moving to the Russian Federation and Crimea, or about applying for state pensions from Kyiv.

The local railway station says everything about the situation in Khartsyzk. Of its fifteen tracks, only two are in active use right now. What is more, probably the only local commuter train comes in on the first track, the Iasynuvata-Ilovaisk, pulling all of four cars. The second track is occupied by a freight train carrying local coal, but the cars are all Russian-made and the coal is heading out to Russia, as well. Indeed, the cars with Khartsyzk coal are marked "RZhD, owned by OAO VZB-Leasing,"[142] followed by a phone number with a Moscow area code.

But, mind you, the remaining tracks are not empty. More than a dozen rusting Ukrainian-made trains are parked here, with the bottoms of some of the cars corroded entirely away, so that coal could not be poured into them. In truth, there is nothing to put into them, anyway, with most of the coal mines shut down at this point. What little coal extraction has been kept up under occupation goes in the new cars to the Russian Federation.

November 4, 2016
Radio Svoboda (RFE/RL)

THAT SWEET WORD, "WAR"

The war in the Donbas is the best illustration of those miles of tunnels that run under Ukraine's political realities today. There is an external enemy occupying Ukrainian territory. As soon as Ukraine tries to take the smallest step in the direction of integration with the EU, the unhealed wound of this occupation opens up and begins to bleed again. That's how this war is seen from the outside.

From the inside, things are far more prosaic. Despite the ubiquity of slogans about patriotism and the national interest, the only villa in Donetsk that has not been occupied by militants is that of their putative antagonist, Rynat Akhmetov, who early in the conflict branded the "republicans" a disgrace. In mainland Ukraine, however, he barely avoided doing time for funding the militants. In a region where every third pensioner survived the winter thanks to care packages from Akhmetov's "humanitarian fund," in contrast to the "love" and "care" offered them by the official government's blockade, things don't seem quite so obvious, and the money siphoned from industrial wells goes toward bullets as often as toward rice.

Here, they hate Poroshenko and respect Akhmetov to the same degree. Here, you can find armchair generals who know all the pathways to victory, and ordinary people who silently send a few dollars from Donetsk to support the Ukrainian army. Despite the blockade, Ukrainian producers manage supply lines pretty well here: back in 2015, you could still find fresh Roshen candies on local shelves.

While only the select few suppliers found their way through the frontline in 2015, now, towards the end of 2016, they are managing to move cheese, juice, chocolates, ketchup, and other goods through Ukrainian checkpoints

President of Ukraine Petro Poroshenko takes part in a peace march in Kyiv as a tribute to the victims onboard a passenger bus that came under fire near the town of Volnovakha (to the south of Donetsk) on January 13, 2015. Twelve civilians were killed in the attack and eighteen were injured.

by the ton, delivering them to the DPR quite easily. In Donetsk's Amstor supermarkets, you can find huge quantities of Sadochok and Sandora juice marked with the address of their Ukrainian producer: Mykolaïv Oblast, Zhovtnevyi Raion, village Mykolaïvske. The one thing about the juice that is not Ukrainian, though, is the hiked-up price: a quart of Sadochok starts at 1.15 US dollars, and a quart of Sandora is almost two dollars at the local exchange rate. Ukrainian chocolate isn't far behind. You can generally find the Korona and Milka brands at Donetsk supermarkets. The production facility address on the Korona chocolate says Trostianets, Sumy Oblast. The price of a one-ounce bar of plain milk chocolate is around 75 US cents, which is unheard of, though it is among the most "economical" selections. In fact, chocolates are one thing that few here can afford, since Ukrainian chocolates with fillings such as nuts or raisins will cost them as much as two dollars a bar.

If you walk around Donetsk Amstor stores, you will see several types of Ukrainian cheeses, among them Pyriatyn, Dobriana, and Shostka. Next to the price, in brackets, is the country of origin: Ukraine. But the barcodes on them are not Ukrainian. In other words, theoretically you are buying a Ukrainian product, but it is being treated as though it were not from Ukraine. In the case of sausage, sometimes there is a Ukrainian barcode, and all the information on the label is in Ukrainian only. But 90 percent of the producers are from the occupied territory.

The most lucrative kind of Ukrainian contraband under occupation is jewelry. What's more, every piece of jewelry sells with two tags: one says "Made in Ukraine" and the other sports a two-headed eagle marked "Ministry of Finance, DPR."

In short, the war in the Donbas seems a kind of happenstance, a cover under which business dealings that connect the occupied region with the "mainland" continue as before.

However, if local "princelings" and underhanded Ukrainian politicians are interested in the war as a source of petty privileges and bribes, the constant stretching of the "Minsk elastic" at top echelons can't help but remind us about the convenience of a fragile peace for Bankova.[143] Understanding that it won't be possible to raise the question of Crimea seriously until the "Lord of the Kremlin" has died, and that Russia will not leave the Donbas but will, in fact, continue to control it, the Ukrainian president and his entourage keep telling us about the inevitable benefits of the worthless scraps of paper that are the Minsk accords. In the DPR itself, they alternate between calling them "legal acts of a foreign state" and announcing their own interpretations of them.

The thing is that, when a society is aware of an external enemy, consolidation frequently takes place precisely around hatred toward that enemy, transferring aggression from internal problems and their sources to the external irritant. However paradoxical it might sound, if this kind of "external enemy" does not take an "all or nothing" approach, but rather maintains a slightly open wound, its presence inside the state can be completely justified by the ruling elite. When this happens, it's always easy enough to nod in the direction of the frontline, tossing into the trenches high utility rates, bad roads, the ever-climbing exchange rate, and even corruption, which after the Maidan had come to be perceived as an immediate, personal injury, a reminder of hundreds of deaths. But psychologically, the war outweighs everything: despite all their dissatisfaction with the current powers that be, even the lips of the far right can be heard to whisper, "Now is not the time to open a second front."

Indeed, now is not the time. But the irony is that in Kyiv they are trying to treat the ambiguity of the Donbas situation as a natural development, getting the public used to the idea that taking thirty hours to get from Donetsk to

Kyiv, cold nights in the fields, bribes and fisticuffs at check-points, and the occasional death of Ukrainian soldiers are par for the course and we have to accept it. This war has long been smelling not only of *russkii mir* and Buriat put-tees,[144] but also of Lipetsk[145] with its innocent boxes of Stri-la Podilska chocolates.[146]

November 6, 2016
Tyzhden

WHERE THE ELITE OF OCCUPIED DONETSK TAKE THEIR LEISURE

These days, it is typical for people to think of Donetsk as a city of artillery fire and rubble. In fact, it's mostly the southern and northern outskirts that suffer from shelling: Trudovski, Oktiabrskyi, Vietka, Staromykhailivka, and the airport. The other side of Donetsk is a city of new Mercedes and SUVs parked in specially marked spots, not shell craters. There is an unspoken list of restaurants and clubs where highly-placed militants and Donetsk's "golden youth" come to have a good time. As a rule, the latter are also connected to the DPR: they are either the offspring of those same militants and the political leaders, or they are the owners of the restaurants and their friends, who are also closely linked to the local elite.

Pushkin Restaurant, located on the boulevard of the same name, takes pride of place on this list. The next cross-street, Maiakovskyi Avenue, is blocked off to traffic and is famous for housing the administration of the DPR leader Zakharchenko, which explains why it is patrolled 24/7 by four armed militants. Two of them are even part of the view from the restaurant window. This does not bother guests one iota, as the Pushkin serves only people from DPR ministries. Not that long ago, I met with a man from the OSCE at the Park Inn Hotel, which is literally 100 yards from the Pushkin. Apparently, the Pushkin is not frequented by the OSCE; the live music and eighteen-dollar salad plate are tacitly considered the fare of local bigwigs alone.

And about those prices. The Pushkin is an expensive restaurant even for some local hotshots. For instance, risotto with shrimp costs over 21 US dollars, or 540 Ukrainian hryvnias, tuna tartar goes for almost 15 dollars, Greek salad is close to six dollars, and an ordinary *vinegret* salad[147] is still over five dollars, or 140 hryvnias. An espresso will set you back 1.20 dollar, while a hot chocolate is a whopping 4.75 dollars. Based on these prices, Donetsk's elite will drop 10–50 dollars for dinner—the equivalent of 300–1,100 hryvnias.[148]

Second on the list is a place that opened not long ago, named after a restaurant in a Russian TV series, the Claude Monet. The Donetsk Claude Monet has already managed to replace its staff completely. The prices on the menu, which were initially quite affordable, quickly skyrocketed beyond the means of most locals, which caused the restaurant's clientele to disappear, along with its profits, and forced an exodus of the staff. The Claude Monet together with the Pushkin are possibly the only establishments that have the appearance of upscale Western restaurants, with quite impressive interiors. Clearly, this is the reason for the high prices. A Greek salad here will cost close to four dollars now, or about 100 hryvnias, foie gras is 13 dollars, a meat platter ranges from seven to nine dollars, while a five-ounce side of plain rice is two dollars, or 50 hryvnias. This, when a two-pound bag of rice costs only 60 cents in Donetsk.

The Golden Lion is another notable establishment on this list. This is where the top bosses of the DPR "Ministry of Finance" traditionally enjoy a breather. It's easy enough to recognize those who operate out of these offices: two black jeeps will be parked at the entrance with identical Ukrainian license plates, while all around the periphery, including the back entrance, you can see four militants armed to the teeth. Prices here are a tad lower than at the Pushkin; one of the most expensive dishes is the tiger shrimp at almost eight and a half dollars, or a bit over 200 hryvnias, while the seafood salad is just over nine dollars. A Golden Lion espresso will lighten your wallet by 80 cents, or 20 hryvnias.

Finally, we have the recreation center of the "golden youth": the Barberry restaurant, which combines elements of a club with a hookah lounge and DJ. A tomato and cucumber salad costs 2.70 US dollars, or about 70 hryvnias, a Caesar with shrimp is 7.60 dollars, foie gras 11.50, and a cheese platter 9.20 dollars, or 230 hryvnias. If you decide you want a plain three-and-a-half-ounce serving of sliced bell pepper as a garnish to your entrée, it will cost you 2.30 dollars, or 60 hryvnias. The Barberry is right in the center of Pushkin Boulevard and its parking area is always full of expensive foreign cars with Russian plates—or local ones in the DPR style.

November 18, 2016
Radio Svoboda (RFE/RL)

DONETSK: A TOUR OF EXPROPRIATED PLACES

Like other cities in the part of the Donbas not controlled by the Ukrainian government, Donetsk has essentially been turned into a big military base at this point, with a number of its administrative buildings transformed into barracks and accommodations for the militant leaders.

A list of the sites in Donetsk that have been expropriated and adapted for military purposes starts with a meatpacking plant that has made headlines on more than one occasion because of its "signature" barbed wire. The main entrance to the plant and the adjoining parking lot are surrounded by wire and adapted for military equipment, as well as for the passenger cars belonging to the militants themselves. The warehouses behind the factory building continue to function as intended and this is where a significant proportion of people work who prefer a safe job loading and unloading cargo to the dangerous life of a mercenary.

The central city district of Voroshylovskyi is a real gold mine for the military guide. The first thing that catches the eye is Maiakovskyi Avenue, which is closed at both ends and where only cars of the "ministries" are allowed. This is where the "administration" of Oleksandr Zakharchenko, the leader of the Russian-controlled DPR crew, is located. It is guarded by four armed militants positioned behind a barrier. Passage is only permitted on the left side of the avenue as you drive toward Pushkin Boulevard.

The part of Rosa Luxemburg Street where the Donetsk University dorms are located was also closed off until a while ago. At that time, there were here concrete blocks, Ural military motorcycles, and a military checkpoint. The dorm buildings themselves were turned into barracks.

More recently, the way was opened back up and the checkpoint removed. Nevertheless, the buildings are all still being used by mercenaries, as testified by the tricolor walls on the main floor of one of the buildings.

Along Bohdan Khmelnytskyi Avenue are the premises of the Donetsk National Technical University, which have also been taken over by the separatists. This is where the "Academy of Internal Affairs"[149] of the DPR "Ministry of Internal Affairs" is now established. Close by, on Vatutin Avenue, is an elite new building whose apartments until recently were given to pro-Russian militants who had distinguished themselves. One of the apartments was reserved for the late "Motorola."

Higher up, at 54-a Universytetska Street, you will see the Optima Hotel, which has been designated for the militants, complete with an armored personnel carrier in its parking lot. The hotel is now furnished with a controlled checkpoint, barrier, and patrol. According to some sources, the hotel regularly welcomes Russian guests. The Viktoriia Hotel next door is no slouch either, having become famous back in 2014. Its entrance boasts one of the most impressively equipped military checkpoints, where all cars entering the hotel premises are checked. Here, you will see mercenaries wearing helmets, bulletproof vests, and Kalashnikovs. Inside the Viktoriia, say unconfirmed reports, the Russian handlers of the DPR leadership hang out.

December 1, 2016
Radio Svoboda (RFE/RL)

IMMERSED IN WAR

An ordinary guy with a nice smile, he looks a bit over twenty, with a tanned face and a blackened fingernail—a common injury for local workers. This is Andrii from Makiïvka. Before the war, he used to sing along to the band Bumboks[150] and work in construction. In 2014, he began to listen to Vladimir Vysotskii's song "Russkii russkomu pomogi" (Russian, help a Russian)[151] and put on camouflage. He's barely smiled since then.

His friend Serhii, like Andrii, was an ordinary worker and not much into politics. He took up a machine gun in the summer of 2014 and ended up in Ilovaisk. Serhii has had nightmares ever since. They were later joined by a common acquaintance named Anton. Anton had done time before the war and got out just as Andrii and Serhii were preparing to join the unit led by Bes. After leaving jail, Anton worked for a while, but he soon figured out that free food, booze, and a Kalashnikov were a good alternative to the spare change he was paid at the coal mine. Literally, there was hardly any paper money circulating in the DPR by mid-2014 and many coal miners were being paid with a pile of coins. It looked impressive, but you couldn't live on it. Worse yet, the miners regularly found their ventilation cut off, 500 yards below the surface, because of the shelling. So Anton eagerly joined the ranks of the defenders of *russkii mir*.

A dozen more joined these three later, all with similar backgrounds and a few with a criminal past as well. Andrii was the only one who was motivated to fight for an idea. The others fought for booze and food—and later for money. Many simply liked the idea of being a soldier of fortune: Serhii, for example, was really excited about wearing a military uniform and carrying a long, expensive knife. They were all borne along on a stream where their parents' stories about the "Great Soviet Union" were mixed in with the *Brat* (Brother) and *Brat-2* films.[152] They were inspired to take up the fight by the cultural icon of the tough guy raised on tradition, often with roots in romanticized prison culture, even if they didn't quite understand what for. Russian propaganda and Russian tanks sped up the choice, and off they went to defend the newly-emerged "people of the Donbas."

In Andrii's old building, twenty-one men joined up. Some ended up with Bes, others with the *kazaki*, and the rest with various units around the Donetsk airport. The lucky ones signed up at neighborhood checkpoints and had an easy time putting the squeeze on the locals for livestock and taking them to Donetsk from Makiïvka.

The romance of the military quickly lost its charm. Of the twenty-one new defenders of *russkii mir*, only three

Volunteers for the DPR forces at a military recruiting office in Donetsk.

were still bearing arms by December 2016. Some resigned, some deserted, and some were laid to rest at the cemetery. Some now live hand-to-mouth, some beg their friends for money, and many drink bitterly. *Russkii mir* doesn't mean a damn. Just like before the war.

Serhii returned to civilian life immediately after the battle at Ilovaisk. He traded his favorite knife for a ticket to Anapa,[153] where he worked hard as a pool-cleaner. But he didn't really fit in, so he came back to Makiïvka. He spent a couple of weeks thinking vaguely about going to Syria to fight, but he ended up at a roadside café, happily swapping his machine gun for kebab skewers. Anton lasted longer, but his departure from the ranks of the "knights of '*Novorossiia*'" was quite the show: he got so drunk on his last leave that it took him three days to regain consciousness. He called up his commander only to learn that he had been reported as a deserter and had better not to show up. They didn't toss him into a basement; they just waved him away, and he wasn't the only one like that.

Andrii has been working loading cargo for almost a year now, his wages down from the soldier's 260 US dollars, or 17,000 Russian rubles, to the laborer's 150 dollars, or 10,000 rubles. Initially, he had migrated from Bes's unit to "republican" law enforcement. He was one of the few people among either the locals or the newcomers who actually dreamt of a great "Little Russian" country. In the fall of 2014, in a uniform with the "*Novorossiia*" insignia, a smiling Andrii was still trying to convince me that they were about to take Mariupol. They would then move to the borders of the Donetsk Oblast and wait for Zaporizhzhia to have a "referendum" so that they could enter there, too.

A year later, he was the only one of the old guard left in his unit. The idealists who had survived were resigning one after another. Yesterday's heroes turned into loading dock workers and epauletted security guards. They provided security for the villas of Zakharchenko's people and regularly unloaded trains with ammunition coming from "Great Russia" to "New Russia." Andrii resigned from the DPR armed forces, saying, "This is not what I went off to fight for." Now he unloads pallets of sausages instead of artillery shells.

Meanwhile, new recruits are replacing him and others like him. They, too, are attracted by the uniform, the machine gun with a grenade launcher, the expensive long knife, and opportunities to extort goods from people. And, of course, a stable income. For many of them, it is the only available job. The peculiar type of the young "republic's" economy ensures that its army has a steady flow of human resources.

After he returned to civilian life, Andrii began to hate all things Ukrainian even more, it seems. But he and others like him hate Zakharchenko and his entourage almost as much. When you ask them about the "republic," they tell you openly that they wouldn't fight for what this war has turned into. "My country is Russia," says an unsmiling Andrii. "It can't go on like this forever. We must become part of Russia one day. There will be a big war."

Many "indigenous imperialists" who have left the militants but dream of returning to the Donbas also believe that a "big war" is coming. "For more than half a year now, there's been a quasi-war going on, in which we don't belong," Oleksandr Vasin, a well-known militant with the Piatnashka brigade, wrote in social media around a month ago. "Our places among the ideological militias have been taken over by money grubbers... Borodai was right when he said that it's time for us to leave, but we won't leave forever! This war isn't over. We're leaving to come back, to come when Ukraine goes on the offensive and all these money grubbers scatter in every direction. That's when we will come back..."

Vasin mentions Borodai for a reason.[154] He runs the Union of Donbas Volunteers, which includes many men in Piatnashka brigade, the military organization with probably the highest share of fighters from all over Russia—from unrecognized Abkhazia to the Far North. This is the power center from which Borodai, Girkin, Bezler, Purgin, and Khodakovskyi play the role of a kind of opposition to Zakharchenko and his entourage, blaming the DPR leadership for "betraying 'republican' ideals." This explains the "republican" leader's hostility and distrust toward the few ideologically-driven individuals who remain in the DPR armed forces. The "leader" of the DPR is now extremely unpopular among veterans. But this discontent does not threaten those in power. The local Chekists always have their ways of shutting up the critics.

Oddly enough, more people in Russia seem to be dreaming of a "big war" and a return to the trenches than in the "new republics." Here, most people are sick and tired of the war. The DPR will always find people happy to dress up in camouflage, though; you see cadets in their new military coats with shiny gold buttons on Donetsk buses all the time. Like their buttons, their eyes sparkle with pride at being cadets of the "DPR Armed Forces," the heirs of the heroic defenders of the republic. It is these cadets who will take the place of Andrii and his cohort.

The cadets' path through the ranks starts with the "republican" flag and coat of arms hanging in every school lobby. The insignia of the "young states" are sometimes placed on other floors, too, so that the students "do not forget them by the time they get to the second floor," as one local teacher has put it. The next step on the path is the exhibit booth featuring "School Graduates–DPR Heroes." It is reinforced with five-minute "civics" lessons dedicated to the Saint George's ribbon; with a curriculum where nothing is related to Ukraine and even geography ends with the Donetsk Oblast; with the incentive of a trip to Moscow, Saint Petersburg, or Rostov (flight loads of students have been taken there since 2015); with "God's Summer" and "Little Russian Bear" competitions; and with shooting competitions and patriotic war games where older schoolmates with combat experience, some of them in wheelchairs, teach the students the correct way to pull a trigger.

All these are the threads that weave that military coat with its fake gold buttons.

Many of those who are fifteen today will readily join up tomorrow, convinced that these are the ranks of "the most distinguished," as their teachers in schools and loudspeakers in shopping malls keep telling them.

Nobody knows who they will become the day after tomorrow: disillusioned, unsmiling loading dock workers, or Cargo 200,[155] in brand-new tactical assault vests adorned with orange-and-black ribbons.

December 16, 2016
Dzerkalo Tyzhnia

THE DONBAS IN 2017: THREE
VARIATIONS ON A THEME

Predicting what will happen in Ukraine has turned into something of a game today: it is both difficult and extremely easy at the same time.

The variables in this kind of forecasting are shuffled like so many cards in a deck by both politicians and the ordinary denizens of social networks. The result, as a rule, often matters less than the process itself. In fact, the former tends to be defined by the latter. This paradox has only become possible because predicting has turned into a separate source of income in Ukraine, and the mass of experts in this is almost turning into a social class of its own.

But simplicity ends where checkpoints begin. The signs for the LPR and the DPR signal not only the lack of basic rights and freedoms and danger to life and limb, but also an uncertain future. This is an outline of three possible futures for the occupied territories based on what is going on today.

Before moving on to the scenarios themselves, we need to answer one question: who populates the occupied territories today? The social profile is fairly simple—mostly working class. Everybody knows that the Donbas intellectual elite for the most part emigrated to other parts of Ukraine with the onset of the separatist storm—not just professors and teachers, but journalists, writers, musicians, and academics—and are now firmly planted in Kyiv and major regional cities. Of course, the occupation almost immediately came up with surrogates like the "DPR Writers' Union," to replace those who had once engaged in intellectual activities in the Donbas.

The nature of ideological beliefs is more complex and important. Paradoxically, the DPR itself has made ideological leanings more ambiguous. The idea of a "'*Novo-rossiia*' from Odesa to Kharkiv" has sunk into oblivion. The idea of merging the LPR and DPR, while less popular, is still afloat here, yet is equally unrealistic: neither of the quasi-formations has reached the boundaries that it imagines for itself, so there is nothing, really, to merge. The desire to feel a part of "Great Russia" is also vanishing, albeit more slowly, like the fantasy of "*Novorossiia*." Endless statements by Russian Minister Lavrov[156] that the Donbas is part of Ukraine and the continued wait for the offer of Russian citizenship[157] have increasingly made yesterday's "republicans" feel betrayed. There's nothing at all to feel proud of in the "young republics": widespread corruption, cynicism, and embezzlement by those in power have exasperated even those who, not that long ago, were bringing sausage and moonshine to their sons in the barracks.

In short, the average inhabitant of occupied Donbas resents the present and dwells in the Soviet past—a past, which surfaces here and there, in familiar rallies and queues. This is nothing new. What is interesting is that the minute anyone mentions returning to Ukraine, the first thing that comes to mind for these people is not "Nazis" anymore but the utility rates. In other words, for those people wandering through the landscape of tricolor flags the first question is not "who?" but "how much?" Economics have come to trump ideology.

Those who have stayed here have already lived through the worst. Although they have various reasons for not leaving this territory—even when the frontline ran right through their homes—their motivations are never purely ideological.

Finally, there are those who have returned. These people are a specific social category, rooted in the local reality even more strongly than those who have "always been here." Unlike the latter, those who have returned have started a new life twice: when they decided to leave everything under the occupation, and when they had to once again abandon everything on the other side of the checkpoints. Their return was no less forced than their flight from here. Most of these people still uphold the idea of a unified Ukraine, although pragmatism quickly supersedes enthusiasm in this and, six months later, it is hard to see much difference between them and the common inhabitant whose attitude can be summed up as "I don't care."

In broad strokes, this is a portrait of the general population. Now, let's look at the "bourgeoisie." In the past few years, the Donetsk establishment has seriously changed its façade. Fashionable suits by Arber have been replaced by the striped navy-style undershirts, and pocket squares by crosses of Saint George. Labyrinths of tunnels filled with designer studios and spas that used to lead to the oblast administration and beyond, running deep into closed-access private estates, suddenly crumbled. Forcing their way through the shower of rockets came people with guns to take their place. That simple thing, the gun, is a symbol of Donetsk business and an instrument of diplomacy. These days, any issue is shadowed by the notorious

A Grad rocket shell in the steppe near Donetsk.

"basement," the terror apparatus that determines someone's place among the elite.

This elite differs from the "Donetskites"[158] of the past in two ways: they have higher-caliber guns, and they could wind up on one of the lists—those same lists that flash "from 7 to 15 years." Ironically, these circumstances lead the elite in navy-style t-shirts to pay no attention to anything at all. Knowing that there is no way back, the people on top, who were yesterday's lumpen, have crudely divvied up everything in the city—things that used to be based on delicate connections and negotiations behind closed doors at places like the Dubok Café in Donetsk. Today, everything in the city belongs to either Zakharchenko or his wife—and, if not his wife, then Tashkent,[159] or other people further down the list: members of the "People's Council," the MGB, the "police," the military headquarters, and various administrative offices. All these make up the fabric of the Donetsk elite today and feature on any number of lists. There is no turning back for these people.

And now for the possible futures of the Donbas.

SCENARIO 1. A MAJOR WAR

Accurate forecasts are impossible for this case. The situation in the DPR today is as follows. The ranks of the military are basically full, and recruitment is ongoing. Equipment comes in far less often than it did before the summer of 2016, but there is a constant inflow of ammunition, fuel, and lubricants. The occupied territory has turned into one extensive military base, with enough equipment and personnel for full-fledged active combat operations. Let us not forget about the uncontrolled border with Russia, through which anything can pass at any time. Still, the option for the separatists and Russia of using sheer force collapses before the logic of numbers: the Battle of Svitlodarsk proved that expanding to the administrative borders of the Donetsk

Oblast and taking over all cities controlled by the Armed Forces of Ukraine would mean crossing the moral red line of the past two years and raising the rate of losses to the level of the Chechen campaigns—or even higher.

Moreover, such a step would also require a *casus belli*. A decision by Russia to recognize the independence of the LPR/DPR and their subsequent integration into the Russian Federation could be one. In that scenario, Russia would be asserting that the territory controlled by the Armed Forces of Ukraine was part of Russia and thus occupied by Ukraine. Russia would be compelled to fight a war over it. Ultimately, these considerations support the notion that Russia will never, in fact, recognize the independence of the LPR/DPR.

If such a major assault were to take place, we would undoubtedly witness a new moment of decisiveness in the population. Those who have been wandering between unrecognized status and Ukrainian passports for the past three years would once again remember the "special path of the Russians," which would now take the shape of the Kremlin star rather than the Donetsk flag. A full-scale war would also offer opportunities to the veterans who are now vegetating in local bars and pubs, and to the Russian volunteers who left the Donbas in early 2016.

For the elite, however, these would not be the best of times. Nobody is more afraid of a war than those same people who dream of taking Kyiv: Zakharchenko and Co. All these people have been rolling in the money they have been able to milk from the status quo. For the elite, a war would bring unnecessary risks, risks they have already undergone. Neither Givi, nor Zakharchenko, nor "Tashkent," nor Kononov are interested in exchanging their warm offices and loose bundles of cash from contraband for a cold, wet trench. But they would not have much of a choice if war came. That is the disadvantage of being enclosed in the "republican" citadel: you cannot go very far.

SCENARIO 2. ELECTIONS

Elections are even less likely than a major war. Zakharchenko's constant talk about "the young state" and his sig-
natures in Minsk as the representative of ORDLO[160] draw
smirks even in Donetsk: no one takes him seriously. Obviously, a single order from Moscow could turn this coach
back into a pumpkin once and for all, and everyone in the
"republic" would be told that it was time for a rally—this
time, to stop a "fratricidal war." The LPR/DPR would not be
the sticking point. The people are used to toeing the line
and would do so again.

The problem for Moscow—and, in fact, the only hope
of Ukraine—is the nascent civil society in our country. Allowing representatives of LPR/DPR to participate in elections, even while adhering to Ukrainian law, is more surreal
than a direct assault on Mariupol. It is hard to imagine how
Ukraine might gain the upper hand over Moscow in this, as
this very issue has driven Ukrainian diplomacy into a dead
end. On the one hand, thousands of people have died so
that people like Zakharchenko and Givi would never have
anything to do with our country—except maybe to be held
in our prisons. On the other, there are hundreds of tanks
and Grads, and tens of thousands of militants in occupied
Donbas, putting pressure on Ukraine to "negotiate directly
with representatives of [occupied] Donbas."

Whatever happened, the locals would surely swallow
the legitimization of LPR/DPR within a Ukrainian legal
framework with a sigh of relief that "the torment is over."
The slogan about the "special path of the Russians" would
await its next "Russian Spring," when the generation of
those who spent three years in cadet uniforms grew up.
Without financial support from Moscow, even the inevitable storm of indignation among local militants, too, would
quickly fade. In fact, things would be just like they were in
2014: everyone would be invited to change colors, while the

hardcore idealists would be forced to do their soul-searching in the vastness of "Great Russia." In practical terms, little would change for the local military contingent: the regular troops would be withdrawn to Russia and all the rest, being covered by an amnesty, would simply change their labels.

The main pebble in the show will still be the "elite," which will irritate everyone else on a daily basis. It's hard to imagine what would become of Zakharchenko, Givi, "Tashkent," and others like them, after an election. If they were to enter Ukrainian politics, however, it would justly be seen as the greatest disappointment in Ukraine in the last twenty-five years.

SCENARIO 3. NOTHING CHANGES

This is the most likely scenario, and not even because "there is no alternative to Minsk": barbed wire for another ten or more years. The reality is that changing nothing is the best option for everyone all around. We already know how the elite feel, wallowing in lawlessness in the LPR/DPR. They don't need change. They are at the very top now, and any movement will inevitably mean going down. Whether it's down to the left or to the right makes little difference to them.

The locals? After two and a half years of war, the patriots who have stayed here and the majority alike are certain that the LPR/DPR is already permanent. The rest have long found their place as residents of a territory for which Wikipedia now has a separate page. On those rare days when they are wide awake, perhaps when they have to queue for eight hours in the freezing cold, they may remember that they live in a made-up place that doesn't exist on the map. But for everything else, this will be over just as soon as they bring their sausage through the checkpoint.

The military? Both sides are busy smuggling contraband worth millions. The next evolutionary link has to wait its turn in the hierarchy. They might profit a little less, but that's about it. And Svitlodarsk only happens once a year. God willing, they may escape it.

What do the politicians say? "The country is at war." This is how they often justify high utility rates, bad roads, and the rapid devaluation of the Ukrainian hryvnia. All this is because of the trenches, so go look for it there. And the streams of contraband start in Kyiv, our capital, before merging into a sea here, in the war zone.

The rest of the country? The war has long been personal and it lives in the homes of those who have a loved one at the front. The rest of Ukrainians see the Donbas only as often as it appears on the evening news. They've come to terms with losing Donetsk, just like they came to terms with the loss of Crimea, about which not one serious expert will risk claiming its return anytime soon.

There could be the fourth scenario somewhere entitled "Miracle." But the title of this dispatch restricts me to three.

December 28, 2016
Dzerkalo Tyzhnia

THE WAR IN THE DONBAS

2017

JANUARY 27

The first leader of the LPR, Valerii Bolotov, dies in Moscow.

JANUARY 29

The battle at Avdiïvka, to the north of Donetsk, intensifies.

FEBRUARY 8

Mykhailo Tolstykh (Givi), deputy commander of the separatist Somali battalion, is assassinated at his office in Donetsk.

FEBRUARY 18

Russian president Vladimir Putin signs a decree to recognize identification documents (passports, birth certificates, university degrees, etc.) issued by the LPR and the DPR to Ukrainian citizens who are residents of these regions as equivalent to the national Ukrainian identification documents that allow visa-free travel to the Russian Federation.

MARCH 15

Ukraine officially terminates all public transportation between the occupied areas of the Luhansk and Donetsk Oblasts and the rest of the country.

2017

MARCH 26

Ukrainian positions are shelled eighty-eight times by separatist and Russian forces, killing nine Ukrainian servicemen.

JUNE 7

Battles at the villages of Zholobok and Krymske in the Luhansk Oblast resume for control of the strategic road between Luhansk and Lysychansk.

JUNE 24

Another agreement for an immediate ceasefire is reached by the members of the Trilateral Contact Group.

JUNE 27

On the eve of Ukraine's Constitution Day, a massive hacking attack from Russia using the virus Petya takes place. A large number of Ukrainian government and private organizations fall victim to the attack, many of which use Russian-developed software for accounting and communications purposes, including the Ministry of Infrastructure, Cabinet of Ministers, Cyber Police, State Service of Special Communications and Information Protection, websites of the Lviv City Council and the Kyiv City State Administration, telecommunication giant Ukrtelekom, state bank Oshchadbank, Ukrainian railway Ukrzaliznytsia, the largest airport in the country Boryspil Airport, the Chornobyl Nuclear Plant, major TV and radio media, and a number of other large enterprises.

AUGUST 25

Another agreement for an immediate ceasefire is reached by the members of the Trilateral Contact Group.

NOVEMBER 23

Following a coup in the LPR, Ihor Plotnytskyi departs for Moscow and is replaced by Leonid Pasichnyk as interim head of the LPR.

DECEMBER 27

Another agreement for an immediate ceasefire is reached by the members of the Trilateral Contact Group.

Russia's war against Ukraine in the Donbas and the occupation of Crimea continue as of the publication date of this book.

THE DPR AND RELIGION

The religious aspect of the war in the Donbas has manifested itself through the military conflict. I have to say that,
by the end of 2016, religious motives among the militants
had receded into the background and no longer have the
kind of overweening power that they had in 2014. As I mentioned earlier, in the spring of 2014, at a Makiïvka militant
checkpoint known as 4/13, an icon of Christ was nailed to
the post—and one of the guys I knew was standing at that
checkpoint. What was striking was that this fellow was
standing with earphones on, and was listening exclusively
to Western rap. But in his pocket, he had one of those little
icons that the *kazaki* regiment was handed by a local priest
during the blessing of their machine guns.

It is no secret that, in the *kazaki* world, Christian Orthodoxy plays a very special role. Those who were still
trudging to the coal mines yesterday and are wearing as-
trakhan hats today have combined rap popular among the
locals with little icons of the Mother of God. But such eclec-
ticism goes much further. Despite the decline in religious
propaganda in local media, Christian Orthodoxy, specifically of the Moscow Patriarchate, is still considered to be one
of the pillars of the "struggle against fascism." Allow me to
remind you again that, in the rare instances that Zakharchenko visits the Holy Transfiguration Cathedral in the center
of Donetsk without warning, the service is interrupted to
acknowledge the presence of the don of the DPR.

This kind of piety is mutual. Zakharchenko has promised to deal harshly with "sectarians" within the territory
under the control of the DPR, including Buddhists. The boss
of a gang that is recognized in Ukraine as a terrorist group
has announced that for him there are only four confessions:

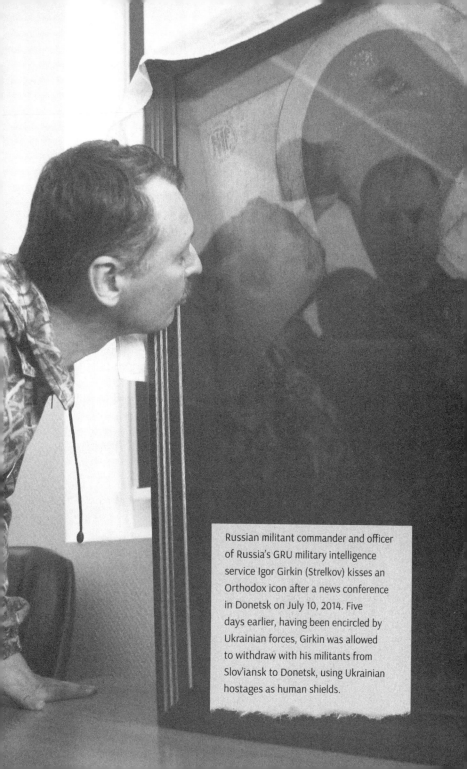

Russian militant commander and officer of Russia's GRU military intelligence service Igor Girkin (Strelkov) kisses an Orthodox icon after a news conference in Donetsk on July 10, 2014. Five days earlier, having been encircled by Ukrainian forces, Girkin was allowed to withdraw with his militants from Slov'iansk to Donetsk, using Ukrainian hostages as human shields.

"I am Orthodox, I go to church, and for myself I believe that the only church for a man who believes in God is the Moscow Patriarchate. I recognize four major religions: Orthodoxy, Roman Catholicism, Islam, and Judaism." At one point, he threw the renowned Ukrainian academician, Ihor Kozlovskyi, into prison, accusing him of founding a "radical religious group" that threatened the security of the DPR. Kozlovskyi was a professor of religious studies.

The clergy who have remained here continue to propagandize for *russkii mir*. I don't often go to church, but when I went to the Easter service in 2015 and 2016, I had to listen to the priest's sermon about the "holy war" that "our people" are waging against "the enemy."

Some of the priests allow themselves to speak directly, among them Andrii Tkachov,[161] an archpriest well known both in the Donbas and among adherents of Russian Orthodoxy, whose evening sermons on the KRT channel[162] were quite popular in the region even before the war. A seemingly well-educated theologian, he suddenly began talking about the real and the false Ukraine and calling upon the faithful to endure the era of tribulation that began with the Maidan. Tkachov himself moved to Moscow in the summer of 2014.

January 6, 2017
Radio Svoboda (RFE/RL)

HOW THE MILITANTS PREPARE CHILDREN TO JOIN THEIR MILITARY ORGANIZATIONS

The DPR gang leaders have organized a powerful system of "military and patriotic" education for young people that raises children up in the ideals of *russkii mir* and in hatred for all things Ukrainian. This kind of work goes on at all levels of the educational process, but there is a set of institutions that directly address how to prepare new trainees for the DPR's military and the front.

The Berehovyi Lyceum Boarding School for Intensive Military and Physical Training, one such institution, operates under the jurisdiction of the DPR "Ministry of Defense." Youngsters join the lyceum after the ninth grade and are trained to replenish the ranks of illegal armed formations.

The DPR allocates considerable funding for this type of military education, even prioritizing it over the funding it provides to existing military units, where basic necessities are sometimes not available. The young students are fed, given a new uniform, and brought up in the "anti-fascist" spirit. Every once in a while, World War II veterans are invited to the lyceum; parallels are drawn between the Wehrmacht and the Ukrainian Armed Forces.

They even organize balls for the lyceeists, who dress in white uniforms, complete with belts in the colors of Saint George and a Soviet star on the buckles. In the fall of 2016, the lyceum was reorganized by merging it with another military institution, the Donetsk Higher General Military Command College, or DonVOKU.

DonVOKU is the next level in the ideological indoctrination of youth by the DPR. Recently, cadets from this college have been seen in large numbers all across Donetsk, and their numbers keep growing. This is hardly surprising, given that, for the locals, this institution is a bit like

Children attend a ceremony to unveil the "Book of Memory,"
a monument to the DPR militants who died fighting against
Ukrainian armed forces at Iasynuvata, north of Donetsk.

a Suvorov military school;[163] even young people from the LPR are trying to enroll at DonVOKU.

The DPR is training cadres for the future command staff in four general areas: intelligence, tank troops, infantry, and the political department. At this point, a cash allowance is being issued at the rate of around 1,500 Russian rubles, or 25 US dollars. Once they have completed their studies, graduates receive the rank of lieutenant. The ideological indoctrination here is already an order of magnitude higher because, after all, these are the young men who will later be training new recruits to fight the mythical "Ukrainian Nazism."

Last but not least, one of the most exclusive institutions is the DPR's Academy of the "Ministry of Internal Affairs," which is located in an appropriated building of the former University of Computer Science and Artificial Intelligence. Here, in addition to future prosecutors and police officers, personnel are trained for the DPR "Ministry of

Internal Affairs." Candidates study here under the patron-age of those who already hold important posts in the DPR inner circle.

This academy not only prepares senior staff and man-agers for the police system, but also teaches methods to be used while interrogating people and getting informa-tion out of them. This guarantees that there is a pipeline of trainees ready to take the places of those who are now seventeen to twenty years old as they themselves move on. Some of these young people are already practicing at checkpoints on days designated as "high alert," when the dons of the DPR are especially "ready" for an infiltration by saboteurs and spies from Ukraine. When this happens, the experienced Chekists are assisted by those who were children just yesterday.

January 10, 2017
Radio Svoboda (RFE/RL)

"I FOUGHT IN THE WAR": LIFE AFTER LEAVING THE DPR MILITIA

For many locals who participated in the conflict in the Donbas in the ranks of illegal military formations, the end of 2016 also marked the end of their military careers. The majority of the "veterans of '*Novorossiia*,'" as many of them prefer to call themselves, have left the militias and returned to their civilian lives. Still, their reasons for donning civilian clothes again and taking up their former lives vary considerably.

In the summer of 2014, nearly all the men between the ages of twenty and forty in our apartment building in Makiïvka joined the ranks of the militants. Their reasons for doing so were not all the same. Some were at the very bottom of the social heap and had no income at all. Others believed in the idea of a "*Novorossiia*" stretching from Odesa to Kharkiv. Still others wanted the easy pickings that carrying a machine gun guaranteed at that time. Altogether, more than two dozen of my neighbors joined the militants back then and nearly all of them stayed in the ranks of the illegal units for more than a year.

But as 2015 drew to a close, many began to abandon the ranks of the separatists. Some of those who had survived the conflict's hot spots like Donetsk Airport and Ilovaisk stated that the war had turned into a means of making money for those who made it to the very top, and they had no intention of fighting for the purpose of making Zakharchenko or Givi rich. Some were unhappy with the inability to take leave, the lousy pay, and pointless duty out in the cold. One way or another, of the two dozen or so from my apartment building who had joined up, only three remained among the militants by the beginning of 2017.

One of those three continues to serve in a tank battalion and has no intention of leaving, even after being seriously wounded. This man is one of the few who still believes in the idea of "the people's lands." The other two are currently in the ranks of the "republican guard," which has turned into a kind of joke at this point: its members rarely show up at the front and mainly serve a decorative function at rallies and ceremonial events.

Adapting to civilian life for those who have returned has been far more painful. For instance, one of the guys I know, who was awarded a "medal" back when Bezler was in charge, now has to work as a simple loading dock worker and openly admits that, after operating a howitzer, loading trucks is really unbearable. What's more, he is constantly blowing up at his parents, accusing them of not giving a damn that rockets were flying at him until not that long ago. The psychological readjustment to civilian life for people like him is often extremely painful.

Other former militants are not faring much better. As I've mentioned earlier, this includes those who resigned from the DPR army and moved to Russia to clean swimming pools, or got a job slinging hash at a local *shashlyk* joint, or lucked into a job with the "Ministry of Emergency Management." But most continue to live an antisocial existence in their old neighborhoods, drinking away what money they manage to scrape together moonlighting on local construction sites.

January 13, 2017
Radio Svoboda (RFE/RL)

BACK IN THE USSR: SOVIET THEMES IN DONETSK EATERIES

The Soviet past is an extremely popular motif in the aesthetics of the DPR. It can be found everywhere—in the educational system, in propaganda, and in the designs of packaging. The service sector is no slouch at incorporating it, either. Some cafés and restaurants in Donetsk have taken to using Soviet themes to attract customers. Some are putting a spin on old Soviet slogans to draw clientele, like the signboards of Café Gourmand on Pushkin Boulevard that use a familiar formula: "Feeling down? Booze it up!"

Among the properly "Soviet" establishments is a café-bar by the unambiguous name of Nasha Rodina SSSR,[164] located not far from the Pivdennyi Bus Station. Strangely, the interior of the café reflects nothing about the Soviet past; like its menu, the restaurant has nothing special other than its name and signboard.

But a café called Olivier-80,[165] which is in a basement on Hurov Street, is something else. When you walk in, you are immediately immersed in the Soviet past. The waiters are dressed in the kind of shirts they wore in Soviet times, with the collar buttoned up to the top. Busts of Lenin, photographs of Soviet actors, Soviet-era diplomas, and even a portrait of Josef Stalin decorate the walls.

At one of the tables, there's a telephone from the 1960s, together with a newspaper from the same period, with articles about a decree of Lenin's. The table is called the "Table of the Party Worker," and is decorated with several four-line poems dedicated to the Soviet era. The table itself is fashioned in the shape of a Soviet sewing machine.

Opposite the table, a pair of skates, an accordion, and a checkerboard with checkers glued to it hang on the wall. There's also a shelf with a series of Soviet books and an assortment of black-and-white photographs. One of the most impressive elements in the decor of this café is a large burgundy banner with Lenin's profile and the slogan "Moving toward the victory of communism under the banner of Marxism-Leninism and the leadership of the Communist Party!" The same style is maintained even in the bathroom, where the walls are covered in Soviet newspapers, and black-and-white photographs are fixed with clothespins to a rope hanging from the ceiling, as if the photos had just been developed.

Sausage on sale in Donetsk. Cheap, low-quality sausage often figures in the nostalgic imagery of the Soviet Union since its collapse in 1991, especially among the older population of the post-Soviet countries.

The menu, on the other hand, is quite varied and lists only a few select Soviet-era items: Gold of Zhiguli vodka,[166] a compote[167] based on cranberry pulp, cucumber lemonade, "Honeycake from the USSR," and, of course, the ubiquitous Olivier salad, which is offered in all of six versions: smoked salmon, shrimp, chicken, and other options. The most expensive version is the "Olivier deluxe" with a salmon fillet; a small portion costs 3.80 US dollars, or a bit more than 100 hryvnias.

The music featured at Olivier-80 also departs from the Soviet theme. Mostly Western performers—Mylène Farmer is a favorite—are on the rotation. When I went there, the guests were anything but poor and the table next to me ordered several versions of the Olivier, along with a bottle of bubbly, which the waiter brought out in a pail of ice. In fact, the service was quite decent—that distinctively Soviet boorishness is something you won't see here, any more than you will cafeteria-quality Soviet cuisine: the food at Olivier-80 is actually good.

January 25, 2017
Radio Svoboda (RFE/RL)

"LOOKING FOR A TUSK TO BUY": ADS IN OCCUPIED DONETSK

The war in the Donbas often coincides with business, even in advertising. A slew of brands has emerged from the concept of *russkii mir* that are now used both for propaganda and for commerce. The Blokpost[168] is one such store in one of the downtown districts of Donetsk. Blokpost not only applies military terms to the goods that it sells but has decorated its interior in military style; the entire shop is painted the colors of a camouflage net. Yet, as of this writing, what Blokpost sells—mostly food items and pet food—has little to do with the war.

The Soviet theme so popular in Donetsk is also used to promote an entire range of goods produced in the LPR using Soviet packaging designs on products such as milk, creamery butter, and ice cream. Not that long ago, sugar joined their ranks.

Narodnyi—"of the people"—is a modifier used in the occupied territories to brand not only politico-ideological organizations such as the DPR and LPR and local newspapers, but also grocery stores and even European-style vinyl replacement windows ("Narodnye okna").

The phrase *iskonno russkii*—"originally, primordially Russian"—can be found in snack bars and cafés like Rasseia and Teremok, with decor replete with Russian samovars and *pliushki*.[169] Similarly, *russkii mir* finds religious expression on the verge of "entrepreneurship" and ideology: the icon of Christ with the inscription "God is with us" that I've mentioned several times already is still nailed to a pole at the site of an old militant checkpoint in Makiïvka, where guards used to earn their keep extorting goods from transiting vehicles. The same image can be seen on the banner of the Berkut Union of Veterans of the Donbas, hanging

near the building of the former Donetsk Oblast State Administration. Incidentally, the administration building itself is still adorned with the word "Russia," and beside it
is a street sign, to which the separatists added an arrow
reading "Kyiv 777 km"—much like the signs that pointed to
Berlin during World War II. Still, just a bit further down, at
the Covered Market, the religious theme becomes commer-
cialized. Here, they sell a huge quantity of imperial Russian
flags with the inscription "We are Russians. God is with us."

The Soviet past has returned to Donetsk with the restoration of the erstwhile Moskva Grocery. Prior to the sei-
zure of the city by separatists, the store had been a shop
selling imported clothing.

Paraphernalia for cars has a special place, starting
with bumper stickers that say "Thanks for the victory,
grandpa,"[170] as well as orange-and-black Saint George's
ribbons, DPR flag decals, and a slogan that became popular not long ago: "Get to work, brothers."[171] This phrase
was first uttered by a Russian policeman named Magomed
Nurbagandov, who died at the hands of Islamic State militants. In the DPR, it has been turned into an expression
of resistance to the Armed Forces of Ukraine. "Motorola"
even managed to photograph himself with this inscription
before he was killed, and now you can find it on the rear
windows of Donetsk taxis.

DPR propaganda uses every possible surface to promote its ideas. You will often see the phrase "Here there
are no Nazis who feel like they are the masters of the country" on billboards.[172] Propaganda is disseminated even at
bus stops. For instance, the Hanzivka stop at the border
between Makiïvka and Donetsk is decorated with the Russian tricolor and the inscriptions "The Donetsk Republic"
and "The Young Republic."

Another form of branding in the retail sector is the
"quality seal" from the "People's Control" initiative, whose
members check the quality of goods in DPR retail chains,

shops, and markets. I have to say that "People's Control" is possibly the only organization in the occupied areas that really does a good job, because they pay no attention to the strict chain-of-command of the occupation or to the connections the owners of retail outlets might have. Many stores and markets in Makiïvka and Donetsk have found themselves facing repeated strict inspections from the "people's overseers." As a result, they have lost customers and some even have closed altogether. Incidentally, the markets in the DPR have long been nationalized and turned into subsidiaries of the "Markets of Donbas State Enterprise."

Finally, last week, even the outlying districts of Makiïvka and Donetsk were papered over with a single solicitation; in some places, you encountered it every ten yards. Given the general situation under the occupation, it came across as a joke: someone was ready to pay a decent price for a saiga horn, a mammoth tusk, a walrus tusk, or a rhino horn. Where local residents might possibly get any of these items is hard to fathom. Still, given the scale of the campaign, the advertiser clearly expects to succeed.

January 26, 2017
Radio Svoboda (RFE/RL)

FOLLOWING THE PATH OF CRIMEA?

"They expelled us from their society, so we made our own, a more durable one—and it works," says one of the heroes in the popular movie *District 13: Ultimatum*.[173] The film at times resembles to a remarkable degree what the DPR has become today: a place where field commanders are incinerated by a Shmel,[174] where grenade-launchers can be shot into a building in broad daylight, where you can find yourself without any rights when confronted by the highway patrol, and where sporadic machine-gun fire is heard during curfew. Add some large-caliber guns and checkpoints into the mix and you get a real-life Ukrainian version of the film. Welcome to Hell, indeed. But more importantly, as in the motion picture, a majority of the people in the LPR/DPR are pleased that they are drifting further and further away from the legitimate center of their country, Ukraine.

In 2017, many pro-Ukrainian patriots in the occupied territories pinned greater hopes on the possibility that the situation with the LPR/DPR would be resolved. After Oleksandr Turchynov's announcement of a "2017 turning point," it looked like the Ukrainian government would finally adopt a firm position and not only stop giving up Ukrainian soil, but also make up its mind to take back what had been taken away. Where exactly this breakthrough was supposed to take place, on the battlefield or at Minsk, was hard to say. But people expected it, and groundless hopes have a way of taking the upper hand over fundamental impasses. Yet hardly a month had passed before everything had turned upside down for the pro-Ukrainian cause. Now, the reclamation of Ukrainian territory disappeared from the agenda. Instead, everyone who had anything to say at all started talking about the supposed integration of the LPR/DPR into

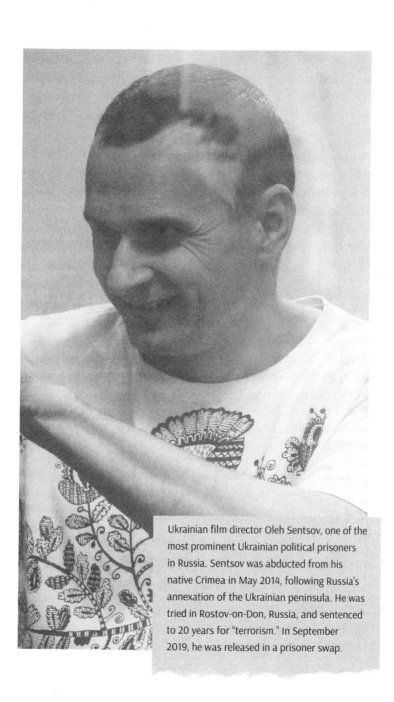

Ukrainian film director Oleh Sentsov, one of the most prominent Ukrainian political prisoners in Russia. Sentsov was abducted from his native Crimea in May 2014, following Russia's annexation of the Ukrainian peninsula. He was tried in Rostov-on-Don, Russia, and sentenced to 20 years for "terrorism." In September 2019, he was released in a prisoner swap.

the Russian Federation. And, on top of that, another topic related to the war appeared out of the blue: the legal definition of what the hell this all was.

The paradoxical nature of the Ukrainian position in this matter has taken everyone by surprise. Let's leave aside for a moment the fact that the importance of having a legal definition for the occupied territory only became clear in the fourth year of this war. What's more, public opinion about it tosses around various terms, like "occupiers," "terrorists," "hybrid forces," and "effective control."[175] Of course, every "expert" in the Ukrainian Facebook community will argue that there are no terrorists in the LPR/DPR, insisting that there are only foreign occupiers. The participants in the "civilian" blockade also talk about foreign occupiers, demanding that the Ukrainian parliament adopt a bill to that effect. Regarding these issues, national hysteria has reached the point where you hear people saying, "Every word spoken on Vodafone[176] is a bullet fired at our soldiers. Don't use products made by the occupier!" If trade is the problem, it is unclear how it is OK to buy coal from the Donbas but not to sell cheese to it: is the blood shed in the name of buying the occupier's coal any less red than the blood shed in the name of selling Ukrainian cheese? The blockade—at least its official version—is a tactical step that, absent a comprehensive strategy, is just as much of a mistake as the absence of a strategy would be. It is wrong to start a blockade using Minsk as a pretext just because some Grishin,[177] or Ivanov, or Petrenko is conducting a blockade of his own.

But then this is all just a prelude to something else. There is a more substantive issue at stake: if Russia is an occupying party, then why are our diplomats so determined to present their case at the Hague as a matter of terrorism? The answer is obvious: it is because the Ukrainians use the term ATO (Antiterrorist Operation) to describe the war. And, then, what kind of a blockade are we talking about? Why are they demanding certificates to get social benefits, even though the UN has openly requested that the requirement be dropped? Kyiv says it is unable to guarantee respect for human rights in the LPR/DPR, while at the same time agreeing to take on this commitment. Ukrainians are insisting on the term "occupiers," but the president agrees under pressure to a blockade, while his diplomats present evidence of "terrorism." So, is it a war with a foreign state, or is it homegrown terrorism? We don't have answers to the most elementary questions about the most important event in the recent history of our country. Somewhere here is the beginning of chaos, when people are forced to buy ten certificates in order to get a Ukrainian pension while living in the DPR.

However, this legal chaos is surpassed by the actual chaos in the LPR/DPR. "Multilevel integration" into Russia, which is so much talked about here and which emerged after the launch of the blockade and Russia's recognition of the DPR passports, has once again persuaded the imaginations of locals of the rightness of the formula "Russia will not abandon us!" The problem Ukraine has in dealing with the people of the occupied territory is that the government is too quick to pull out the calculator and reduce the problem to how much it would cost in freight-car loads to support their people there. Therefore, nobody in the government in Kyiv gives a damn what a thousand patriotic Ukrainians who have lived for three years under Russia's "effective control" might say about the Ukrainian state—people who have lost their jobs and who are ashamed to look in the eyes of their hungry children in the morning. Ukraine proposes to them, "Come on over, abandon your home, your school, your college," but it is an offer with no deadlines or dates. The DPR counters, "Wait. Soon you'll have everything. Ukraine has abandoned you, once and for all."

Everyone knows that the more you struggle to pull yourself out of a swamp, the more deeply you sink into it. The DPR is often compared to a swamp, but few notice that the Ukrainian government itself helps ensure that people are trapped in it. Ultimately, any problem that Kyiv tries to attach to the LPR/DPR only leads to the greater integration of locals into the "republican" system. Sure, for a while you wave your arms around and gulp the air chaotically, trying to understand what to do after the blockade, missing your lost job and the 24-hour shifts at a checkpoint. But after a while, you get used to it. The curfew no longer bothers you and the blown-up elevator makes you think, "Yeah, I've been living like this for three years already." The problem has become habitual, the habit has become normal, and this ghetto is your familiar home.

In terms of the socioeconomics, you'd have to look long and hard to find some aspect of the DPR that *isn't* integrated into all things Russian. So, what do locals really have in mind when they talk about integration? And what does the majority really want? You'd have to say that the local residents are fairly unassuming. The needs of the majority are defined by the field of vision open to them in their day-to-day lives. The most "fortunate" in this sense turn out to be the local pensioners: most of them get both a Ukrainian and a Russian—read "republican"—pension, and, until recently, an official care package as well. Their television and fifty years of Soviet life long ago convinced them that on the other side are the fascists they didn't manage to finish off during World War II. Still, that doesn't get in the way of the old ladies' smiling politely at Ukrainian soldiers when they cross the frontline to get their pensions or shop for Ukrainian sausage. Chronic resentment for these last three years has been evident only around the fact that the Ukrainian pension is higher and that Zakharchenko is "robbing the people." But when the hryvnia-to-ruble exchange rate was set at one to two, the difference in the pensions was nearly eliminated. As of 2017, this part of the population feels completely at home in the DPR, with the exception of those who are too sick to go for their Ukrainian pensions and so have to live on just one. But even in these cases, the difference in prices between the LPR/DPR and Ukrainian-controlled territory is somewhat balanced out by cheap utility rates in "republican" areas.

Here it's all about Russian rubles, Russian wages, and a Russian model of government, along with "cheap sausage"—that is, low utility rates—and basement prison cells.[178] Some of the laws are cribbed from Russian Federation. Here, it's also about the Russian army and special forces. In schools, Russian history and the Russian version of reality. Even geography is limited to the Donetsk Oblast, as I've mentioned earlier. And we pro-Ukrainians are all so pleased that "nobody's going to annex them." That's probably quite true. Why? Because Russia doesn't need to legally absorb some lump of territory that would entail "liberating" Mariupol and a wider war, not to mention that the sanctions would be more severe. The issue lies elsewhere: could its national strategy be based on the dog-in-the-manger principle "I can't eat it, but I won't let anyone else have it, either"? What do we gain from making fun of the "republican" passports, reassuring ourselves that "they certainly won't be able to travel to the West with them"? After all, they may not need to, especially since many of the locals, even those now outside Donetsk Oblast, have never travelled in their entire lives.

Another layer of society is the local youth, who have long since adopted the "republican" colors, so integration with Russia is not a threat to them, either. Yet other young locals have gone into the militia. However, the steady flow into the ranks of the militants only lasted until the end of 2015. In the past year, the DPR "Commissariats" have done nothing more than call for new recruits through the intercoms of trolleybuses, as they continue to do to this day. There are almost no takers. As one former militant noted back at the end of 2016, "Anyone who wanted to is already fighting." The rest join the militias only as a last resort, when they are out of options. Nevertheless, this part of local life is always available and is a kind of guarantee of at least a subsistence-level income of 15,000 Russian rubles, or 250 US dollars, in monthly wages.

School kids and students don't worry too much about "republican" diplomas. Some, surprisingly enough, engage through Skype with Donetsk National University faculty now in Vinnytsia, to prepare for Ukrainian state exams. They, also, should not be forgotten. Most of them plan to work in the LPR/DNR after finishing their post-secondary education. Those, such as the graduates of medical universities, who are looking for a serious future and good prospects, move to Russia from the universities in the DPR that have signed agreements with Russian universities. Acceptance of "republican" diplomas happened long before the whole business with the passports, although this was not government practice, but was based on private agreements. These days, the pathway to Russia is open to all.

As for the passports themselves, there is a kind of integrational component with Russia, for sure. Firstly, Russia's recognition of the LPR/DPR passports as equally valid next to Ukrainian national ones solved the problem of the local militants who were unable to add a new photo to their Ukrainian passports when they turned twenty-five. This act rendered their Ukrainian passports invalid. Given that none of these people even intended to show up in Ukrainian-controlled territory, they turned their attention entirely to the Russian Federation, where they wouldn't have been able to travel with invalid Ukrainian papers, anyway. Even if someone had managed to resign from the illegal military formations and "break through" to Russia for work, the job would have disappeared quickly, the minute the question of documents came up. Now all these people have "republican" passports. By recognizing the LPR/DPR passports on a par with national Ukrainian ones, Russia has managed to integrate the militants into its own society by providing them this manner of a spare parachute.

Anyone who has not obtained a Ukrainian passport yet has also received a ticket to the Russian Federation: most of the young people now boast about their "republican" piece of paper in preference to the Ukrainian colors. Needless to say, this generation won't be linked to Ukraine even legally. The services provided by Russian banks have only strengthened this process. It's true that the LPR/DPR passports do not offer any advantages over Ukrainian ones, but if you consider demand for them among the locals, you get a proper measurement of how much people here are "waiting" for the Ukrainian government to return.

The only remaining bridge between the LPR/DPR and Kyiv was industry: thousands of people continued to receive Ukrainian hryvnia and delivered goods on the "mainland," but now, with the blockade, this has been cut off—a bridge properly burned. Once again, thousands are faced with a choice: remain in the LPR/DPR or start a new life. Something tells me that only a handful will go for the new life, having decided that our country has ultimately turned its back on them, which they will no doubt be persuaded of around here. Despite all the complications, the DPR really has started to look for markets and to deliver raw materials to Russia. And the Russian Federation, with some backtracking and the finishing off of some local industry, is in a position to resolve this last issue of the integration, as well.

Once a year, Ukrainians remember Crimea. It's ours, they say, and, if we don't bring it back into Ukraine, then our children (or maybe great-grandchildren) will. Between the blockade, the Hague, chaos in the Ukrainian parliament, and the war among the oligarchs, the only thing left is to announce the day for remembering the Donbas—no doubt with energetic saber-rattling, or rather computer-mouse-rattling on Facebook.

March 31, 2017
Dzerkalo tyzhnia

Relatives and friends meet the released Ukrainian hostages at the airport of Boryspil, Ukraine.

US AND THEM

Even before 2014, I often heard people talk about "us and them" in what is now the occupied part of the Donbas. "Us" meant the residents of Makiivka and Donetsk (since they were the ones talking), and "them" meant the "westerners,"[179] by which Makiivites referred not to residents of western Ukraine but to everyone who spoke Ukrainian. Of course, this factor, language, moved the geography of "us and them" to the right bank of the Dnipro, where those "strange" people lived who were hard for simple laborers to understand. Often, the differences among us were made along historical lines and went no further than some words about Stepan Bandera and recollections of how our grandfathers fought each other on the frontlines of the Second World War.

Not that long ago, I happened to find myself in one of the Ukrainian hinterlands. Spending not quite two days in a Ukrainian village (I won't name it for the sake of my personal safety in Donetsk) gave me innumerable impressions and thoughts about what it is that nevertheless distinguishes and unites us.

1. LANGUAGE

Despite popular opinion, the residents of the central and northern oblasts of our country (where I also had a look) speak a language that is not quite Ukrainian. Just like here, in Makiivka and Donetsk, they don't know Russian, either. The Donbas bogeyman about "Ukrainian-speaking Banderites" does not withstand quantitative or qualitative criticism. The language people speak in this little town is classic Surzhyk. In a single sentence you're likely to hear five to six Ukrainian words mixed with two to three Russian ones, spoken with Ukrainian pronunciation. It's like speaking Spanish with Italian pronunciation. For instance, the lady of the house might use the word "obizhena" (in Russian, offended) instead of "obrazhena" (in Ukrainian, offended). However, the language factor coupled with the small size of the place immediately sets visitors apart from locals. Donbas Russian would not be confused with the Russian language here, although some locals speak Russian, as well.

2. WORK

The second factor that struck me was local attitudes toward work. Given that, prior to the war, I went through hell at many Makiïvka and Donetsk factories, this aspect always bothered me. I remember how people went to their shifts in Makiïvka: at 6:30 am, the minibus was filled with what looked like forced laborers, their gray, exhausted faces reflecting depression and a hopeless life. That was how it was when I worked loading railcars: twelve-hour shifts plus two hours commuting there and back turned people into creatures without feelings or emotions, people whose physical fatigue was coupled with weariness about their day-to-day existence. Nothing interested them anymore: not politics, not sports, and not the arts. Many of my "colleagues" barely made it to the evening, when they were paid for their shift, went home, and drank so heavily that the next morning on the bus they felt as though they had been booted in the face all night.

I saw something completely different here in the Ukrainian village. Most of the residents commute to the oblast capital for work. True, they don't have the same kind of heavy industry as in the Donbas. However, the trip is more than an hour each way and people have to get up at around 5 am. Everything is the same here as in Makiïvka, except for one thing: you don't see sadness in their faces. As the bus fills with fellow villagers, the impression is that they are all on their way to some kind of concert. I wouldn't say that these people are somehow different from us, either: like us, they are dressed pretty plainly and enjoy about the same level of income, but everyone is smiling, courteous, and pleasant. Oh, and there is one more difference: as they get off the bus after work with their pitiful wages, everyone thanks the driver for having driven them home. You get out of the overflowing, stuffy minibus in complete darkness (there is no outdoor lighting at all) in some godforsaken village and find the strength for a smile and a "thank-you." In Makiïvka, other than the hour-long accompaniment of Butyrka[180] in the cabin of the bus, passengers can only count on maybe a short obscenity from the driver because they quietly called for their stop.

3. INSIGNIA

It's no secret that, in the DPR, all the companies have been forced by the government to fly the "republican" flag on their premises. This "little duty" irritates many here, even those who support the DPR. But everybody has to display something "republican." Even if you don't want to spend the money for a large flag, there has to be a small one behind either the counter or the bar. In this remote village, I saw two Ukrainian flags, each hanging outside a private home, next to where the hay was stacked and turkeys were running around. I wondered who really needed this here? There was no holiday, no TV camera, and no militants who might stick you "in the basement" if you didn't display the flag. And yet, the flags were flying. Beyond this, some cars had a bumper sticker reading "Glory to Ukraine!" just below the license plate. In this, Donetsk was about the same: flags of the USSR and "*Novorossiia*" and orange-and-black ribbons are also displayed in cars without the threat of an AK-47.

But here's yet another interesting detail: the gates to many private buildings not only are painted, but they also depict flowers, swans, grapevines, and even trees. You won't find anything like this in the private sectors of Makiïvka or Donetsk: most gates have no images on them at all, although occasionally you might see a red star, which gives the impression that this is a base for the DPR militia.

In short, it's a completely different view of the world, a special attitude toward the soil (in the literal sense), more optimism, more satisfaction and confidence in the future—that's how I would describe the Ukrainian hinterland that I happened to visit. Though there is one thing we do have in common: "mainland" Ukraine does not have any decent roads either.

May 7, 2017
Ukraïnskyi tyzhden

A burnt-out car at the destroyed Donetsk Airport.

A KNACK FOR LOSING THINGS

In the last three years, the course of Ukraine has experienced development that took other nation states decades, if not centuries, to achieve. The revolution at the end of 2013, the annexation and loss of Crimea, and the war in the Donbas—all these events squeezed into the tight knot of a few months that turned the next three years into a political infinity.

But this all had a very tangible beginning, and the geometry of losses is striking. We gave up Crimea without a fight, ostensibly for "political expediency." We convinced ourselves that withdrawing from administrative buildings in Donetsk and Luhansk was "to prevent a panic" and to keep the situation "under control." We firmly believed that the entire Ukrainian army was incapable of handling Girkin and a few dozen mercenaries, and that by letting that gang of terrorists go free to return to Donetsk, we would save the hostages they were using to cover their retreat.[181]

In the end, in less than six months, from spring to fall 2014, Ukraine gave up Crimea and the industrial heart of the Donbas, and somehow rationalized each of these losses. The calculus was pretty straightforward: "Russia is to blame." However, they also included among those deemed guilty the population who were themselves hostages, stuck in the newly-built fictional world between the blocks at checkpoints. The country has shown a rare talent for abandoning its own.

For three years now, a few million people living behind those concrete blocks under the tricolor have been in an informational vacuum. One of the most powerful, possibly the most powerful, events in the history of modern Ukraine has already become overgrown with barbed wire, mines, and ... silence.

It's hard to believe that, over this entire time, the war and occupation of the Donbas has not been adequately discussed on national airwaves—not a single presidential address on television has been delivered to those who remain behind the checkpoints. Not a single realistic deadline for ending the occupation has ever been announced. There is, in fact, no strategy for returning these lands. There is no alternative to Minsk simply because its non-implementation suits everybody, to one degree or another. Indeed, this opinion is widespread even among those who are fighting for the "people's lands" here today. After all, if the return of the Donbas to Ukrainian control has been stalled for objective military and political reasons, it is absolutely unclear why the government has so easily and quickly abandoned those it considers its own. Supposedly, over the past three years, our secret services have been hard at work, wracking their brains over how to break through the informational blockade in the occupied areas, which is revealing of—perhaps a lack of ability? Of resolve? Or something else? It is revealing because occupied Donbas is like a ghost in the awareness of the majority on the other side of the checkpoints: empty and depopulated. Yet, the people themselves—the human "component" of this conflict—cross the contact line by the hundreds of thousands every month and never feel any kind of informational input from the Ukrainian side.

The mass of Russian and local propaganda in the DPR that crowds the airwaves 24/7 really is impossible to counter in any technical sense. The fact is that people are as much an information product as is a text. They will actively absorb any geopolitical meaning that is repeated n number of times. In this regard, the "republic" is highly proficient. They may cut corners on pensions and wages, but they are not stingy when it comes to promises for the future. Russia's political manipulators know very well—and they are absolutely correct in this—that any social evil, up to a certain point, can be drowned out by excess information. It all depends on how the "main course" is presented in the hourly news.

How surprising is it, then, that the majority of the "remainers"—a term that has already become quite common here—under occupation have become indifferent toward Ukraine and do not react to developments that have taken place since the Maidan, afraid of what they do not understand? The DPR has placed its bets on the future, while we are fighting on the fronts of the past. At the same time as the busy agenda of Ukraine's information—and political—arena is preoccupied with the question of blocking Russian social networks and celebrations of May 9, the "republics" are busy 24/7 raising a new generation of fighters and are thus entrenching the occupation without gaining a single mile of new land.

What do we see on the home side? Nothing. The Ukrainian mainstream behaves as though it did not notice a war going on. As if there weren't tens of thousands of people freezing or sweltering at checkpoints for the fourth year in a row, while shuttling back and forth for Ukrainian products and pensions. Afterwards, they will all return to the DPR and continue to curse everything connected to Ukraine. The DPR's lack of a defined position, its haphazardness, and the shortcomings of life in the "republics" might, one would think, offer fertile ground that would spur Kyiv to launch a real reoccupation process in the region, starting with the hearts and minds of the people. During the course of this conflict, the press, volunteers, and special forces have gathered an enormous body of evidence that could undoubtedly take the local perception of the conflict beyond the old tropes of "Nazis" and "sausage" and help the population see the situation more clearly.

When it all comes down to it, the question is what this system imagines itself to be, what kind of people are in it, what Donetsk had prior to the war, and what it is left with now. The fact is that here, in the DPR, people mean no more than dust, no matter what role they play. The system will always grind the individual down and turn them into powder if they go against the status quo. "And if there are those who come to you, then there will be those who will come for you, too."[182] This is a classic paradigm of Soviet thinking and its view of the individuum. Proclaiming another *peremoha*[183] all too soon, maybe we ourselves are caught up in a pattern of exaggerated triumphs, as, for example, when radio broadcasts from Ukraine that barely reach the farthest suburbs of Donetsk are in all seriousness presented as an achievement. At the same time, right under our noses, a one-thousand-person queue continues to make its way to the checkpoint, the people despising the past twenty-five years and seeing no future for themselves. What do the places where the blue-and-yellow flag is flying have to offer them? A cheaper brand of cheese, which fills the shelves in Donetsk, anyway? Here in the DPR people are offered something much bigger: a myth. Whether it is Soviet or Russian does not matter. The main thing is that it can sustain them for many years, even as they keep travelling for food once a month to those strange, increasingly incomprehensible "beings" on the other side.

Of course, things are not always easy. The "argumentum ad morti,"[184] as many call it here, isn't going anywhere. Those who have lost their loved ones in this war are unlikely ever to be able to accept the flag flown by those whose bullets hit them. If we try to imagine the impossible—that the Ukrainian government simply returned to the occupied Donbas right now—we would find ourselves in a greater mess than under the occupation itself. No one, not the government, not those who live in free Ukraine, nor the locals who are pro-Russian, is prepared for such a coming together. If we were handed back an area where people had been taught systematically for three years to hate those on the

other side of the barricade, it would just launch a count-
down to the next war. Sooner or later, everything would
repeat itself—repeat itself to deprive us of our land once
and for all. Isn't this why the infamous Minsk process is
uncontested? And isn't this why the future will be made up
not of bullets, but of every lost day—every day in which our
country will remain so creatively silent?

(Written in captivity)

May 26, 2017
Dzerkalo tyzhnia

76413

Stanislav Aseyev at a welcoming ceremony in Kyiv for Ukrainian hostages released from the DPR in a prisoner swap.

NOTES

PREFACE

1   Lviv: Staryi Lev Publishers, 2020.

THE LOST GENERATION OF THE "FABLED NOVOROSSIIA"

2   Literally "New Russia"—a historical term used in the eighteenth cen-
     tury imperial Russian conquest of today's southern Ukraine and in
     the annexation of the Zaporozhian Sich, revived by Russian propa-
     ganda for a brief time during the 2014 aggression against Ukraine in
     the Donbas and in the occupation of Crimea (editor's note).

3   The flag of Ukraine represents a banner of two horizontal bands of
     equal size, blue on the top and yellow on the bottom, symbolizing
     the blue sky and the yellow fields of wheat. The color combination
     was used on the banners of the Kingdom of Galicia-Volhynia (today's
     western Ukraine) as early as the twelfth century and as a national
     symbol during the 1848 Spring of Nations (ed.).

4   *Opolchenie* is a historical term that refers to the defense of the Slav-
     ic homelands from culturally and religiously distinct invaders arriv-
     ing from the South or the West during a period that stretches from
     the Middle Ages to World War II. The use of the term by Russian
     propaganda in Ukraine's Donbas was meant to introduce the notion
     of the homeland defense similar to that during the Nazi attack on So-
     viet Ukraine in World War II, thus effectively marking the Ukrainian
     government in Kyiv after the 2014 Revolution of Dignity as a "fascist
     coup" (ed.).

5   Russian propaganda TV channel that was in operation in 2013–2017
     (as Life in 2016–2017) and which engaged in pro-Russian reporting
     on the ground during the Donbas military aggression. The channel's
     reporting was criticized for manipulations, including an episode in
     which supposedly the business card of Dmytro Iarosh, the leader of

the Pravyi sektor paramilitary organization, was filmed among the personal effects of a deceased Ukrainian fighter. The role of the far right Pravyi sektor during the Revolution of Dignity in Ukraine was routinely exaggerated and demonized by Russian media in an attempt to portray the entire popular uprising as far right, "neo-Nazi," and xenophobic, and these efforts extended to the military hostilities in the Donbas and their portrayal (ed.).

6 A reference to the Order of Saint George, the highest military order of the Russian Federation. Originally established by Catherine II in the Russian Empire of the 18th century, it was revived in 2000 in Russia. The ribbon of the order is orange with three black stripes. Ribbons of the Order of Saint George were adopted in 2005 by Russian state and state–sponsored organizations in celebration of the "Russian victory" against the German forces in World War II. Since 2014, Russian propaganda has promoted the use of the ribbon in the Donbas as a symbol of resistance to the Ukrainian forces, an implicit parallel to the Soviet struggle against Nazi Germany during World War II (ed.).

7 "Russian Spring" is a term credited to Egor Kholmogorov, a Russian far-right ideologue and writer, one of the authors of the "*Novorossiia*" project. The term was meant to establish a parallel between Russian-sponsored anti-Ukrainian actions in Ukraine's east and the pro-democracy movements known as the Arab Spring (ed.).

8 Grad (in Russian, "hail") is the name of BM-21, originally a Soviet 122-mm multiple rocket launcher (MRL) that later received several modifications in Russia, including systems with satellite navigation and automated target aiming (MRLS). The launcher is capable of firing up to 40 rockets in 20 seconds, reaching targets as far as 19 miles away. The system is generally considered imprecise and is used for blanket shelling of an area, usually resulting in a high casualty rate (ed.).

9 *Ukrop* is a Russian ethnic slur for Ukrainians that was used for pro-independence Ukrainians after the Revolution of Dignity (2013–2014) and adopted during the Donbas aggression as a derogatory reference to the Ukrainian forces (ed.).

10   A reference to the unlawful referendum in the DPR on May 11, 2014, universally seen as an attempt to legitimize the separatist "republic" in a process that would imitate free and open elections by the local population. A similarly bogus referendum was held on the same day in the "Luhansk People's Republic" (LPR) (ed.).

11   A reference to the snap presidential elections in Ukraine on May 25, 2014 that were held following the ousting of the pro-Russian president Viktor Yanukovych after the Revolution of Dignity (ed.).

12   A reference to Pavlo Hubariev, a pro-Russian activist who proclaimed himself the "people's governor" of the Donbas (March–November 2014) but was soon sidelined by other leaders of the militia forces (ed.).

13   The alias of Igor Girkin, a Russian nationalist and officer of Russia's GRU military intelligence service who played a key role in Russia's occupation and annexation of Crimea and the later military aggression against Ukraine in the Donbas, where he briefly held the position of "defense minister" in the DPR. In 2019, the Dutch state prosecutors charged Girkin along with other co-conspirators for murder in the downing of the MH17 flight that killed all 298 people on board (ed.).

HOW I BECAME A SHADOW IN MY OWN LAND

14   Anti-Terrorist Operation (ATO) is the name Kyiv gave to the war operation in the country's east, because admitting that it was a war would have had considerable unwanted repercussions for civilian institutions and foreign aid (translator's note).

15   A reference to the "parade of captives" in the city of Donetsk organized by the militants on Ukraine's Independence Day, August 24, in 2014, in which captive soldiers of the Ukrainian armed forces were led in a humiliating procession between two rows of militants armed with rifles with bayonets. Human Rights Watch and other organizations have maintained that the "parade" violated the Geneva Convention ban on humiliating and degrading treatment of soldiers captured during military conflicts. The "parade of captives" in Donetsk also clearly referenced the World War II march of captive German soldiers in Moscow in July 1944 (ed.).

16   The "Cossacks," Vostok (from Russian, "East"), and Somalia are the names of some of the battalions of the Russian-sponsored militants in the DPR (ed.).

17   SMERSH is a term coined by Joseph Stalin, a portmanteau of the phrase "Death to spies" in Russian (*smert´ shpionam*), as the name of a military counter-intelligence organization in World War II, originally focused on subverting German intelligence operation in the Red Army and later expanding its mandate to squashing all kinds of "subversive activities" in the Soviet military (ed.).

18   Smerch (in Russian, "tornado") is the name of BM-30, originally a Soviet heavy multiple rocket launcher that is known for its long range (43 to 56 miles) and low precision. The first confirmed use in combat was in Syria by the Syrian military forces and in Ukraine's Donbas in 2014. Bellingcat has established the use of several Smerches by the Russian-sponsored militants in the DPR near Makiïvka (ed.).

WHO HAS JOINED THE DPR MILITANTS AND WHAT ARE THEY FIGHTING FOR?

19   From Ukrainian and Russian, *oplot* translates into English as "bulwark," "bastion," or, more broadly, "reliable support," usually used in idioms such as "the last bastion." Oplot is also the widely known name of a modification of the T-84, a Ukrainian-made tank (ed.).

20   Oleksandr Zakharchenko (1976–2018) was a Donetsk-born pro-Russian separatist, the head of the DPR state and its "prime minister." In 2010, he headed the Kharkiv-based pro-Russian organization and martial arts group Oplot, whose branch later operated in Donetsk and formed the militia group described here that actively participated in the takeover of the Donetsk city council in April 2014. At the end of August 2018, Zakharchenko was killed in a bomb explosion in the Separ Café on Pushkin Boulevard in Donetsk (ed.).

21   For clarity, all amounts given in Ukrainian hryvnia have been converted to US dollars following historical exchange rate charts. The hryvnia devalued sharply in 2014 when it went from just over 8 hryvnias for 1 US dollar in January, at the height of the Revolution of Dignity (EuroMaidan Revolution), to almost 16 hryvnias per dollar at the end of that year, after Russian aggression in Ukraine's east (parts of Donbas) and annexation of Crimea. In 2015, the currency sharply fell again reaching an average rate of 23–24 hryvnia per US dollar (with rates as low as 28–29 in February-March 2015). Since then, the currency has been devaluing slower, averaging from 24 to 28 hryvnia per US dollar, with the current exchange rate of about 28 hryvnia per US dollar (ed.).

22   In Ukrainian and Russian, sword (ed.).

23   Igor Bezler (b. 1965), known under his pseudonym Bes (from Russian, demon), is a Simferopol-born leader of the pro-Russian separatists whose group actively participated in assisting the Russians in the takeover of Crimea and later participated in the war in the Donbas. Security Service of Ukraine (SBU) identified Bezler as an operative of the Russian military intelligence service GRU. Bezler went into hiding in 2014 and later issued statements denouncing Russian-sponsored separatists. According to Bellingcat, he has been living under a different name in Russian-occupied Crimea (ed.).

24   From Russian, the east (ed.).

25   Oleksandr Khodakovskyi (b. 1972 in Snizhne, Donetsk Oblast) is former "security minister" in the DPR and creator of the Vostok Battalion, the majority of whose fighters he later lost to Igor Girkin (Strelkov), and former "secretary" of the "DPR Security Council" (dismissed in 2015). In media reports, Khodakovskyi has sometimes been tied to the Ukrainian oligarch Renat Akhmetov, who owns large industrial plants in the Donbas and had significant influence in the region before and after the breakout of the war (ed.).

26   Prokofiev International Airport, named after the Soviet composer and pianist Sergei Prokofiev who was born in today's Donetsk Oblast, better known as Donetsk Airport, that was the scene of long and fierce defense by the Ukrainian armed forces that ended with the airport's complete destruction. The Ukrainian soldiers defending the airport were nicknamed "cyborgs" for their seeming invincibility (tr.).

27   Motorola was the *nom de guerre* of Arsen (Arsenii) Pavlov (1983–2016), a Russian citizen born in Ukhta and the leader of the Sparta

Battalion. Based on circumstantial evidence, Motorola likely participated in the Russian takeover of Crimea before arriving in eastern Ukraine where he was noticed for his participation in the Rymarska Street standoff in Kharkiv (March 15, 2014), the battles for Slov'iansk and at Ilovaisk, and the storming of the Donetsk Airport. Motorola and his Sparta battalion were allegedly involved in the torture and execution of the DPR prisoners and internal rivals. He was assassinated in October 2016 and died from a bomb explosion in the elevator of the apartment building where he lived (ed.).

28　Givi was the *nom de guerre* of Mykhailo Tolstykh (1980–2017), an Ilovaisk-born leader of the separatist militia in the DPR. He participated in the battles for Slov'iansk and at Ilovaisk, and in the Donetsk Airport siege; he allegedly participated in the torture and inhumane treatment of prisoners, including humiliation and abuse of captive Ukrainian soldiers that are supported by video footage. Tolstykh died in early February 2017 after being assassinated with a portable rocket-assisted flamethrower in his own office (ed.).

29　Kalmius is the name of the river that runs from north of Donetsk into the Black Sea at Mariupol (tr.).

EXECUTED AS AN "ENEMY OF THE PEOPLE" OF THE DPR

30　*Russkii mir* (Russian world) is a broad and ambiguous concept adopted by the Russian government under Vladimir Putin as a framework to implement policies of neoimperialist revanchism in the independent countries that were formerly parts of the Russian Empire or the Soviet Union. In attempting to appropriate the heritage of the Kyivan Rus, pre-1917 Russian Empire, and the Soviet Union, the concept appeals to the common cultural, religious, and linguistic roots of East Slavic peoples living in Ukraine, Russia, and Belarus. The "defense of the brethren" of the common *russkii mir* from an alleged assault was used by Russia as a pretext for the takeover of Crimea, the incursion into Ukraine, and military and financial support of the war in the Donbas (ed.).

31　This is a reference to the beheadings of international journalists, local residents, enemy soldiers and their own fighters by the members of the Islamic State of Iraq and the Levant (ISIL) as an instrument of intimidation, terror, retaliation against Western powers and regional rivals, and as a tool for the recruitment of new followers. Footage of the beheadings was posted by the ISIL members to social media starting in the summer of 2014, receiving extensive coverage in international media and wide condemnation by the international community (ed.).

32   Reference to the chemical factory in Sievierodonetsk near Lysy-chansk in the Luhansk Oblast of the Donbas region; the plant produces products for the chemical industry and agriculture (liquid ammonia, ammonium nitrate, potassium nitrate, crude methanol, various acids and polymers). Since 2011, the factory is part of OST-CHEM, which belongs to Group DF of the Ukrainian gas and titanium oligarch Dmytro Firtash who has close ties to Vladimir Putin. As the co-owner of RosUkrEnerho, Firtash was the middleman buying gas from Russia at below market prices and selling it to Ukraine, amassing a large fortune in the process. He owns seven TV channels in Ukraine, including Inter, one of the most-watched channels in the country, as well as a news agency, thus wielding considerable political influence in Ukraine. In 2014, Sievierodonetsk was the site of a bitter battle between Ukrainian forces and Russian-sponsored militants; it is currently under Ukrainian government's control and some Ukrainian activists have argued that the frontline conveniently loops around the factories of the Ukrainian oligarchs such as Dmytro Firtash and Rynat Akhmetov (ed.).

THE CHECKPOINT: "I'M ALIVE BECAUSE OF THE WAR"

33   *Kvas* is a traditional refreshing brew made of fermented rye bread that is a very popular summer drink (tr.).

HOW TO DEFEAT THE DPR

34   Ukry is an ethnic slur for Ukrainians in the Russian language. Similar to other slurs, there have been attempts at appropriations by Ukrainians, including the novel *Ukry* (2015) by the prominent Ukrainian

writer Bohdan Zholdak which describes the war in the Donbas from the view of Ukrainian forces. Ukry emerge here as the modern-day Cossacks defending their homeland, modeled on Eneïda (1798), Ivan Kotliarevskyi's mock-heroic poem and the first literary work published in the modern Ukrainian language (ed.).

35   Okean Elzy is a Ukrainian soft-rock band that became very popular in many post-Soviet countries while singing entirely in Ukrainian. Its leader is Sviatoslav Vakarchuk, who is also the founder and former leader of the Holos political party represented in the Ukrainian parliament (ed.).

YOUNG PEOPLE IN THE DPR AND THE LPR: WHAT DOES THE FUTURE HOLD?

36   The use of the term "republic" and "republican" in the DPR and Russian state propaganda since 2014 refers primarily to the DPR and the LPR, both claiming to be the "people's republics," but it also alludes to the Soviet past, in which the Soviet Union comprised—as of 1989–15 Soviet republics. Though nominally autonomous, the Soviet republics were strictly subordinated to the political and economic center in Moscow where the main decisions were made (ed.).

37   The flag of "Novorossiia" was proposed in two versions: one appears as a blue cross with a thin white boarder on a red field, and the other shows a white-yellow-black tricolor and resembles an upside-down Romanov flag (ed.).

THE DONETSK "UPRISING" A YEAR LATER: THE FUTURE OF AN ILLUSION

38   In Ukrainian and Russian, Pasha is often the diminutive form for Pavlo (Pavel), and the first name here refers to Pavlo Hubariev. See also notes 12, 43, and 77 (ed.).

39   Reference to the Russian propaganda campaign depicting the Revolution of Dignity (EuroMaidan Revolution, or simply the Maidan) as

a coup by a junta comprising primarily Ukrainian far right groups, labeled by Russian-sponsored media as either "Nazi" or "fascist" in an allusion to the Soviet struggle against Nazi Germany in World War II (ed.).

40   Reference to the European Square (Ievropeiskyi Maidan) in Kyiv, the epicenter of the Revolution of Dignity in 2013–2014, which is also often dubbed EuroMaidan Revolution, or simply the Maidan (ed.).

THE VOICE OF THE DONBAS: HOW FIVE THOUSAND VICTIMS ARE "HEARD"

41   Amstor is a chain of shopping and entertainment centers in Ukraine largely owned by Smart Holding Group, which belongs to the influential Russian-Ukrainian oligarch Vadim Novinskii (Vadym Novynskyi). A Russian citizen who made a fortune on privatizing large state enterprises in Ukraine during the tumultuous 1990s, Novinskii was granted Ukrainian citizenship in 2012 by the then President Viktor Yanukovych and is currently a member of the Ukrainian parliament from the pro-Russian party Opposition Bloc "Pro Life," a successor to Yanukovych's Party of Regions. In the course of the war in the Donbas, Amstor lost control over eleven of its thirteen centers located primarily in central and eastern Ukraine, while Novinskii was banned from entering Crimea which he used to represent as an MP before its occupation by Russia (ed.).

42   Uragan (in Russian, hurricane) is the name of BM-27, originally a Soviet self-propelled multiple rocket launcher system. The system can deliver high-caliber rockets and mines, and has been used by Soviets in Afghanistan to lay minefields (ed.).

43   Denys Pushylin (b. 1981) is the "head of state" of the DPR and former deputy to "governor" Pavlo Hubariev after the latter's arrest by the SBU, the Ukrainian secret service. Pushylin also represented the DPR at the Minsk accord negotiations as part of the DPR/LPR delegation (ed.).

44   Feliks Dzerzhinskii (1877–1926), nicknamed Iron Feliks, was a Polish-born Bolshevik and Soviet official who founded two notorious

Soviet secret police services, the Cheka and the OGPU (the latter one was responsible for planning and organizing the Soviet Gulag system in the 1930s). Dzerzhinskii was one of the architects of the Red Terror that earned its name for the mass summary executions, including in public places (ed.).

45   Comrade Artem was the moniker of Fedor Sergeev (1883–1921), a prominent Russian and Soviet revolutionary and politician who in 1918 founded the Moscow-controlled Donetsk-Kryvyi Rih Soviet Republic in the Donbas, which challenged the Ukrainian People's Republic (UNR). The legacy of the Donetsk-Kryvyi Rih Soviet Republic was revived in 2014 as a political project when the DPR declared itself a successor to it (ed.).

46   Taras Shevchenko (1814–1861) was the national poet of Ukraine, artist and political figure who has created the foundation of modern Ukrainian literature. Born a serf, Shevchenko dedicated the bulk of his work to depicting the suffering of his fellow men and women, inspiring whole generations of Ukrainians to fight for independence from Russia and for democracy (ed.).

CHRONICLE OF DECLINE AND FALL: THE DONETSK OBLAST STATE ADMINISTRATION BUILDING

47   Hryfon was the name of the special subunit of the court police of the Ukrainian Ministry of the Interior, whose task it was to provide security to judges and other court employees, including those participating in hearings and members of their families. Hryfon was dissolved and its tasks transferred to the National Police of Ukraine and the National Guard of Ukraine in 2015 in the course of the police reform (ed.).

48   This reference to the Revolution of Dignity (EuroMaidan Revolution) reflects the spread of propaganda about alleged destruction and vandalism on and around the European Square (the Maidan) in Kyiv. In actuality, the protests were peaceful and there was no destruction of property until the government forces of President

Yanukovych began a violent crackdown against unarmed protesters, most of whom were young students of local universities (ed.).

GRENADES AREN'T A BIG DEAL ANYMORE: EVERYDAY TRAGEDIES IN MAKIÏVKA

49 Petro Poroshenko was elected Ukraine's president after the ousting of Viktor Yanukovych following the killing of protesters by the Yanukovych regime at the height of the Revolution of Dignity (EuroMaidan Revolution). Poroshenko and his team assumed office in June 2014 and faced the consequences of Russia's occupation of Crimea and Russian-sponsored separatist movement in the Donbas, devising a strategy of rebuilding Ukraine's military while relying on volunteer battalions and soliciting Western help without defining Russian actions as a war (ed.).

WHY THEY LIKE "TSARS" IN THE DONBAS

50 From Russian, "cotton or wool wadding" (vata); vatnik is a pejorative term that arose (often ascribed to Anton Chadskii) in Russia in 2011 to describe opponents of the pro-democracy, anti-government and anti-Putin protests sparked by elections to the Duma seen as fraudulent. Initially the term was used by Russian liberals to describe other Russians who held pro-government views in line with the disinformation spread in the state-run Russian media. From the time of the Euromaidan protests in late 2013, the term began to be applied more broadly to people who blindly accepted Russian disinformation broadcast in Russia, Ukraine, and neighboring countries. The concrete meaning of vatnik is the quilted coat commonly worn by laborers and people who live in small villages (ed.).

51 A reference to the Colorado potato beetle used as a slur for the pro-Russian residents of the Donbas. The beetle has orange and black (sometimes white and black) stripes on its back, which in the slur alludes to orange and black ribbons of Saint George's cross that are worn as a pro-Russian symbol (tr., ed.).

52   Adjective based on the Ukrainianized form of *russkii mir* (Russian world). Mir can also be translated as "peace," thus *russkomirnyi* is an ironic pun in Ukrainian meaning "Russian-minded" and "Russo-peaceful," i. e., the Russian conception of peaceful as the opposite of it (tr.).

53   Aseyev idealizes the democracies of Europe and the United States here. In fact, his first-hand experience of a government based on the sovereignty of the people was arguably more democratic than anything in the West: the grassroots shadow government of Ukraine that arose in the spring of 2014. This movement of private citizens organized and supplied an independent armed resistance to the Russian-backed militants in the Donbas and Crimea at a time when the official government of Ukraine was paralyzed by corruption and, in many cases, loyalty to Russia (ed.).

54   The Christian Orthodox Church, the absolute power of the emperor, and the focus on the age-old, conservative traditions of the Russian people (as a way to reject such Western ideas as individualism, rationalism, and civic rights and freedoms) were the three components of the imperialist ideological doctrine of the Russian emperor Nicholas I, who reigned from 1825 to 1855. This ideology experienced a revival after the collapse of the Soviet Union, especially during Vladimir Putin's rule (ed.).

55   Reference to a series of illegal referendums on May 11, 2014 in the parts of the Donetsk and Luhansk Oblasts under Russian-sponsored separatist control on the status of the DPR and LPR as "republics" (ed.).

56   Ihor Plotnytskyi (b. 1964) was the "Defense Minister" and the head of the "Council of Ministers" of the "Luhansk People's Republic" (LPR) in 2014–2017 and was forced to flee to Russia after being ousted by Leonid Pasichnyk (an SBU operative who defected to the LPR). Plotnytskyi was one of the masterminds behind the shelling of the Ukrainian armed forces at Zelenopillia in July 2014 by Russian artillery from Russian territory, the first such direct attack during the war in the Donbas. See also notes 134 and 136 (ed.).

WHAT IS UKRAINE TO ME? THE VIEW FROM MAKIÏVKA

57   See note 50 for a definition of *vatnik (ed.)*.

58   At the time, 1 US dollar cost around 55 Russian rubles. 28 rubles for two pounds (one kilogram) of potatoes is considered a very high price for Ukraine, given that potatoes is the main staple food in the country and is grown both privately in the gardens in the countryside and on an industrial scale by agricultural firms (ed.).

59   Ukraine's parliament is called Verkhovna Rada Ukraïny–from Ukrainian, the Supreme Council of Ukraine (ed.).

A LETTER TO THE RUSSIANS

60   Between 1946 and 1991, the Soviet Union occupied nearly 8,650,000 square miles, one-sixth of the Earth's land surface–a fact that was often repeated in Soviet propaganda (ed.).

WHO LIVES OFF THE RESIDENTS OF OCCUPIED DONBAS?

61   In July 2015, the market exchange rate of the US dollar was about 21–22 Ukrainian hryvnias or 55 Russian rubles for 1 dollar, and the exchange rate of the Ukrainian hryvnia was 2.6–2.7 Russian rubles for 1 hryvnia (ed.).

THE "ESPERANTO" OF VLADIMIR PUTIN

62   Pilar Bonet Cardona has spent most of her professional career as the Moscow correspondent for the newspaper *El País* (tr.).

THE HALF-LIFE OF THE *SOVOK*

63   *Sovok* (from Russian, dustpan) is a pun on the word "Soviet." In the late-Soviet period sovok was used as a derogatory term for those Soviet citizens who uncritically supported Soviet ideology and bought into Soviet propaganda (ed.).

64   Komsomol (in Russian, an abbreviation meaning All-Union Leninist Communist League of Youth) was a Soviet youth organization for those between ages 14 and 28 that was used as a political organ to expose Soviet youth to the Communist ideology and to prepare future members of the Communist Party (ed.).

65   Reference to the series of removals of Lenin monuments, dubbed *Leninopad* (Leninfall), as well as monuments to other Soviet leaders, in the Ukrainian capital and the regions, which took place at the height of the Revolution of Dignity (EuroMaidan Revolution) in early 2014, which included a strong anticolonial current next to the main pro-democracy and pro-Western motivations (ed.).

66   Lenin was the better-known alias of Vladimir Ulianov (ed.).

67   As the leader of the Bolshevik revolution and the founding head of the Soviet Union, Lenin embraced the use of violence to crush internal opposition, including among the members of his own party. Under Lenin's leadership and with his emphatic approval, the Cheka—the Soviet secret police created on Lenin's orders—unleashed in 1918 the Red Terror against real and imagined enemies of the Soviet state and administered Soviet concentration camps, which were established in April 1919, imprisoning tens of thousands of people who were used for slave labor under horrific conditions. See Anne Applebaum, *Gulag: A History* (New York: Anchor Books, 2004) for an accessible study of the development of the Soviet concentration camps (ed.).

IRRECONCILABLE DIFFERENCES

68   In the battle at Mar'inka in June 2015, separatist forces temporarily occupied a part of the town, representing some of the heaviest fighting in the Donbas after the signing of the Minsk accords (ed.).

69   Oleksandr Turchynov, Ukrainian politician, economist, Baptist minister, and member of the parliament. He became the chairman of the Verkhovna Rada, Ukraine's parliament, following the shooting of EuroMaidan protesters on February 18–20, 2014, and became Ukraine's acting president on February 23, serving until Petro

Poroshenko assumed office in early June 2014 after the snap presidential elections (ed.).

70   The 130 victims who perished during the Revolution of Dignity are referred to as the Heavenly Hundred, a name that alludes to the historical military unit of an infantry *sotnia* (hundred) and suggests that those who were killed by the Yanukovych regime during the revolution are now fighting for Ukraine in heaven (ed.).

71   Gopnik is a term that arose in the late Russian empire and was in use in the late Soviet Union as well as in the post-Soviet states. It now refers to hooligans, or generally men and women who come from working-class, poor, or low-education backgrounds, engage in alcohol and substance abuse, and are known for wearing tracksuits and squatting in groups in the yards of apartment buildings (tr., ed.).

A FEW FAIRYTALES ABOUT THE DPR

72   New Russian, referring to "*Novorossiia,*" meaning New Russia in Russian (ed.).

73   Berdychiv is a small city with population of around 75,000 residents in Vinnytsia Oblast, which is in right-bank Ukraine, nearly 550 miles away from Donetsk (tr.).

74   This is precisely what happened to the author, who was arrested, tortured, and later sentenced to a lengthy prison term on accusations of "spying" for the Ukrainian government (ed.).

75   Pryp'iat was the town in Soviet Ukraine that was built from scratch and once housed Chornobyl nuclear plant employees. It was abandoned after the Chornobyl nuclear disaster (tr., ed.).

DONBAS: SEVEN HUNDRED DAYS OF SOLITUDE

76   Ilich is the patronymic of Vladimir Ulianov, better known as Lenin (ed.).

77   Russian-language book about "*Novorossiia,*" the DPR, and Ukraine by Pavlo Hubariev, published in 2016 (tr., ed.).

78   A patriotic march, written by composer Vasilii Agapkin in honor of the Slavic women seeing off their men in the First Balkan War in

1912. The song gained an iconic status during World War II, after it was performed on the Red Square in November 1941, sending Soviet soldiers to defend Moscow from the German attack. The use of the song in the DPR is a clear parallel to that (tr., ed.).

79 *Pelmeni* are boiled dumplings filled with minced meat and popular in Russia, Ukraine, and Poland (ed.).

80 Bogatyrs were members of the *druzhyna* (group of elite warriors) during the reign of Volodimer the Great of Kyivan Rus´ (980–1015) and later became characters in East Slavic legends similar to knights-errant in Western European tales. They were loosely based on real individuals but highly idealized. Russian painter Viktor Vasnetsov produced perhaps the most iconic portrait of three famous bogatyrs in his painting "The Bogatyrs" (1881–1889) (tr.).

81 MAR is the private military company headed by Aleksei Marush-chenko, while E.N.O.T. is an abbreviation for Edinye narodnye ob-shchinnye tovarishchestva (United People's Communal Associations; in Russian, *enot* also means "raccoon"), another private military company (ed.).

82 A battalion of Russian citizens who served as mercenaries in the war in the Donbas. The Troia (Troy) battalion came into conflict with the leadership of the DPR at the end of 2015. On December 31, 2015 their headquarters near Horlivka were surrounded and stormed by various units of the DPR after a month-long siege, allegedly killing several members of the battalion and kidnapping one of its leaders, thus disbanding the battalion (ed.).

83 Evgenii Shabaev is the leader of the Khovrino *kazaki* paramilitary group in Russia and a sometime mercenary with ties to Russian military contractors (tr.).

84 Donetskaia Respublika (in English, the Donetsk Republic) is a pro-Russian political organization founded in 2005 by Andrii Purhin. Its declared goal is the restoration of the Donetsk-Kryvyi Rih Soviet Republic of 1918. The organization participated in the storming of the building of the Donetsk Oblast State Administration in March 2014. Purhin (b. 1972) served as the head of the "People's Council" of the DPR in 2014–2015 and was succeeded by Denys Pushylin. Donetskaia

Respublika is considered a terrorist organization in Ukraine and its activity is prohibited (tr., ed.).

85 *Prizrak* in Russian means "ghost" (ed.).

86 A police academy (tr.).

87 This was a classic slogan from Soviet times, reflecting the importance of this heavily industrialized region to the entire Soviet Union (tr.).

88 Oleksii Mozhovyi (1975–2015) was one of the leaders of the "Luhansk People's Republic" and the leader of the Prizrak battalion. He was assassinated after accusing the leadership of the LPR of treason (ed.).

89 A reference to the battle for Ilovaisk in August 2014 that ended in the Ukrainian forces being encircled by the Russian military that crossed the border and joined the battle on the side of the separatist forces. The Ukrainian troops reached an agreement to retreat from the city, but the agreement was not honored and the retreating troops were shelled, resulting in a massacre that was often described as a "meat grinder" and in the capturing of several hundred Ukrainian soldiers and fighters of the volunteer units (ed.).

WHAT COMES NEXT?

90 A reference to the fabricated story broadcast by Channel One, Russia's main TV channel, in July 2014, alleging that Ukrainian forces crucified a little boy after retaking the city of Slov'iansk. Journalist investigations by the BBC and other independent media have shown that the story had little to do with reality and the segment itself was filmed in Rostov-on-Don, the Russian Federation. A similar propaganda campaign was launched by Russia in April 2021, accusing Ukrainian armed forces of killing a boy near Oleksandrivske in the Donetsk Oblast using a drone (ed.).

91 A reference to President Petro Poroshenko, whose main business is the Roshen confectionary brand (tr.).

92 A sergeant in the Donbas Battalion of the Ukrainian National Guard, Mykhailo Zaiets (1975–2015; *nom de guerre* Kosyi) was killed when his vehicle struck a mine in October 2015 (tr.).

93 Rynat Akhmetov, the Ukrainian billionaire oligarch who controls most heavy industry in the Donbas (tr.).

94   The nickname of Oleksandr Zakharchenko, the DPR leader assassinated in 2018 (tr.).

95   Dozhd and Ekho Moskvy are considered the last of nation-wide independent media in Russia that sporadically engage in criticism of the Russian government under Vladimir Putin (ed.).

96   Aleksandr Nevzorov (b. 1958), Soviet and Russian journalist, politician, former MP and television personality, and a bitter critic of the Russian government under Putin (tr., ed.).

97   Lev Shlosberg, a Russian politician, human rights activist, and journalist, leader of the Pskov regional branch of the oppositional Iabloko party, and a critic of the Russian government under Putin. On August 25, 2014 he published an investigation about the suspicious deaths of members of the Pskov division of the Russian Airborne Troops, drawing attention to the involvement of the Russian regular army in the war against Ukraine. Following the publication, Shlosberg and other journalists investigating the secret burials of Russian troops became victims of violent assaults (ed., tr.).

98   Vladimir Zhirinovskii (b. 1946) is a Russian politician of Ukrainian-Jewish heritage and the leader of the Russian Liberal Democratic Party. He embraced ultra-right and nationalist political positions, blending them with populism and a cult of personality in what strongly leans toward fascism. In his provocative statements over the years, Zhirinovskii advocated for Russian imperial politics such as annexing the independent states that were once parts of the Russian Empire or of the Soviet Union, including Ukraine and the Baltic states, using violence and war as necessary (ed.).

99   The author refers to the Golden Horde, which subjugated medieval Rus´ from the middle of the thirteenth century to the end of the fourteenth. The association of medieval Mongol and Turkic states with barbarism is a commonplace in popular culture of Russia and Ukraine (ed.).

CULTURAL LIFE UNDER OCCUPATION:
THE CITY OF DONETSK

100 In Soviet times, *dom kultury* (house of culture) was the local club house where recreational activities, from sports and hobbies to the arts, took place (tr.).

101 "*Ded voeval*" is a popular post-Soviet propaganda slogan meaning "Grandpa fought in the Great Patriotic War," known in the rest of the world as World War II (tr.).

CITIZENS WITHOUT CITIZENSHIP

102 A reference to Ramzan Kadyrov (b. 1976), the head of the Chechen Republic. A former member of the Chechen independence movement and son of the Chechen president Akhmad Kadyrov, Ramzan Kadyrov made a political bargain with the Russian government under Vladimir Putin and became the absolute ruler of the once-rebellious republic, accumulating an enormous fortune in the process. Kadyrov has been responsible for well-documented cases of torture, abductions, and abuse of women and members of the LBTQI community in the Chechen Republic. He has also been connected to the participation of Chechen mercenaries in the war in the Donbas and has been placed under Ukrainian and US sanctions (ed.).

103 "There is no God but Allah" (tr.).

104 *Krymnash* (from Krym—nash, meaning "Crimea [is] ours" in Russian), the celebratory slogan expressing Russia's claim on Crimea (tr.).

HOMO DONBASUS, OR THE CHANGES
BROUGHT BY THE WAR

105 Sergei Kirov (*né* Kostrikov, 1886–1934) was a Soviet politician and Bolshevik revolutionary, a personal friend and an alleged rival to Joseph Stalin himself. Kirov's assassination in December 1934, in

which both Stalin and the NKVD may have had a hand, was a major milestone in Soviet history, as it served as a pretext for Stalin to cement his totalitarian rule over the Communist Party and the country by initiating the first Great Purge (the Great Terror), a campaign of murderous repressions in 1936–1938, in which about 1 million people perished (ed.).

106 In Russian, *subbota* means "Saturday." Soviet workers were required to come out on the weekend to engage in community clean-ups for no pay (tr.).

107 This anecdote from Brodsky's life is part of a conversation with directors Aleksei Shishov and Elena Iakovich, recorded in Venice in 1993 during the shooting of the film *Progulki s Brodskim* (Walks with Brodsky). This conversation was transcribed and published in *Progulki s Brodskim i tak dalee: Iosif Brodskii v filme Alekseia Shishova i Eleny Iakovich* (Moscow: Corpus, ACT, 2016) (ed.).

108 The author quotes Brodsky here, continuing from the above quote (tr.).

109 A reference to the advisory referendum in the Netherlands on the Ukraine-EU Association Agreement that was held on April 6, 2016. Only slightly over 32 percent of eligible voters participated in the non-binding referendum, of which 61 percent voted against approving the Agreement by the Dutch government, which was an EU requirement. The vote resulted in the Dutch government's insistence on an addendum to the Association Agreement that postulated that Ukraine would not be receiving an EU candidate status, any guarantees of military aid or security guarantees, or increased financial support, among other things. The campaign was mired in financial irregularities and marked by propaganda slogans from Russia's playbook that together worked in favor of the opponents of the Association Agreement. The campaign's messaging painted Ukraine as "the most corrupt country" in Europe, a bigoted accusation later adopted by Donald Trump as he pressured the newly elected President Zelenskyi to open an investigation into Hunter Biden (ed.).

110 A reference to the illegal mining of amber in the Volhynia, Zhytomyr, and Rivne Oblasts of Ukraine, dubbed the Amber Fever, or Amber Wars. A labyrinthine system of licensing for the use of natural resources in Ukraine has made it possible for a number of local criminal organizations to control the illegal mining of amber, in which they have often clashed with local and national police (ed.).

ABOUT EASTER... AND MORE

111 A reference to Ihor Kozlovskyi (b. 1954), a Donetsk-born prominent Ukrainian scholar of religion who was abducted from his apartment in Donetsk on January 27, 2016. The abduction took place in the course of indiscriminate retributions against "Ukrainian nationalists" in the city for the unsolved attempt to blow up the Lenin monument in Donetsk the night before. Kozlovskyi stayed behind in occupied Donetsk to take care of his paralyzed son and, following his obduction, spent almost two years in an illegal prison run by separatist militants, where he was tortured (ed.).

112 Paskha is the name both for Easter and for a sweet, tall, cylindrical yeast-leavened bread baked for Easter, made with an extravagant number of eggs and plenty of raisins, akin to Italian *panettone* (tr.).

113 A broad reference to the war against the Ukrainian government, conflated here with the "Great Patriotic War," the Soviet name for World War II (ed.).

114 Skewered and grilled pieces of marinated meat such as pork, lamb, or beef, similar to shish kebab; the word also signifies the grilling parties and picnics at which shashlyk is prepared (ed.).

WHAT PYGMALION LEFT UNSAID

115 The unrecognized legislature of the DPR (ed.).

116 Russian soldiers caught by the Ukrainians at the beginning of war claimed that they weren't serving in the Russian army at all and had come to the Donbas for a vacation. That was the official line used by those who ended up captured. This is similar to another claim—namely, that the Donbas militants had bought their uniforms and heavy arms in local sporting goods stores rather than receiving them from Russia (tr.).

117 Ukraine launched a nationwide "decommunization" process where-by place-names associated with the Bolsheviks and the Soviet regime, as well as some of the place-names referring to the Russian Empire, were replaced by either their historic antecedents or by names the local community preferred, such as "Dnipro" for "Dnipropetrovsk," which, before the Soviets, was called Iekaterynoslav, after Catherine II (tr., ed.).

118 The Serbian Chetniks originated during World War II as a royalist-nationalist movement. In March 2014, Serb volunteers calling themselves Chetniks, led by Serbian ultra-nationalist Bratislav Živković, supported the pro-Russian side in Crimea and claimed to be returning the favor of Russian volunteers who had fought on the Serbian side of the Yugoslav Wars (1991–2001) (tr.).

EVENING STROLLS THROUGH AN EMPTY CITY

119 A reference to the torture chambers in the DPR, which were typically in the basements of buildings, similar to Stalin's times (tr.).

120 A reference to the Immortal Regiment (in Russian, *bessmertnyi polk*), a propaganda organization in Russia, founded in 2011, that organizes marches on May 9 (Victory Day in the former Soviet Union and today's Russia), during which people carry the portraits of family members who fought or perished in World War II. In 2016, such marches received state support from the Russian government. In 2017, in Donetsk, Simferopol, and Moscow, portraits of Russian soldiers and separatist militants who were killed in the course of the Russian-supported war against Ukraine were displayed next to the portraits of people who fell during World War II (ed.).

QUID PRODEST?

121 In Latin, "what is the benefit," often interpreted in the manner of *cui bono, "who benefits?"* (tr.).

122 The battle at Zelenopillia took place on 11 July 2014, when three Ukrainian army brigades, the 24th Mechanized Brigade, the 72nd

Mechanized Brigade and the 79th Air-Mobile Brigade, were attacked and destroyed by Grad and artillery fire (ed.).

123 Beginning in 2014, the Ukrainian Armed Forces initiated reforms that would bring their rules of engagement into conformity with the policies of Nato. The officer in this account apparently refers to Nato rules for authorizing long-range strikes on military targets (ed.).

124 The author is invoking the principle *inter arma silent leges*, first attributed to Cicero. The idea that "in time of war, the law is silent" has long been used to excuse or justify the abrogation of civil and human rights in time of war. The idea that the trauma endured by soldiers gives them moral immunity from judgment by peacetime society maintains popular currency around the world despite international law defining war crimes and urging their punishment (ed.).

THE "REMAINERS:" THE UNDISCOVERED BOSCH OF THE DPR

125 Kurgans are ancient burial mounds that can be found throughout the steppe in Ukraine and Russia (tr.).

126 "Remainers" is the name given locally to people who strongly identify with Ukraine but have remained in occupied Donbas for different reasons (tr.).

127 Stepan Bandera (1909–1959) was the leader of the militant wing of the far-right Organization of Ukrainian Nationalists (OUN) and one of the leaders of Ukrainian ultranationalists who were involved in terrorist activities in western Ukraine and elsewhere, fighting against both the German and Soviet powers for Ukraine's independence. Bandera and his wing of the OUN (OUN-B) initially cooperated with Nazi Germany, but he was arrested following the OUN-B's declaration of Ukraine's independence after the arrival of German troops. Bandera was kept in Berlin and, after he was briefly released from custody, arrested again and transferred to the Sachsenhausen concentration camp where he remained until the end of World War II. Bandera, as well as OUN, were demonized by Soviet propaganda and used as a scarecrow of Ukrainian nationalism and

Ukrainian independence movement on the whole. Since 2014, these images and messages have been reanimated in the course of Russian aggression against Ukraine, in which the present-day Ukrainian government has been portrayed as a far-right, ultranationalist "junta" that is allegedly the modern-day incarnation of Nazism (ed.).

128 MGB (from Russian *Ministerstvo gosudarstvennoi bezopasnosti*, Ministry for State Security) is the DPR security service, modeled on the predecessor of the Soviet KGB (tr., ed.).

SCREECHING IN THE THORNS

129 This is a play on the Russian title of the Australian writer Colleen McCullough's 1977 novel *The Thorn Birds*, which was published in Russian as *Poiushchie v ternovnike* (Those who sing in the thorns). The novel gained significant popularity in the late Soviet Union after the broadcasting of the US mini-series under the same name in 1983 (tr., ed.).

130 The source for this quote is Joseph Brodsky's (Iosif Brodskii) collection *Menshe edinitsy: izbrannye esse* (Moscow: Nezavisimaia gazeta, 1999), previously published in English as *Less than One: Selected Essays* (New York: Farrar, Straus, and Giroux, 1986) (ed.).

131 Aleksei Smirnov, a Russian citizen from Moscow, the head of the Angel "peacekeeping" battalion, who was later arrested by the DPR. After the arrest, a video recording of Smirnov surfaced in which he admitted his guilt and showed repentance in the self-accusatory style of the Soviet show trials (ed.).

132 Ievhenii Kosiak (b. 1971) is a former colonel of the SBU, the Security Service of Ukraine, who defected to the DPR. He was arrested in August 2015 by the SBU and exchanged for captive Ukrainian citizens in September 2016 (ed.).

133 Donetsk was known as "the city of a million roses" for its vast beds of rosebushes (tr.).

134 Oleksii Kariakin (b. 1980) actively participated in the anti-Ukrainian demonstrations and the violent takeover of the building of the Security Service of Ukraine (SBU) in Luhansk in April 2014. He then served as the chairman of the "People's Council" of the LPR but was

removed from office in March 2016. Kariakin left for Russia immediately after his dismissal and was later accused by the Plotnytskyi
group of an attempted coup. He returned to the LPR in 2017 following Plotnytskyi's resignation as the head of the LPR and assumed
the position of the first chairman of the newly formed LPR "Public
Chamber" (ed.).

135 Rostov-on-Don, Russia, is on the Azov Sea, south of Luhansk and
east of Mariupol (ed.).

136 Plotnytskyi resigned in late 2017, citing ill health, while Zakharchenko was assassinated in August 2018 (tr.).

"PRIMARIES" UNDER THE OCCUPATION

137 Ihor Martynov (b. 1969) is a former member of the Donetsk city
council from the Party of Regions, the former director of the Shcher-
bakov Culture and Recreation Park, and a member of the DPR "People's Council." He was installed as the mayor of Donetsk by the DPR
leadership in October 2014 (ed.).

PROPAGANDA ON THE STREETS OF DONETSK

138 A reference to the "humanitarian convoys" from Russia to the LPR
and the DPR in which goods for civilians and military equipment,
arms, ammunition, motor fuel and oil, among other items, were
transported through the Ukrainian border without allowing an inspection by the Ukrainian customs or international organizations
such as the Red Cross or OSCE. According to reports, the convoys
often transported back to Russia stolen machinery from Ukrainian
defense factories (Topaz radiotechnology factory and the Luhansk
Cartridge Works are the most well-known examples) that were dis-
assembled and moved to operate in Russia, sometimes along with
their employees, as well as the bodies of the Russian soldiers and
mercenaries who were killed in action (known as *gruz 200*). The convoys were broadly condemned by democratic Western governments
and organizations as such that violate international law, especially
against the background of the refusal of the DPR and LPR leadership

to accept humanitarian aid from such organizations as the International Committee of the Red Cross. The first convoy took place on August 22, 2014 and immediately preceded the direct involvement of the Russian regular army in battles against the Ukrainian armed forces and volunteer battalions. Between 2014 and 2018, 74 such "humanitarian convoys" were sent to Ukraine with a total of over 7,200 trucks (ed.).

139 Oles Buzyna (1969–2015) was a Ukrainian journalist, writer, politician, and TV host. He gained notoriety with his book *Vurdalak Taras Shevchenko* (Taras Shevchenko, the vampire), which was criticized for its anti-Ukrainian stance, and *Vernite zhenshchinam garemy* (Bring back harems for women), which was condemned by Ukrainian women's and LGBTQI organizations for spreading misogynistic and homophobic views. Buzyna held broadly pro-Russian views and condemned pro-democracy uprisings such as the Orange Revolution and the Revolution of Dignity in Ukraine. In 2012, Buzyna ran for a seat in the Ukrainian parliament from the Russian Bloc party but failed to win sufficient support. On April 16, 2015 he was found shot dead near his apartment building in Kyiv and Russian media have been spreading conspiracy theories about his murder by "Ukrainian nationalists," while Vladimir Putin condemned the murder as "political" only minutes after it was announced by a Ukrainian government official. The murder of Buzyna—as well as other pro-Russian political activists around the same time period—was attributed by the Ukrainian government to Russian efforts to destabilize the political situation in Ukraine and discredit the country with Western partners at a time when it direly needed internal unity and international support in the face of Russian occupation of Crimea and aggression in the Donbas. Buzyna's murder remains unsolved (ed.).

OCCUPATION AS IT IS: KHARTSYZK

140 In Russian, "glutton" (tr.).

141 ATB is a Dnipro supermarket chain that has rapidly expanded into the rest of Ukraine in recent years (tr.).

142 RZhD is the Russian-language abbreviation for Russian Railways (tr.).

143 Bankova is the street in Kyiv where the presidential administration is located (tr.).

THAT SWEET WORD, "WAR"

144 Many of the soldiers used by Russia in the Donbas and Crimea are Buriats, a northern Mongolian people in Russian Federation (tr.).

145 Lipetsk is a city in Russia where controversy raged for years over a Roshen plant that Russia took over.

146 Strila Podilska (Podillia arrow) is a very popular chocolate made at the Lipetsk factory that was at the time owned by President Poroshenko's Roshen confectionary holding (tr., ed.).

WHERE THE ELITE OF OCCUPIED DONETSK TAKE THEIR LEISURE

147 Deriving its name from the French vinaigrette, an oil and vinegar dressing, and featuring such ingredients as boiled and diced potatoes, red beets, carrots, pickles, and finely chopped onions (with local variations including other ingredients such as beans and sauerkraut), this hearty salad is a staple food in Russian, Ukrainian, and Belarusian cuisine (tr., ed.).

148 Here and elsewhere the author provides prices in both Russian rubles and Ukrainian hryvnia, since the Russian ruble was introduced by the DPR and the LPR as one of the accepted currencies in the areas of the Donbas under their control. The prices in Russian rubles have been converted here to US dollars according to the exchange rate at the time to allow the reader to better understand the price levels in relation to the average income of the population. According to the State Statistics Service of Ukraine, the average salary in Ukraine as of June 2016 was below 5,000 Ukrainian hryvnias, or approximately 200 US dollars. Average salaries were the highest in

large cities such as Dnipro, Kharkiv, Odesa, and Lviv (160–180 US dollars), with Kyiv topping the list (320 US dollars) (ed.).

DONETSK: A TOUR OF EXPROPRIATED PLACES

149 The police academy (tr.).

IMMERSED IN WAR

150 Bumboks (from the English "boombox") is a popular Ukrainian hip-hop and funk band whose lead singer is Andrii Khlyvniuk (tr., ed.).

151 Vladimir Vysotskii (1938–1980) was an iconic Russian Soviet singer, song writer, poet, and actor whose songs and poems expressed criticism of the stagnation-era Soviet Union using the familiar language of the street. As an artist who positioned himself against the "official" Soviet culture, he achieved a legendary status in the Soviet Union, not least also because of the rumors surrounding his death, and he continues to be an important figure in Russian popular culture today. "Russkii russkomu pomogi" expresses largely Russian nationalist views with lyrics that allude to Russian defense against external enemies ("We wouldn't have crossed this threshold, / if it weren't for our enemies"), appeal to the legacy of Rus´ ("Rising from the darkness of past centuries, / Rus´ stood its ground on Rúsian might"), and to the Russian soul that is to be defended just as the land itself ("Save the Rúsian soul. / Save Rúsian land"). It is worth noting that Rúsian refers to the peoples of Rus, the medieval state with the center in Kyiv that later gave rise to the modern Ukrainian, Russian, and Belarusian nations. "Rus´" and "Rúsian" (*russkii* in Russian, as opposed *to rossiianin* [citizen of Rossiia, i. e. modern-day Russia]) were reinterpreted later in the Russian Empire, the Soviet Union, and post-Soviet Russia as a synonym for "Russian" and the heritage of the Kyivan Rus´ was claimed almost exclusively by Russia as a means to legitimize itself vis-à-vis Western royal houses and the Western culture. Such notions were also employed in the recent Russian attempts to promote *russkii mir* as a unifying paradigm for East

Slavs under Moscow's leadership and to justify Russia's aggression against Ukraine (ed.).

152 *Brat* (1997) and *Brat-2* (2000) are Russian neo-noir crime movies written and directed by Aleksei Balabanov. Both films reflected the rise of nationalism in Russia in the late 1990s, against the background of state corruption and the economic decline after the collapse of the Soviet Union. The films included a strong anti-Western and anti-American message, as well as an appeal to the conservative and isolationist Russian notions (ed., tr.).

153 A resort town on the northern coast of the Black Sea and close to the Sea of Azov in the Krasnodar Krai of the Russian Federation, just south of the Kerch Strait (tr., ed.).

154 Aleksandr Borodai (b. 1972) is a Russian citizen, pundit, political strategist, journalist, and one of the ideologues of *russkii mir*. Borodai is closely familiar with Igor Girkin (Strelkov), he participated in the Russian takeover of Ukraine's Crimea and was installed as the first "Prime Minister" of the DPR in May 2014 (until August of the same year, when he was replaced with Oleksandr Zakharchenko). Borodai also leads the Union of Donbas Volunteers, an organization founded in 2015 in Russia and claiming to provide assistance for Russian volunteers who fought in the Donbas as well as to the families of those who died in action in the Donbas (ed.).

155 Cargo 200 (in Russian, *gruz 200*) is the code name used in the Soviet and Russian military for transportation of casualties, originally referring to the corpses of soldiers that were transported in zinc-lined coffins and later used broadly for all types of casualties. The term itself gained prominence in the course of Soviet involvement in Afghanistan in the 1980s. The term received international attention with the onset of the Russian aggression against Ukraine: the OSCE Special Monitoring Mission reported many Russian vehicles in the Donbas with the inscription "Cargo 200." *Gruz 200* (2007) is also a popular neo-noir thriller by Aleksei Balabanov (the director of *Brat* and *Brat-2*) that presents a grim view of the war the Soviet Union waged in Afghanistan (ed.).

THE DONBAS IN 2017: THREE VARIATIONS ON A THEME

156 The Russian Minister of Foreign Affairs, Sergei Lavrov (tr.).

157 This changed in April 2019, when Vladimir Putin suddenly announced that Russia would fast-track passports for those living in occupied Donbas. In July 2019, that offer was extended to all Ukrainian citizens living in the Donbas, including the areas under the control of the Ukrainian government. Official Ukrainian statistics report a total of close to 406,000 of residents of the Donbas who received Russian passports as of the end of 2020, while Russian officials claim that number to be close to 640,000. Due to the conditions in the occupied areas of the Donetsk and Luhansk Oblasts, there is no reliable data as to the total size of the population remaining there: estimates range from 1.6 million (Ukrainian government) to 2.8 million (the United Nations) and to 3.77 million (the DPR and LPR data) (tr., ed.).

158 A reference to *donetskie* (in Russian, Donetskites)—a political and economic elite that moved into the offices of the national government of Ukraine and large state companies following the pro-Russian then-president Viktor Yanukovych. The management style of this group was often compared to a steamroller and close connections to organized crime have been reported for many of them (ed.).

159 *Nom de guerre* of Aleksandr Timofeev (b. 1971), a Russian citizen and then the DPR "Deputy Prime Minister" and "Minister of Revenues and Fees." Timofeev was badly injured in the blast that killed Zakharchenko in August 2018 and, once Denys Pushylin took over as the head of the DPR, he was accused of theft and later sentenced to 14 years in prison by the DPR (tr., ed.).

160 ORDLO is the official abbreviation for Select Raions of the Donetsk and Luhansk Oblasts (in Ukrainian, *okremi raiony Donetskoï i Luhanskoï oblastei*). ORDLO is the formal designation of the LPR/DPR (ed.).

THE DPR AND RELIGION

161   Andrii Tkachov (b. 1969) is a Christian Orthodox priest from Lviv, Ukraine. For a time he studied at the Moscow Suvorov Military School and at the Military Institute of the USSR Ministry of Defense in the Department for Special Propaganda, from which he was expelled. He later studied briefly at various religious educational institutions in Ukraine (as non-resident student at one, expelled from another) and in the early 1990s was ordained a deacon and then a priest of the Ukrainian Orthodox Church of the Moscow Patriarchate in Lviv. He is known for his aggressive anti-Western stance and his sermons directed against civic rights, the rights of women, and science. In June 2014, he moved to Russia where he served in a church near Moscow, occasionally writing about Ukraine as a "quasi-state" and the Ukrainian people as "false brothers," "possessed," and "insane" (ed.).

162   The now defunct KRT (Kyivan Rus´ TV channel) was a pro-Russian Ukrainian channel. The ownership of the channel is disputed and some reports have argued that it was owned by Vitalii Zakharchenko, the Donetsk-born former Minister of Interior Affairs under President Yanukovych (Zakharchenko is accused of sanctioning the use of firearms against the Maidan protesters; he reportedly escaped to Russia) (ed.).

HOW THE MILITANTS PREPARE CHILDREN
TO JOIN THEIR MILITARY ORGANIZATIONS

163   The system of Suvorov military schools was organized in the Soviet Union during World War II to provide boys of school age with an education that focuses on military subjects. These boarding schools existed in many Soviet republics, including the one in Kyiv, Ukraine, which after the collapse of the Soviet Union was reorganized and came under the auspices of the Armed Forces of Ukraine (ed.).

BACK IN THE USSR: SOVIET THEMES
IN DONETSK EATERIES

164 In Russian, Our USSR Motherland (tr.).

165 Named after the eponymous salad that was invented by a French chef Laurent Oliver for the Hermitage restaurant in Moscow in the 1860s and became a staple Soviet and post-Soviet menu item (tr.).

166 The Zhiguli was the Volkswagen of the Soviet Union, in that it was a small, cheap car that ran forever but had little else to recommend it. It was rebranded as the Lada in foreign markets, with the ability to withstand extreme cold its main selling points (tr.).

167 Compote here refers to a drink made from stewed fruits or berries (tr.).

"LOOKING FOR A TUSK TO BUY":
ADS IN OCCUPIED DONETSK

168 In Russian, checkpoint (tr.).

169 Heart-shaped millefeuille buns (tr.).

170 The slogan rhymes in Russian: *spasibo dedu za pobedu*. This is a reference to the victory in World War II, which in the Soviet Union and in post-Soviet Russia has been primarily interpreted as the Soviet (and Russian at that) victory over Nazism (ed.).

171 In Russian, *rabotaite, bratia* (ed.).

172 The slogan takes a swipe at both the Ukrainian government elected following the Revolution of Dignity (called by Russian propaganda a "Nazi junta," among other epithets), and at Ukrainian president Petro Poroshenko, a wealthy businessman and an oligarch before his election as president. It thus combines an ideological message with a popular anti-elite sentiment that is widespread in most of Ukraine and which accuses the country's ultrarich of causing the poverty of the working class (ed.).

FOLLOWING THE PATH OF CRIMEA?

173 A 2009 French action thriller directed by Patrick Alessandrin, the sequel to the 2004 film *District 13*, which was directed by Pierre Morel. Both films depict events in a poor and overpopulated ghetto on the outskirts of Paris which the authorities have surrounded with a fence of barbed wire as they are unable to control it, and where violent gangs rule without any regard for the law (ed.).

174 Shmel (Bumblebee), is the name of RPO-A, a Soviet infantry rocket launcher (tr.).

175 "Effective control" is a term from international law referring to the way in which responsible authority in an occupied zone is determined (ed.).

176 Vodafone Ukraine is Ukraine's second largest mobile operator. The network was originally known as UMC Ukraine and was the pioneer of mobile communications in Ukraine. In 2003, UMC was acquired by Mobile TeleSystems (MTS), Russia's largest mobile network operator with headquarter in Moscow, and renamed MTS Ukraine. In 2008, MTS and the British Vodafone Group PLC signed a strategic partnership agreement, which was expanded in October 2015 and resulted in the rebranding of MTS Ukraine as Vodafone Ukraine. The rebranding was largely seen in Ukraine as a move aimed at continuing operation in Ukraine despite the Russian ownership of the company, including in Crimea and the Donbas. The company continued operating in the occupied areas of the Donbas, both the LPR and the DPR, until January 2018 when the service was interrupted following a fiber optic line cut. Although the service was restored soon after, Vodafone remained unavailable in the DPR following the demands from the "republic" to pay taxes to their "treasury" (ed.).

177 Grishin is the real name of Semen Semenchenko (b. 1974), a military volunteer and one of the initiators of the blockade. In March 2021, Semenchenko was accused by the Security Service of Ukraine (SBU) of being the leader of a private military company engaged in contraband and sale of spare parts from Russia for military equipment in Ukraine, and was arrested following a court hearing (tr., ed.).

178 Shortly after the outbreak of the war in the Donbas, Russia has been supplying energy (natural gas and oil, etc.) to the LPR and the DPR at prices well below market, or entirely for free, at times trying to charge the Ukrainian government for it. The low utility rates are used by the separatists as one of the "carrots" for people to stay on the occupied territory. The author puts this on the balance sheet along with the complete lack of the rule of law, terror, and torture in the republics (ed.).

US AND THEM

179 From Russian, *zapadenets* (westerner), which in the Soviet period was a derogative term that generally applied to Ukrainians from the western part of Ukraine (tr., ed.).

180 Butyrka is a Russian band that plays prison pop. The name is based on a remand jail in Moscow (tr.).

A KNACK FOR LOSING THINGS

181 On July 5, 2014, Girkin and a group of militants who had been occupying Slov'iansk withdrew to Donetsk despite being encircled by Ukrainian forces. The Kyiv government claimed that Girkin was allowed to escape because he and his men were holding hostages as human shields (ed.).

182 A line from the song "Skovannye odnoi tsepiu" (Those who are chained together) by the Russian band Nautilus Pompilius (ed.).

183 In Ukrainian, *peremoha* means "victory," while zrada means "betrayal." The Ukrainian media, including opinion makers on social media, have been oscillating between these two radical evaluations of the events surrounding the political events in the country, while in reality neither was entirely the case (ed.).

184 In Latin, "appeal to death" (tr.).

ILLUSTRATION CREDITS

All images are reproduced in this volume by permission from the copyright holders.

Road signs for Makiivka and Donetsk, with Msta-B 152 mm howitzers
　　on the road. February 24, 2015. Photo: Valery Sharifulin,
　　ITAR-TASS News Agency / Alamy Stock Photo · **x**
Graffiti in Donetsk reading "*Novorossiia*! Putin." June 10, 2015. Photo:
　　Celestino Arce, ZUMA Wire / ZUMAPRESS.com / Alamy Live News · **1**
The destroyed building of the new terminal of the Donetsk Airport.
　　Photo: Tommy Trenchard, Alamy Stock Photo · **5**
DPR military recruiting office in Donetsk. February 10, 2015. Photo: Mikhail
　　Sokolov, ITAR-TASS News Agency / Alamy Stock Photo · **15**
The "parade of captives" in Donetsk. Captive soldiers of the
　　Ukrainian armed forces are led between two rows of militants
　　armed with rifles with bayonets. August 24, 2014. Photo:
　　Alexander Ermochenko, Xinhua / Alamy Live News · **18**
The "parade of captives" in Donetsk, staged on Ukrainian Independence
　　Day, in which Ukrainian servicemen captured by DPR militants were
　　led through the city streets in a humiliating procession. August 24,
　　2014. Photo: Maxim Shemetov, REUTERS / Alamy Stock Photo · **23**
A separatist fighter with typical Christian Orthodox icons at an LPR
　　checkpoint near Stanytsia Luhanska. January 25, 2017. Photo:
　　ITAR-TASS News Agency / Alamy Stock Photo · **28**
A local boy with the DPR militants as they stand guard outside a regional
　　administration building in Kostiantynivka, Donetsk Oblast, seized in
　　the night by separatists. April 28, 2014. Photo: Sandro Maddalena,
　　NurPhoto / ZUMAPRESS.com / Alamy Live News · **35**

Children celebrate a farewell bell event at Donetsk school number
   30, where the DPR anthem is played for the first time instead
   of the Ukrainian anthem. May 2015. Photo: Pacific Press
   Media Production Corp. / Alamy Stock Photo · **40**

Pro-Russia demonstrators celebrate and occupy the streets after
   attacking Ukrainian police and violently dispersing a peaceful
   pro-Ukraine unity demonstration. April 28, 2014. Photo:
   Idealink Photography / Alamy Stock Photo · **47**

A road sign for Donetsk damaged by shelling. Photo
   courtesy of *Radio Svoboda* (RFE/RL) · **50**

A pro-Russia demonstrator holds an anti-Nazi sign in front of a barricade
   outside the building of the Donetsk Oblast State Administration.
   April 11, 2014. Photo: REUTERS / Alamy Stock Photo · **57**

Pro-Russian demonstrators with icons and Russian flags on their way
   to a memorial in Donetsk. March 30, 2014. Photo: Romain Carre,
   NurPhoto / ZUMAPRESS.com / Alamy Live News · **63**

An apartment building partly destroyed in a night shelling attack in the
   city of Horlivka (north of Donetsk) and blamed by DPR militants
   on Ukrainian armed forces. Photo: Alexander Kravchenko,
   ITAR-TASS News Agency / Alamy Stock Photo · **71**

The building of the Polit (Flight) Hotel near the Donetsk airport, destroyed
   by heavy shelling. Photo courtesy of *Radio Svoboda* (RFE/RL) · **75**

Nadiia Savchenko, a military bomber and helicopter pilot, one of the
   most prominent Ukrainian hostages captured by the Russian
   military. She was abducted from Ukrainian territory and tried in
   Moscow, Russia, on the charge of "illegally crossing" the Russian
   border. Savchenko was exchanged in a prisoner swap in May 2016
   and went on to become a controversial politician in the Ukrainian
   parliament espousing pro-authoritarian views. *February 10, 2015.*
   Photo: Maxim Zmeyev, REUTERS / Alamy Stock Photo · **80**

From left to right: Ukrainian pro-Russian politician Viktor Medvedchuk,
   whose daughter's godfather is Vladimir Putin himself; Russian
   Orthodox Church Patriarch Kirill of Moscow and All Russia; DPR head
   Oleksandr Zakharchenko; and LPR head Leonid Pasichnyk talk to the
   media following their meeting in Moscow. December 25, 2017. Photo:
   Sergei Bobylev, ITAR-TASS News Agency / Alamy Stock Photo · **84**

Russian mercenary Arsen Pavlov ("Motorola") at his marriage ceremony in
    Donetsk with Olena Kolenkina of Slov'iansk, which was attended by
    DPR leaders Igor Girkin (Strelkov) and Pavlo Hubariev. The wedding
    received a great deal of attention in the media. Motorola was
    assassinated in his own apartment building in October 2016. July 11,
    2014. Photo: Maxim Zmeyev, REUTERS / Alamy Stock Photo · **88**
"Immortal Regiment" at the Victory Day parade in Donetsk. May 9,
    2015. Photo: Artem Povarov, Alamy Stock Photo · **94**
At a base near Slov'iansk, members of the Ukrainian National Guard carry
    munitions as they prepare to move in the direction of Donetsk. July 15,
    2014. Photo: Gleb Garanich, REUTERS / Alamy Stock Photo · **98**
Joseph Stalin portrait and a flag with Saint George ribbon's colors at the
    Victory Day parade in Donetsk on May 9, 2014. The totalitarian
    Soviet dictator was the mastermind behind the Holodomor, a
    genocidal famine in Ukraine and other parts of the USSR, that
    took the lives of millions of Ukrainians in 1932–33. Photo: Tali
    Mayer, NurPhoto / ZUMAPRESS.com / Alamy Live News · **103**
Pro-Russia militants in Donetsk attack peaceful demonstrators rallying
    for the preservation of Ukraine's unity. The pro-Russian group,
    mostly youths in balaclavas, subsequently celebrated their actions
    by screaming that they had smashed "the fascists." April 28, 2014.
    Photo: Idealink Photography / Alamy Stock Photo · **106**
From left to right: DPR "defense minister" Vladimir Kononov, Donetsk-born
    Russian singer Iosif Kobzon, and the commander of the Somali battalion
    Mykhailo Tolstykh (Givi) on Russian holiday known as the Defender of
    the Fatherland Day, February 23, 2015. Tolstykh was assassinated in
    February 2017. Photo: Russian Look Ltd. / Alamy Stock Photo · **117**
People queue for humanitarian aid in the town of Debaltseve,
    north-east of Donetsk. March 17, 2015. Photo: Marko
    Djurica, REUTERS / Alamy Stock Photo · **129**
Female DPR fighters pose on stage in Donetsk during a beauty pageant
    to mark the upcoming International Women's Day. March 7, 2015.
    Photo: Marko Djurica, REUTERS / Alamy Stock Photo · **134**
Putyliv Bridge near Donetsk Airport, destroyed by heavy shelling.
    Photo courtesy of *Radio Svoboda* (RFE/RL) · **137**

Coal miners near Donetsk are evacuated from under the Zasiadko
          mine after shelling caused a power outage. Photo: Alexander
          Ermochenko, REUTERS / Alamy Stock Photo · **140**
Trucks of a Russian "humanitarian convoy" heading for an illegal crossing of
          the border to Ukraine. The convoys were used by Russia to transport
          goods for civilians and equipment, arms, ammunition, motor fuel and
          oil for the militants in the DPR and the LPR. On the return trip, they
          often transported to Russia machinery stolen from Ukrainian defense
          factories and the bodies of Russian soldiers and mercenaries (*gruz 200*).
          Photo: Alexander Demianchuk, REUTERS / Alamy Stock Photo · **151**
DPR militants vote at a polling station in Kramatorsk during the unrecognized
          referendum on DPR's independence from Ukraine. May 11, 2014. Photo:
          Tali Mayer, NurPhoto / ZUMAPRESS.com / Alamy Live News · **153**
Wreckage of the Malaysia Airlines Boeing 777 plane (flight MH-17) is removed
          by a crane at the site of the plane crash near the settlement of Hrabovo,
          north of Torez (now Chystiakove), in the Donetsk Oblast. The airplane
          was downed on July 17, 2014, by DPR militants using a Russian-army
          Buk ground-to-air missile system, killing all 298 people on board.
          November 16, 2014. Photo: REUTERS / Alamy Stock Photo · **156**
The building on Zlitna Street in Donetsk where DPR militants took up a
          position. Photo courtesy of *Radio Svoboda* (RFE/RL) · **163**
A banner in Donetsk portraying Oleksandr Zakharchenko and Saint
          George's ribbons, ahead of Defender of the Fatherland Day
          (February 23). February 19, 2017. Photo: Viktor Drachev,
          ITAR-TASS News Agency / Alamy Stock Photo · **192**
President of Ukraine Petro Poroshenko takes part in a peace march in Kyiv as
          a tribute to the victims onboard a passenger bus that came under fire
          near the town of Volnovakha (to the south of Donetsk) on January 13,
          2015. Twelve civilians were killed in the attack and eighteen were
          injured. Photo: Gleb Garanich, REUTERS / Alamy Stock Photo · **198**
Volunteers for the DPR forces at a military recruiting office in
          Donetsk. February 10, 2015. Photo: Mikhail Sokolov, ITAR-
          TASS News Agency / Alamy Stock Photo · **208**
A Grad rocket shell in the steppe near Donetsk. Photo:
          Dmytro Pylypenko, Alamy Stock Photo · **215**

Russian militant commander and officer of Russia's GRU military intelligence
service Igor Girkin (Strelkov) kisses an Orthodox icon after a news
conference in Donetsk on July 10, 2014. Five days earlier, having been
encircled by Ukrainian forces, Girkin was allowed to withdraw with his
militants from Slov'iansk to Donetsk, using Ukrainian hostages as human
shields. Photo: Maxim Zmeyev, REUTERS / Alamy Stock Photo · **225**

Children attend a ceremony to unveil the "Book of Memory," a monument to
the DPR militants who died fighting against Ukrainian armed forces
at Iasynuvata, north of Donetsk. August 22, 2017. Photo: Valentin
Sprinchak, ITAR-TASS News Agency / Alamy Stock Photo · **228**

Sausage on sale in Donetsk. Cheap, low-quality sausage often figures in the
nostalgic imagery of the Soviet Union since its collapse in 1991, especially
among the older population of the post-Soviet countries. February 19, 2017.
Photo: Viktor Drachev, ITAR-TASS News Agency / Alamy Stock Photo · **233**

Ukrainian film director Oleh Sentsov, one of the most prominent Ukrainian
political prisoners in Russia. Sentsov was abducted from his native Crimea
in May 2014, following Russia's annexation of the Ukrainian peninsula.
He was tried in Rostov-on-Don, Russia, and sentenced to 20 years for
"terrorism." In September 2019, he was released in a prisoner swap.
August 25, 2015. Photo: Valery Matytsin, TASS / Alamy Live News · **239**

Relatives and friends meet the released Ukrainian hostages at the
airport of Boryspil, Ukraine. December 27, 2017. Photo: Serg
Glovny, ZUMA Press, Inc. / Alamy Stock Photo · **246**

A burnt-out car at the destroyed Donetsk Airport. March 4, 2015. Photo:
Valery Sharifulin, ITAR-TASS News Agency / Alamy Stock Photo · **250**

Stanislav Aseyev at a welcoming ceremony in Kyiv for Ukrainian hostages
released from the DPR in a prisoner swap. December 9, 2019.
Photo: SOPA Images Limited / Alamy Stock Photo · **256**